RUNAWAY DEVIL

RUNAWAY DEVIL

How Forbidden Love Drove a 12-Year-Old to Murder Her Family

Robert Remington
Sherri Zickefoose

McCLELLAND & STEWART

Copyright © 2009 Robert Remington and Sherri Zickefoose

Library and Archives Canada Cataloguing in Publication
Remington, Robert
Runaway devil : how forbidden love drove a twelve-year-old to murder her family /
Robert Remington and Sherri Zickefoose.

ISBN 978-0-7710-7360-1

1. Juvenile homicide – Alberta – Medicine Hat. 2. Murder – Alberta – Medicine Hat.
3. Preteens – Alberta – Psychology – Case studies. 4. Runaway
children – Alberta – Psychology – Case studies. I. Zickefoose, Sherri II. Title.

HV6535.C33M43 2009   364.152'3083520971234   C2008-907570-6

We acknowledge the financial support of the Government of Canada through the Book Publishing
Industry Development Program and that of the Government of Ontario through the Ontario Media
Development Corporation's Ontario Book Initiative. We further acknowledge the support of the
Canada Council for the Arts and the Ontario Arts Council for our publishing program.

Cradle of Filth lyrics are reprinted with the permission of Dani Filth.
Typeset in Garamond by M&S, Toronto
Printed and bound in Canada

This book is printed on acid-free paper that is 100% recycled,
ancient-forest friendly (100% post-consumer recycled).

McClelland & Stewart Ltd.
75 Sherbourne Street
Toronto, Ontario
M5A 2P9
www.mcclelland.com

3   4   5   13   12   11   10   09

To our families.
Writing about this tragedy has made you more precious than ever.

*"We shall flit through the shadows
Like a dream of (were)wolves in the snow,
Under deadly nightshade
Still warmed with the kill's afterglow."*

– Cradle of Filth
"Dusk and Her Embrace"

CONTENTS

Authors' Note

As journalists we rarely get to choose our subject matter. It chooses us. Such was the case on April 23, 2006, when three bodies were discovered inside a home on a quiet suburban street in Medicine Hat, Alberta. We quickly realized that this was a dramatic and sensational story, incomprehensible not only in its brutality, but because one of the perpetrators was a 12-year-old girl. She would become the youngest Canadian convicted of multiple homicide and one of the youngest females anywhere to commit familicide, the annihilation of one's entire family. Killed along with her mother and father was her brother, an innocent boy just eight years old.

The girl's identity is protected under Canada's *Youth Criminal Justice Act*, which shelters offenders under the age of 18 by ensuring their anonymity. Canadian law gives additional protection to those under 14. Older teens can have their trials moved to adult court, but children under 14 must be dealt with as youths, with softer penalties. Anything that may identify a young offender, such as the last name of a family member or relative, cannot be publicized. For these reasons, the girl and her family are identified in this book as they were in the judge's written ruling at her sentencing in November of 2007. Her father, mother, and brother are referred to by first name only, as they are in the court record, and she by her initials, JR. We also use her online username and a nickname she gave herself in one of her many online identities. Names of some family friends and surviving relatives are also not used, nor are some other of their identifying details.

Names of underage teens who testified at the girl's trial have been changed, also in keeping with Canadian legal restrictions. We have also respected the wishes of the parents of a little boy who was traumatized when he discovered the bodies of the victims and have used a pseudonym for him. The names of police investigators, court authorities, and legal experts have not been changed, nor have the names of witnesses who were 18 or older at the time they gave testimony in court.

Some conversations and dialogue have been recreated from court proceedings and interviews. Although the exact words may differ somewhat from what was said, they are the best recollections of those involved and, in many cases, were given as testimony under oath. Internet messages sent between JR, her friends, and her accomplice have been reproduced as they wrote them, without corrections for spelling, punctuation, or grammar.

This work is not meant as an indictment of any particular subculture, style of music, or belief system. Rather, it is an attempt to understand the sudden, downward spiral of a middle-class 12-year-old girl from honour student to complicit killer, and to serve as a warning, perhaps, to others.

It is also an effort to celebrate the lives of the victims, who inspired many to better their circumstances in life. In keeping with the wishes of the victims' families, a portion of the proceeds from this book have been donated by the authors to Rockhaven Recovery Centre in Sudbury, Ontario and to the victim assistance unit of the Medicine Hat Police Service.

This story became personal and, at times, emotional for Robert Remington. Unbeknownst to him at the time of the murders, a longtime acquaintance was a close friend of the victims. A participant in the 12-step recovery program Narcotics Anonymous, she is referred to here as Judith.

May 2009
Calgary, Alberta

RUNAWAY DEVIL

1

ALL HELL FOR A BASEMENT

"Mommy, there's bodies with blood on them."

Jacob and Gareth were inseparable that spring, playing ball hockey, wrestling, and pretending to be Jedi knights engaged in a galactic struggle to save the universe. The afternoon of April 23 was a particularly good time to be a little boy. Bright, sunny, and warm, it hinted tantalizingly at the long summer days to come. Soon, the prickly pear cactus would be in yellow bloom, an anomaly in a country known for ice and snow but part of the normal cycle of seasons on the semi-arid southeastern Alberta prairie, where deep coulees hide dinosaur bones and rattlesnakes nest amid eerie outcroppings of sandstone sculpted by wind and rain.

For Gareth, it was certainly no day to be cooped up at grandma's house. There were pretend hockey games to be won in sudden death overtime and home runs to be hit in the bottom of the ninth inning. Darth Vader's Death Star had to be attacked, the Dark Side confronted, Imperial storm troopers vanquished, the republic restored.

The six-year-old boy gazed out the window and sighed. "Mommy, can I please go to Jacob's and play?"

Sarah Penner looked at her son. He had been patient all morning, tagging along as she ran errands with his little sister in tow. Now, as they ate lunch at her mother's house, he was growing restless and bored. He wanted desperately to see Jacob, his next-door neighbour and best friend.

The previous day, the two boys had played together all day, as usual. Gareth was supposed to sleep at Jacob's house Saturday night, but instead he went with his grandmother to the hockey game between the hometown Medicine Hat Tigers and the Moose Jaw Warriors, who were battling for the Eastern Conference championship in the 2006 Junior A Western Hockey League playoffs. It was the hottest ticket in town, and the last-minute chance to go to the game was not to be missed. In lieu of a sleepover, Jacob's dad, Marc, had cooked the boys hot dogs on the backyard barbecue. Sarah called Gareth home at 5:30 in the afternoon, bundled him off to the hockey game with her mother, and went out with a friend.

When Sarah got home at 10:30 p.m., Gareth was already home from the game, which the Tigers lost 4–3 in overtime, and sleeping soundly. Sarah parked her car in the driveway and noticed that the lights next door at Jacob's house were off. Everything seemed normal.

On Sunday morning, after breakfast, Sarah headed to her mother's house with the kids. Now, with lunch finished and Gareth beginning to fidget, Sarah agreed it was time to leave. She told her son to phone Jacob to see if he could play. If not, she would take him to the movies. Gareth darted to the phone and dialled Jacob's number.

The family's answering machine picked up. On the recording, Gareth heard the cheerful voice of Jacob's mom, Debra: "Hello, you've reached the very happy home of –"

Gareth hung up, disappointed.

"I'll take you to the movies instead," Sarah promised.

Sarah left her daughter with her mom, gathered up her son, and made the short drive back to their house in Ross Glen, a tidy, suburban, middle-class community of mid-1970s bungalows and split-level homes in Medicine Hat, a city of 57,000 located 300 kilometres southeast of

Calgary. It was about 1:15 p.m. when Sarah pulled into the big common driveway they shared with their next-door neighbours Marc, Debra, Jacob, and their 12-year-old daughter, JR.

Gareth's face brightened when he saw Jacob's dad's white truck sitting in the driveway. He raced next door as Sarah walked into her house, set down her keys, and began looking for the discount matinee movie coupons she would use that afternoon.

Within a minute, Gareth was back in the front entrance, calling to his mother. "Mommy, there's bodies at Jacob's with blood on them. I saw them through the basement window," he said in an urgent voice.

Sarah looked at him in disbelief. Six-year-old boys have active imaginations, but Gareth wasn't one to make up a story like that and his voice was remarkably even and calm. "What did you say?"

"I think I saw bodies with blood on them. Come quick."

Gareth ran back to the house next door, with Sarah following across the driveway. "You better not be lying, Gareth," she warned. This was not something to joke about.

As Gareth pressed his face and hands to a ground-floor window, Sarah did the same. She nervously peered into the downstairs family room of her neighbours' split-level home, shielding her eyes against the reflections on the glass. A wave of nausea hit her. She saw the body of a man lying face-up on the floor, clad in black boxer shorts. His legs were smeared with blood and he appeared to be reaching out with his arms, as if in motion. But something was wrong. He wasn't moving. There was also blood coating his face, so much blood that she couldn't tell if it was Marc. Behind a couch, she saw the body of Debra lying on the floor, almost on her back and in an oddly bent angle. Her legs were also smeared with blood.

Sarah gasped, grabbed Gareth by the arm, and hurried the few steps back to her house. She stopped at the front door, afraid to go inside, fearful an attacker might be lurking. She pulled out her cellphone and called her mother. "Something bad has happened next door. You need to come over," she said, describing the gruesome scene.

"You've got to call 911," her mother replied. "I'll be right there."

Sarah trembled as she dialled. Talking rapidly, she told the dispatcher what she had seen. Her heart was beating hard. Could an attacker be close by, watching? Could he have broken into her house while she and the kids were at her mother's?

Too nervous to stay in her home, Sarah loaded Gareth in the car, backed out of the driveway, and parked on the street, waiting for her mother. She couldn't get the horrible thought out of her head that Gareth had wanted to sleep over at Jacob's on Saturday night.

It didn't hit her at the time, but with all the lives lost that day, Sarah would later come to realize that something in her little boy died that bright Sunday, too. Killed in Gareth was his innocence, the thing that mothers fight so very hard to protect.

Phyllis Gehring was puttering around the house in her flowered muumuu when the phone rang. It was her neighbour across the street, telling her that police were swarming around the house beside Phyllis's with guns drawn. Phyllis looked outside. She saw Sarah and her mother directing a policeman with a riot shield to the house of the nice family next door.

Phyllis yelled for Vernon, her husband of 49 years, to come in from the backyard, where he was tending to the flowers and vegetables in their greenhouse. "Get in the basement," she said. It was the safest place she could think of.

"But I need to water the plants," he answered.

A police officer approached Vernon and ordered him to stay away from the fence that separated the Gehrings' house from their next-door neighbours'.

What could be wrong? Phyllis fretted. Everything seemed fine the previous evening when she saw Marc barbecuing on his back deck. The house next door had been unusually quiet, however, that morning. Normally, Jacob would be up early, playing in the backyard. Phyllis and Vernon were forever tossing his baseballs back over the fence after an errant throw, but they didn't mind. It made Phyllis, 68, and Vernon, 71, feel young.

Phyllis and Vernon huddled in their house, wondering if all the commotion had anything to do with the noise they had heard in the night. Teddy, their shih tzu/bichon cross, had barked at what sounded like a thumping sound on the side of their house. Both got up to investigate, saw nothing, and went back to bed. When she awoke Sunday morning, Phyllis began filling her bird feeders to attract the finches, sparrows, and starlings she knew would help keep her plants bug-free during Medicine Hat's notoriously hot and dry summer months. She and Vernon were looking forward to transplanting flowers from their greenhouse into their garden, along with their tomato, eggplant, and pepper plants.

Phyllis had fried some bacon, their typical Sunday breakfast treat. She filled Teddy's bowl with dog kibble and then fed their cats, Buster, a 17-pound male, and the blind Frosty. After breakfast, she did the morning dishes and began mopping the kitchen floor and tidying the living room of the Ross Glen home where she and Vernon had lived for 21 years. It was a good neighbourhood, with driveways lined with pickup trucks, the favoured vehicle of the many working middle-class people who lived on the street.

Vernon was retired from his job at a building supply company. Like many old-timers in Medicine Hat, he had once worked at the now silent clay manufacturing plants in the industrial flats along the South Saskatchewan River. The steep banks of the river valley were rich with red clay deposits, but the city might have remained just a railway stop on the Canadian prairie if not for another crucial commodity, an abundant supply of natural gas.

The Medicine Hat gas field, at a depth of between 300 and 600 metres, is one of the largest in North America, estimated to measure 250 square kilometres. At the turn of the last century it allowed Medicine Hat the extravagance of gas-fired streetlights, which the city kept lit day and night. It was cheaper to keep them burning than to pay someone to turn them off. Because natural gas burns hotter than coal, the local clay could be fired in giant beehive kilns at temperatures hot enough to make it impermeable to water – perfect for the manufacture of tile, brick, and pipes for the emerging cities of the Canadian West.

Today, the old brickyards and the once world-famous Medalta Potteries factory is a museum in the city's Clay District, a national historic site, where the old brick factories and giant kilns stand ghostly silent. It is a sanitized version of the hot fires and sweat that were the reality of the brutal work in the brickyards, where men toiled in unrelenting summer temperatures that regularly pushed 40 degrees Celsius, making red bricks for the homes of the wealthy across the Prairie West. Flares from the factory and the surrounding local gas wells burned into the night, creating a Dante-like inferno that illuminated the dark prairie sky.

Author Rudyard Kipling, who visited the region in 1907, wrote, "This part of the country seems to have all hell for a basement and the only trap door appears to be Medicine Hat."

Like many "Hatters," as local residents are known, the Gehrings have some antique plates and cups from Medalta Potteries. Their cozy split-level is lined with knitted throws, cushions, and other small treasures. It is the perfect place for a pair of pampered cats to enjoy their afternoon naps. Phyllis and Vernon would often join them in slumber.

But on this afternoon, there would be no sleep.

Norm Boucher, the chief of police, was en route to a house he was renovating when he heard the 911 call on the radio of his unmarked police cruiser. "Is this a prank?" he thought. "This isn't April Fool's Day."

Sergeant Brent Secondiak, a young Medicine Hat police officer, was the first on the scene at 1:34 p.m. He was not far away, patrolling on the highway, when the police dispatcher relayed that a little boy and his mother had seen bodies through a basement window. "I kind of had a gut feeling it was a bigger call. It's kind of surreal. I just had a gut feeling," he said later.

Secondiak screeched his cruiser to a halt facing the wrong way in front of the Gehrings' house. Several people were looking at him and pointing, indicating the house next door to the Gehrings. He peered into a basement window and saw a body on the floor, covered in blood. Secondiak wasn't sure what he was dealing with, only that a neighbour had reported two bloody bodies inside. Was this a violent domestic dispute? A murder-suicide? A homicide? If so, was the killer still in the house?

He called for backup, retrieved a protective tactical shield from the trunk of his cruiser, pulled his gun and waited.

Three other young Medicine Hat police officers – Constables Ian Scrivener, Jason Schiebelbein, and Todd Hodgins – arrived within minutes. Scrivener, a member of the tactical unit, had special training in clearing rooms deemed to be "high-risk situations." It fell to him to break down the locked front door of the house using a 35-kilogram battering ram. Secondiak, Schiebelbein, and Hodgins positioned themselves behind Scrivener in a "stack" – a configuration in which the men moved as one, like a rugby scrum.

As they prepared to enter the house, they could hear whimpering.

The four policemen breached the door at 1:45 p.m. Immediately, they saw blood smears on both walls of a stairwell leading to the upstairs bedrooms. More bloody swipes were in the adjacent stairwell leading to the basement of the split-level home, where Secondiak had seen the bodies. Ahead, they had a clear view of the living room, which appeared undisturbed. A quick look into the kitchen revealed a red smear near the handle of the back door.

Secondiak and Hodgins stood with guns drawn at the foot of the stairs leading up to the bedrooms while Scrivener and Schiebelbein cautiously headed down to the basement. At the foot of the basement stairs, Scrivener saw the body of a woman. She was lying on the floor in an unnatural position, partly on her side and back, her head slightly propped on the back of a couch with her light-brown hair dishevelled over her face. Her blue nightgown was askew, hiked up, showing her naked from the waist down. There was a large bloodstain around her body on the carpet and blood smears all over her legs.

A little black dog at her side barked and let out a plaintive whine.

Beyond the woman, to the left, a burly, dark-haired man in black boxer shorts lay face up on the floor in a dark pool of blood, not moving. His legs, too, were smeared with blood. Nearby, a railing separating the basement from a sublevel of the house was broken.

Scrivener and Schiebelbein turned on the basement lights for a better look.

The man's hands were clenched upward as if ready for a fight. His right eye socket was a gaping red wound, and there were multiple slices, punctures, and cuts all over his face and body. On the floor next to him lay a screwdriver. Nearby, Scrivener noticed a black-handled knife. Its tip was bent like a hook and the blade was buckled in the middle.

Unsure whether the man was a victim or a wounded assailant, Scrivener cautiously approached, intending to handcuff him. As he touched the man's hand, Scrivener realized he was dealing with a corpse. The man's arms were frozen upward in rigor mortis.

Rigor mortis, from the Latin words for "stiffness" and "death," begins three to fours hours after death, depending on environmental conditions, and lasts about a day. It is an unreliable indicator of time of death, but the officers suspected this was a relatively fresh crime scene. Still-wet blood was splattered and sprayed across nearly every surface in the basement, including exercise equipment, a TV set, and even the ceiling.

Kipling's words, so familiar to everyone in Medicine Hat, suddenly took on a sickening new meaning. On that bright Sunday afternoon, all hell seemed to be in the basement of the home in Ross Glen.

Guns drawn, Secondiak and Hodgins followed the blood trail on the walls leading to the upstairs bedrooms. The carpet in the second-floor hallway was sticky wet with blood. In the bathroom to the right, they saw a knife lying on the counter in a pink puddle, apparently from being rinsed of blood.

Secondiak looked to his left, into a girl's pink bedroom. The bed was unmade and the room cluttered with stuffed animals, but there were no signs of violence. The officers moved on.

What Secondiak saw in the next bedroom has never left him. On the bed lay the body of a little boy in his underwear, on his right side, with a large gash in his throat. His eyes were wide open. Blood was everywhere – on the bed, the floor, the purple walls, on the boy's Pokemon trading cards, on his wrestling figurines, and on a toy *Star Wars* light sabre on the floor.

Secondiak winced. *No, not a little boy. Please be alive. Please be alive.* But the attack had been fierce. The child had died in his own bed – a place where little boys are supposed to be safe – with no way out and no means of defence. His toy light sabre would have done him no good.

Secondiak, a father with a daughter and two sons, felt sick as he looked around the boy's room at the bloodied toys. The death of a child shakes to the core even the most hardened emergency responders. It takes men like Secondiak back to that wonderful time in their lives when they, too, were eight-year-old boys, when they imagined themselves as cowboys or superheroes or soldiers or Jedi knights.

The only living thing in the boy's room was a hamster in a cage, in the closet.

Secondiak collected himself and walked into the master bedroom. The bed was dishevelled, as if the covers had been quickly thrown back. A purple pillow on top of the duvet seemed out of place. Had the little boy run into the room alone, scared, and picked it up, hugging it for comfort? Secondiak was trying to piece the events together in his head, but deciphering what happened here would be the work of crime scene investigators. Secondiak and the officers focused on the job at hand – to secure the premises and make sure that anyone left alive was safe, and that the perpetrator or perpetrators were not still in the house, all the while trying to preserve evidence and avoid contaminating the scene.

The four officers met on the main level, preparing to regroup outside the house. As they walked toward the front door, they saw a framed portrait sitting on a coffee table of a mom, a dad, a daughter, and a son. They resembled so many happy families in picture frames in countless homes, posed in perfection. The officers stared at it briefly. There were four people in the photo. Three were among the dead. The adolescent girl was missing.

They began questioning the neighbours.

Phyllis answered a knock on her door from a police officer.

"What has happened?" she asked, bewildered.

"What do you think has happened?"

"A death?"

"More than one."

"Oh my God, no."

The officer asked about the missing girl in the photo. Phyllis told him it must be the daughter, JR.

"You wouldn't happen to know where she is?"

Phyllis and Vernon couldn't offer much information. They weren't close to the family next door. They only made casual conversation across the fence and wouldn't have known JR's whereabouts that night. Phyllis told the officer that she sometimes saw her walking down the lane with another girl, but she didn't know many of her friends.

Then she thought of something that might help. "She's 12 but looks a lot older," she told the officer.

"Oh, she does?"

"Yes, 16 or older."

Phyllis and Vernon hadn't known the family next door for very long. Marc and Debra and their two children had arrived in Medicine Hat three years earlier from Okotoks, near Calgary. They were full of life, and Phyllis enjoyed living next door to them. They seemed like the perfect suburban family, although Marc had mentioned that they had been having some problems with JR – which she took to mean the normal rebellious "teen stuff."

Now, with the officer at her door, Phyllis went completely numb. How could something like this have happened in their quiet neighbourhood?

Who would have wanted to hurt the family next door? Just last night, she had made small talk with Marc as their dogs played with each other through the fence, and now there were policemen with guns asking questions.

Dog teams and detectives soon descended on the scene. After interviewing the neighbours, Secondiak and the other officers were no further ahead on the whereabouts of the missing girl. The officers did a second search of the house, praying that she was not dead. Perhaps they had missed a body. The officers searched closets, thinking the daughter might be cowering in fear. They called out but got no response. "We searched high and low, underneath beds, looking for where a kid would hide," Scrivener said later.

Schiebelbein returned to the girl's bedroom and saw a quilt crumpled on the floor. He approached with trepidation, slowly reaching down, swallowing hard. He moved the quilt aside, thinking there would be a body underneath.

There was nothing.

Back in his cruiser, Police Chief Boucher was listening intently to the chatter on the police radio. He could detect the stress in Secondiak's voice. "I can't find the girl," the officer said.

Secondiak checked the garage, the backyard. Nothing.

Had the girl been staying overnight with a friend, perhaps? None of the neighbours knew.

"Thank God she wasn't here to see this," Secondiak thought. And then, it hit him: "Oh my God, what's she going to do when she finds out about this?"

The police began to fear that the girl might have been abducted by the killer. Was he holding her somewhere? Marc, Debra, and Jacob were dead. But the girl was missing. The police were frantic.

Where was JR?

2

THE ALMIGHTY JAXZ

"Other people live in my head with me."

Medicine Hat was a hard-earned prize for Marc and Debra. After 15 years of marriage, the couple finally owned their own home – a four-level split on a tidy suburban street with a tree house in the backyard and a fireplace where they roasted marshmallows with their children. Marc, an instrumentation technician in the oil and gas industry, had been promoted to a new job. His pretty wife Debra, known for her megawatt smile and irrepressible, effusive personality, was poised to launch her own home business. They loved exploring their new surroundings, taking family trips with their children on their cherished motorcycles to the unworldly hoodoos of nearby Dinosaur Provincial Park, a UNESCO World Heritage Site, and having backyard barbecues with the kids on hot summer nights. Described by neighbours as a "Norman Rockwell family," they looked to have a bright future.

But life was not always so perfect for the couple. Marc and Debra had been in recovery programs for substance abuse when they met in 1990 while working out at a gym club in Sudbury, Ontario, a hardscrabble nickel-mining community of 157,000 once known as Canada's ground zero of acid rain due to its sulphur-belching ore-smelting plants.

Marc identified his substance abuse early, entering a 12-step rehab program two months before his twenty-third birthday, in 1986. He is remembered as "a good-looking man with dark hair" by staff at Sudbury's Rockhaven Recovery Home for Men. Although the residential treatment centre has assisted 2,000 men with substance abuse problems in its 40 years of operation, Marc made an impression in his short time there. "He knew exactly what he wanted," says Patricia Delyea, Rockhaven's director. "He came into Rockhaven motivated and prepared to do the intensive inside work that is required in order to succeed with addiction recovery."

Marc admitted to his new co-workers in Medicine Hat that he had been a "wild child" in his motorcycle-riding younger days. "When you get a bunch of guys together, you always compare notes on who did what and Marc was always the showstopper," says Wayne Chopek, who worked with him at a natural gas storage facility near Medicine Hat. A bear of a man with a bushy moustache and thinning black hair, Marc didn't mind sharing stories of his younger days. "He'd laugh about how he and some of his buddies would just go crazy when they were smoking up and driving each other's bikes – harmless fun, not hurting people or causing problems. You just had to sit and laugh with him. He had kind of a haunting chuckle."

By the time Marc met Debra, who was six years older, both were free from addiction and had vowed to change their lives forever. They married in Ontario in 1991. In October of 1993, Debra gave birth to their first child, JR.

Three years later, near the end of Debra's second pregnancy, the family moved to Okotoks, Alberta, a once sleepy agricultural centre that had grown into a bedroom community to the booming corporate oil and gas city of Calgary, a confident Houston-of-the-North with 1 million people and proud of its newfound sense of self-importance on the world energy stage. Marc and Debra were conventional and hard working, just like the thousands of others who were flooding into Alberta to take advantage of the opportunities fuelled by an energy boom in a province with oil reserves second only to Saudi Arabia's.

They named their second child Jacob. His christening in Okotoks was "a picture-perfect moment," according to Reverend Paul Orritt, pastor of a local Anglican church the couple attended regularly. "Jacob never made a fuss. Marc held him tight in his arms and Debra looked on. It was a special day for a family who had overcome some of life's struggles."

JR adored her little brother. "Jacob and her would play all the time," says Judith, a close friend of Marc and Debra's from Calgary. "When I first met her, Jacob was still in diapers. She had amazing eyes. That kind with the dark eyelashes. She was just a pretty little girl in dresses."

In Okotoks, the family lived in an older townhouse. "Times were a bit tough at first," recalls Judith. "Debra went to the food bank, but she was not embarrassed. She didn't care. She was really excited about the cookies that she made or the treats that she made for the kids. She was always stretching a dollar and making good meals for the kids."

Debra soon became a mentor and sponsor at Narcotics Anonymous, a 12-step substance abuse recovery program adapted from Alcoholics Anonymous. She spoke at meetings, which were attended by up to 30 people, and always tried to be an inspiration. "Marc and Debra devoted their lives to helping people get off drugs and alcohol," says Marc's older sister, Monique. They were models of recovery success, says Judith, who became close to Debra through the NA meetings. Debra and Marc applied the principles of NA to their entire lives, constantly taking small steps to better themselves.

NA has a don't-ask-don't-tell policy about the substances members once took: "We are not interested in what or how much you used, but only in what you want to do about your problem and how we can help." And that's how it was with Debra. Judith says: "You get a lot of old-timers in the program who talk about what it was like. But she talked about what it was like *now*. That's what you're supposed to do. Working the program, working the steps, you know. Shit hits the fan, well, then you go to step four, or you go to step five, and laughing at it, which I thought was awesome – not taking it too seriously. You know, everybody hits speed bumps in their life. So she stops, she identifies it, works through it, trips and falls and gets back up, and will laugh about it. I guess she knew she would get out the other end of it sometime." Diane Bob, a family friend, agrees: "Debra did not seek to remain in the problems of life, but always chose to live in the solution."

NA is based on a strong system of fellowship and support, something Debra excelled at, according to Judith: "Sometimes she would just call me up and say, 'Don't need a phone call back. Just wanted to let you know I love you until you love yourself.' *I love the bones and the skin you're in.* That was her famous saying."

Judith loved Debra, but sometimes found her ebullience overbearing. "She would see you and you would get the biggest hugs you ever got. . . . She would stone you sometimes she was so happy. Sometimes I wasn't sure. I thought it was a little too much, a little awkward."

Moreah Ragusa, a Calgary family mediator, life coach, and psychotherapist, acted as a spiritual advisor to Debra. According to Ragusa, Marc and Debra kept their commitment to lead a sober life together and stayed that way to raise their family. "Their search was for a deeper spiritual life. Debra's spiritual motivation was for a unified, spiritual-based family," she recalls.

Marc was raised in a French-speaking Catholic family. Debra was captivated by native spirituality and was interested in sweat ceremonies and medicine wheels – circular stone patterns laid out on the open prairie for sacred ceremonies. She always kept a dream catcher – a traditional North American Indian spiritual object – on a prominent wall leading to the family bedrooms. Dream catchers are made from willow hoops woven with a loose web and traditionally decorated with personal sacred items. According to legend, bad dreams are trapped in the web, while good dreams pass through the centre. Passing by her dream catcher before retiring each night, Debra perhaps believed that the memories of her once tumultuous past would be ensnared.

"Debra was always open to seeking what her Creator's will was for her and her family," says Diane Bob. "She cared for her family, especially her children, in a balanced way. She nurtured them emotionally, spiritually, physically, and mentally."

Over time, Marc and Debra made steady progress in their lives. Marc was adept at mechanics and skilled in multiple trades, including welding. "That was one of his first jobs," says his father, Arthur. "He went in for an apprenticeship. One day, he said, 'I want a job' so he went back to school." People skilled with their hands were coveted by employers in Alberta, which had an almost unending need for trades people to work in its oil and gas fields and booming construction industry.

In Alberta, it was easy to make quick money and burn through it just as fast, but Marc and Debra were patient and deliberate as they gained headway. "It was just slow, steady progress, like the [12] steps," Judith says. "First they were in the townhouse and going to the food bank. He took some classes and got a promotion at work and they got a condo and she did some housecleaning. They put their money away. Life was good there."

They were described by their Okotoks neighbours as a model family. Gail, who lived next door to them for three years, says she couldn't have asked for better neighbours. "They were a loving family through good and bad times. Marc and Deb treated each other and their kids with respect and love that most people would envy. I sure did. In all the time I shared a wall with them, I never once heard a harsh word spoken," she recalls.

"As Marc and Debra always treated each other with respect, they treated their children with the same respect and love," another neighbour says. "They were fair and caring and not overbearing. They did everything as a family. One thing is certain – the kids did not come from a bad family background."

"They were just a regular family," says Bob Grodin, another former neighbour. "They were the family we all wished we had. Debra was the cement who built a pleasant, happy home and Marc's only plan in life was to do right by his family. I lived vicariously through those parents and really admired their devotion to family."

Debra always worked hard to make sure her kids had fun. "She would have dates with Jacob, and [JR] would have dates with her dad where she would get dressed up. Every weekend was family stuff," says Judith. The family took trips on their motorbikes. Marc would ride with Jacob; Debra would ride with JR.

September of 2003 brought good fortune for the family. Marc had upgraded with courses in electrical engineering, and was promoted in his career with EnCana Corporation, a large Canadian oil and gas company. The company paid for the family's move from Okotoks to Medicine Hat, where Marc filled the critical role of instrument technician at the company's natural gas storage facility near Suffield, a town about 50 kilometres west of Medicine Hat that is also home to a military base. He was very precise in his work, which involved installing, calibrating, and maintaining the gauges and other instruments used to control the vital pressure, flow, temperature, and chemical composition of natural gas at the plant.

"He was a guy who took interest in anything he got his hands on. If he had to calibrate an instrument or something, everything, he just got into it," says co-worker Wayne Chopek.

The family purchased a 1,014-square-foot three-bedroom home in the suburban neighbourhood of Ross Glen for $169,000. It was a momentous occasion for Debra, who had gone from getting butter at the food bank and scrimping on every penny to the unimaginable luxury of having workers pack her belongings. "She knew she had arrived because one of the things we both hate is moving," says Judith. "We were really excited that the moving company was coming to pack everything." Here, at last, was a real home with a fenced yard, a back deck, a detached garage, and no walls to share with neighbours.

Medicine Hat was a perfect place to raise a young family – a small, friendly prairie city with hot, dry summers, bright, sunny winters, and an extensive network of recreational pathways that wind through deep coulees carved into the prairie landscape. In places, the geography of the area, located near the dinosaur-rich Alberta Badlands, is reminiscent of the American Southwest, as are portions of the city itself. On the Trans-Canada Highway that runs through town, three motels – the BelAire, the Satellite, and the Ranchmen – feature 1950s-era signs that are the closest thing one can find in Canada to what you see on America's fabled Route 66. The sign at the BelAire was once referred to as "a national treasure" and described as resembling "a robot with two skinny legs, bow-tie torso, stubby arms, and great head." The Satellite Motel sign features a rocket taking off in a vapour cloud, while the Ranchmen features a giant cowboy with one word: "Howdy!"

The motels are located near Medicine Hat's most photographed roadside attraction, the Saamis Teepee, a steel-and-concrete relic from the 1988 Winter Olympics in Calgary, where it towered above the Olympic Cauldron during the opening and closing ceremonies. Billed as the world's largest teepee, it stands above Seven Persons Coulee, an important archaeological site where hundreds of bison were butchered and their meat processed by the Blackfoot people. It is capable of surviving 240-kilometre-per-hour winds and stands not far from a waterslide where passersby are beckoned by a giant cutout of a pinup girl, faded by the sun, in a high-waisted polka-dot bikini and a sailor hat with one leg coyly raised in a flirtatious pose. She is perched atop another sign advertising "Go-Karts and Mini Golf" at the attraction.

With her interest in native spirituality, Medicine Hat would have held a special attraction for Debra. The oases of springs and cottonwood groves in its dry coulees were powerful places to the Blackfoot, who would camp there and make offerings to the pantheon of spirits that guided them as they followed the paths of their ancestors across the open prairie. The Blackfoot often said prayers before crossing rivers, which they approached with both trepidation and awe. One point on the South Saskatchewan River that never froze over in winter was believed to be a breathing hole for underworld spirits who controlled the availability of bison and, therefore, the survival of the people.

Rather than settling near the city's historic downtown, where older neighbourhoods of brick houses on tree-lined streets attract a mix of working-class people and professionals, the family chose a suburb close to schools and the convenience of the Medicine Hat Mall. "Debra, she was so excited," Judith recalls. "Everything about it was family – it was a house and there was a backyard and there were bike paths."

The children were especially thrilled with the big tree in the backyard. It became a centre of activity, with a rope swing and a wooden platform that required a stepladder to reach it. Some mornings, Jacob would squeeze in play time before school, climbing up to the tree fort or playing ball hockey. Once, the playful Jacob broke a basement window next to his backyard deck. "Marc insisted that his youngest child learn responsibility by doing chores to pay for the repair," says neighbour Phyllis Gehring.

Jacob was growing into an energetic, sometimes rambunctious soul. He adored the hard-nosed hockey player Dave "Tiger" Williams, a scrappy, Saskatchewan-born forward who played for five teams in a 14-year career in the National Hockey League. Jacob also liked to mimic the heroics of *Star Wars* Jedi. "He was the most joyful, energetic kid I've ever met," says another neighbour, Danielle Swain. Jacob would often come over to visit her little sister. "We played tag with him over and over again." At school, teachers referred to Jacob as the class clown. In his kindergarten yearbook he wrote: "When I grow up, I want to be a policeman or a soldier. The thing I like best about me is that I have a family and I'm very fast."

It was easy to root for Marc and Debra, who had worked so hard and remained so focused on their goals of succeeding as a family. Marc impressed fellow workers in his new job at the natural gas plant. "He was meticulously detailed about his work," says Wayne Chopek. "You can tell that he settled down. He met Deb and I think Deb may have changed his life and that he saw a different side of life with Deb. She was the primary focus of his life."

Debra started an at-home business as a reiki practitioner – a Japanese stress reduction technique – and had a small holistic therapy studio in a lower level of the family's home. To hone her business skills, she enrolled in a two-month entrepreneurs' course, where she met Nathalie Pepin. Like nearly everyone who encountered Debra, Pepin was instantly struck by her bright personality. Smiling and always engaging, Debra was impossible to ignore. "She always said, 'Hi! How are you today? Need a hug?'" Pepin recalls.

Despite her sunny disposition, Debra was no pushover. "I would never mess with her," Pepin says. It is a sentiment echoed by others. "Debra would have been a lioness with anyone around her children, especially if she felt her child was at risk," according to another family friend.

Debra was a determined student, full of questions and not at all reluctant to interject during class. "I don't get it," she would say, and would reiterate the concept back to the teacher to make sure she had grasped it. "No one got annoyed because it helped us learn better," Pepin says. Once the teacher joked: "Debra, any questions?" before moving on. The tight-knit group laughed together.

When Nathalie met her, Debra was one of a group of women who won a radio station's makeover contest. Debra's transformation was scheduled for the same day as her entrepreneur class graduation, which Debra skipped so she could indulge herself in "some *me* time," as she told her classmates. A black stretch limousine from the city's best hotel, the Medicine Hat Lodge, picked up Debra and the other winners, who began the day dressed casually in sweat pants, jeans, and matching radio station T-shirts. They were pampered with new hairstyles, makeup, and manicures and pedicures, outfitted in new clothes and jewellery, and posed for studio portraits. They also mugged for radio station promotional photos, including one where they posed as Charlie's Angels, holding their fingers and hands together like guns, as the Angels did in the opening credits of the popular 1970s TV series. Debra was interviewed on the radio: "I feel gorgeous!" she bubbled. In the photos, Debra is dazzling with layered shoulder-length hair and honey-coloured highlights.

Debra's luminous smile was shared by her pretty 12-year-old daughter. JR's delicate features were draped by glossy, long dark hair; her clear blue eyes were thickly lashed, and she radiated a wholesomeness that could have graced the cover of *Seventeen* magazine.

JR decorated her new bedroom in Medicine Hat with treasures typical of preteen innocence. On a shelf above her window perched a carefully arranged menagerie of stuffed animals – a winged unicorn, multicoloured bunnies, stuffed kitties, and three bears nuzzled together like a contented family. A sheer white fabric draped from a wrought iron wall hook formed a graceful canopy over her single bed. Dangling from the hook was a pink-and-green huggy monkey, his head cocked toward his animal friends on the shelf.

Next to her bed on some black shelves, she'd organized a collection of slim books, a reading lamp, and the usual girlish clutter – an empty soda bottle, a pink scarf, a silver bowl, a pen, body lotion, and a small wooden armoire jewellery box with glass doors.

When the family arrived in Medicine Hat, JR was entering grade 5, just a month shy of her tenth birthday. She went to a Catholic school and was a studious, quiet, well-scrubbed honour student in what was an uneventful school year. She was a normal, well-adjusted girl who was easily making new friends.

"When I met JR in grade 6, she was kind, gentle and made an effort to befriend me and make me feel welcome," one classmate says. As the grade 6 school year progressed, JR was the girl in the crowd who seemed to skip the awkward stage and instantly become a young woman. Her girl-friends admired her, especially one of her best friends, Aubrey.

The two girls were typical preteens. "We practically lived at each other's houses on weekends," Aubrey says. They watched movies, incessantly groomed each other's hair, walked to the nearby 7-Eleven for Slurpees and hung out at the Medicine Hat Mall, not far from JR's home, eating New York Fries and Mexi-Fries from Taco Time.

Both were in their school's fine arts program, which included music and art. They often doodled in class. "We used to draw a whole bunch. We used to draw our band teacher as a duck," Aubrey says. "JR was an understanding, decent, outgoing, absolutely amazing person." Another grade 6 friend, Nora, says, "We did the regular things, went to the mall and movies, went swimming and to water parks." JR also took judo and was in a local swim club.

JR seemed to absorb her mother's New Age interests, including reiki, crystals, and meditation. She also became interested in Wicca, the nature-revering, neo-pagan belief system that rejects the paternalistic, monotheistic structure of Christianity. Wicca embraces a variety of gods and goddesses and uses the pentagram, a star within a circle, as its main symbol. JR was so taken by Wicca that she fashioned a pentagram out of black tape on her bedroom wall opposite the foot of her bed. She framed the five-pointed star with four triangles, also made from black tape, two on each side of the pentagram, with two triangles pointing down and two pointing up. It stood in odd contrast to her little-girl collection of stuffed bunnies.

As the grade 6 school year progressed, JR and some of her friends began to question the formal religion taught at their school, including the concept of hell. "If God was so loving, why would he torture people?" says Nora. "All of us shared our frustrated feelings about this. JR did also. It was clear she had no desired belief in God at all."

Entering early adolescence, JR and her friends began testing the limits of authority. At the Medicine Hat Mall, JR and her young girlfriends were drawn to teens from the local goth crowd, a small but easily identifiable community of perhaps a few dozen who dressed in black, wore black nail polish and eyeliner, used black hair dye and sometimes white face makeup – all symbols of the alienated, and often eroticized, androgynous movement that began as an offshoot of the punk rock scene of the late 1970s.

Goth took root in the Batcave, a nightclub in London, England, in the early 1980s, where people came dressed in black clothing as a backlash to the glittery wardrobe that went with the disco music of the 1970s, which they saw as vacuous. Early goth bands included UK Decay, the Banshees, and Bauhaus. The latter took its name from the German Bauhaus art movement and came to widespread attention with their song "Bela Lugosi's Dead," a nine-minute single released in August 1979. The band's passionate lyrics and dark, gloomy sound set the tone for the genre, which was influenced by philosophical movements like existentialism.

A highly intelligent "A" student, JR was attracted to the cerebral side of the goth subculture. As a member of the school's fine arts program, she was also drawn to the theatricality of goth and identified with its artistic roots. Soon, she and her friends began wearing more black than the other girls at school. JR occasionally wore a choker and an oversized black hoodie with the logo of a heavy metal band. One of the group's favourites was The Misfits, a horror-punk band whose promotional clothing features a human skull. JR saw the dark lyrics of goth and metal music not as violent, but as creative. "It's expressive and it lets out a feeling. It's not all about killing people," she would say later.

JR's small circle of school friends began to drift apart from others in their class. "Whenever we travelled from room to room, everyone seemed to separate themselves into two groups," Nora says. "The first group consisted of myself, JR, and three or four others who we hung out with. The second, of course, was the rest of the class. Our side was labelled the 'dark' side even though most of us dressed appropriately."

Nora and JR felt shunned by their former friends. They became labelled as the "bad" group, which made them angry. "They were judging us by appearance and who we hung out with. From then on, we kept in our tight clique," Nora says.

One picture of the group shows them happily huddled together in a locker room, all dressed in dark clothing with dark eyeliner – a tight-knit clan on the verge on teenhood, feeling more like young women than kids, and bonded inseparably. There are four in the photo, all wearing little red paper hearts for a Valentine's Day dance. Aubrey, with dark eyeliner, is wearing a pink tank top, short denim skirt, and straight, streaked hair. JR is lying on a bench on her back, looking up at the camera, dressed in black with leather wrist straps, a lollipop stuck seductively in her open mouth.

It is clear from the photo that JR was maturing more quickly than the others. By the summer of 2005, between grade 6 and grade 7, she was physically more mature than most of her friends. Although only 11, she could easily pass for 15 or 16, and she was troubled by her development. "There was this big girl, boobs, you know, and it just made her feel so awkward," says Debra's friend Judith. One day, after dropping JR off at a friend's house to go to a birthday party, Debra looked at her rapidly maturing daughter and told Judith: "Oh, she struggles so much with that. My poor honey."

Research has shown that girls who reach early puberty are at risk for delinquency and aggressive behaviour. Studies show that young girls who develop early are also more likely to be depressed, socially withdrawn, moody, and sexually active. JR began to exhibit some of these traits that summer when she joined several social networking websites, where she fashioned an online alter ego that was sexually potent and menacing.

On August 27, 2005, just a few months shy of her twelfth birthday, JR registered on MindViz.com, a website with heavy teen content that offers instant messaging and online chat areas. Like other social networking sites, it allows users to accept online "friends" – other members of the same network that you can connect with by either accepting or rejecting when contacted with a "friend request." These sites also allow members to post profiles of themselves. Often these profiles are exaggerated to the point of creating an alternate identity, according to Sergeant Timothy Schottner, a computer forensics expert with the Medicine Hat Police

Service who is also a member of ICE, Alberta's Integrated Child Exploitation unit. JR's friend Aubrey, for instance, claimed on one of her web profiles to be 60 and from Finland.

On her MindViz page, JR listed her sexual orientation as bisexual and described herself as single with a dog. She gave no age, but with her straight dark hair and makeup, looked much older than a girl creeping up on 12. In the black-and-white profile picture she posted, she is holding a realistic-looking replica handgun in her right hand, pointing it up to the ceiling.

On another site, MySpace.com, she began listing her age as older than she really was. On MySpace she adopted the username "x_madness_x" and claimed to be 16. Among the interests she listed on her profile were hatchets, serial killers, criminal psychology, blood, moonlight, human anatomy, and "kinky shit." For her heroes, she listed American serial killer and cannibal Jeffrey Dahmer, who murdered 17 men and boys between 1978 and 1991. She also listed Batman, illusionist and musician Criss Angel, and heavy metal artists Marilyn Manson and Dani Filth, the founder, lyricist, and lead singer of the extreme British heavy metal band Cradle of Filth, which would become her favourite band. She listed few friends on MySpace.

When JR returned to classes in grade 7 in the fall of 2005, Sandra Richard, JR's school counsellor, noticed a dramatic change. "She was always a very quiet girl. There wasn't anything that really stood out about her." But in grade 7, "We noticed a change in her. The skirts getting shorter, the chains."

Richard had several conversations with JR about breaching the school's dress code. In addition to short skirts and chains, JR wore fishnet stockings, spiked collars, black mesh tops, and heavy makeup featuring eye accents that looked like teardrops and stars drawn in black eyeliner. Rather than scolding girls about their appearance, the counsellor attempted to engage students by talking to them about self-esteem.

"One time I pulled her into the music room to talk about her short skirt. I told her she was a beautiful girl, a very smart girl, had a great personality and didn't need to dress that way. I told JR that even though she felt physically and mentally older than her age, she still had to respect her parents' rules."

Marc and Debra were called about their daughter's fashion choices at school. Her parents, JR said, weren't terribly concerned about her dress and eyeliner. But at school, she admits she and her friends "got lectured a lot about makeup and skirts," whose hemlines, the rules said, could not be higher than the tips of their fingers when their hands were at their sides.

Early in the grade 7 school year, just weeks before her twelfth birthday, JR and her friends got ready for their all-important class photos. JR arrived at school dressed according to school rules but she swapped fashion accessories with Aubrey before sitting for the photographer. She tilted her head and smiled sweetly for the camera. With her straight, white teeth and long, shimmering hair, it was a perfect teen-magazine moment. But a closer inspection of the photo reveals a black, see-through mesh top and spiked dog collar around her neck, in cheeky defiance of the school's dress code. It was one of the first signs that the middle-class suburban teen was waging war with the rules around her.

The goth-wannabe girls wore black hoodies with logos of Marilyn Manson, the shock-rock artist who had been given the title "Reverend Manson" by Church of Satan founder Anton LaVey and whose 1996 album *Antichrist Superstar* infuriated some staunch Christians. "They didn't like that," JR said of her Catholic school's reaction.

At the Medicine Hat Mall, JR and her friends had already found the next best thing to Marilyn Manson – the dark, brooding members of the local goth community. Among them were two young men – a theatrically flamboyant 19-year-old known as Raven, and another young man known as Trenchcoat, who was about 20 or 21. The mature-looking JR quickly befriended Trenchcoat and Raven, who represented everything her world was not. Like many adolescents, JR resented her conventional, middle-class life. She liked the complicated, older teenagers who were pierced and tattooed and unafraid of consequences, and felt affinity for the much older Raven and Trenchcoat, who were well outside the mainstream.

Such age differences weren't unusual among the goth mall crowd. "Our group of friends doesn't discriminate based on age. It's just a number. It shouldn't inhibit friendship. Most of us have very alike backgrounds so we get along perfectly. It's just friendship," says one 14-year-old girl who was part of the scene.

JR could easily pass herself off as older, and she apparently never shared her true age with older guys. With her dark features, makeup, and advanced development, nobody suspected she was a kid of 12.

Raven, described by JR as simply a good friend, wore black lipstick, eyeliner, black clothing, and a black fingerless glove. Just above the knuckles were tattooed the letters e-f-i-1. "It's 'life' upside down and backwards, which tells you what I think of it," he explains. Except for his ghostly white face, everything about Raven was black, even his Djarum clove cigarettes, a favourite goth brand.

On November 10, 2005, JR joined the website VampireFreaks.com. Although barely 12, she listed her age as 15 and adopted the online name "x-killer-kitty-x." She posted about a dozen sultry photos of herself, including one where she is wearing a surgical mask and several others with falling tears drawn in black eyeliner. She found and accepted 12 people as online friends. Two weeks later, on November 26, 2005, she joined Zorpia.com and adopted an online username she would stick to – Runaway Devil.

Around this time, JR began dating a 16-year-old named Devon Wenaas, a cook at a Medicine Hat pancake house. Because of JR's mature look, Wenaas, a nice-looking, shaggy-haired teen with glasses, says he had no idea the grade 7 girl wasn't yet a teenager. "I could have sworn she was in grade 9. She acted older. She was much more mature than other girls. We hung out for two to three weeks maximum. We were definitely together, not really exactly dating, hanging out at the mall with all of our friends, just having a good time."

When Debra learned that JR was seeing Devon, she insisted on meeting with the two at a local tea shop. "She was really nice. She was definitely really open-minded," but protective, Devon said. For JR, the experience was embarrassing: "It was awkward. She asked him all these questions." The meeting probably taught JR that it would be easier to avoid future humiliation by sneaking around behind her parents' backs. She says she went out with Devon for about a month, going to movies and hanging around the mall scene. Devon, however, was growing jealous of the intense heart-to-heart talks JR was having with her older goth friend, Raven, whom she regarded as a soulmate. Devon spotted them hugging and confronted her.

"He said if I couldn't trust him with my feelings about what was going on, he was out," JR says. "I wasn't too upset. It wasn't really serious." She and Devon broke up.

On December 28, 2005, JR joined Nexopia.com, a popular teen social networking website based in Edmonton, Alberta, where she also adopted the name Runaway Devil, claimed to be 15, and chose the e-mail address "dying resurrection." The same e-mail address was used to register a profile on Geocities.com under the username "meow_mix6six6" – the three numbers associated with Satanism – but nothing was ever posted on the Geocities site. It was on her Nexopia profile that she began to reveal more of herself, or at least the invented image she wanted to present to the world:

"I am the almighty Jaxz. Bow down," she wrote. "I think deep thoughts. I am quite emotional and my mood is ever changing although I can be very good at hiding my feelings. I don't trust easily. I either have lots of energy or very little. I like to make attempts at poetry and anime. I make wookie noises and often scare small children. I am afraid of llamas. I am told I am mentally retarded. Often I am loud and bounce a lot. When I'm hyper, I like to dress up and want an Edward Scissorhands outfit. Other people live in my head with me. I like random questions. I like to pretend I'm a gangster sometimes . . . don't worry I'm not. Yeah, I sometimes watch

Teen Titans [an animated TV series] because I'm that cool. I play guitar and I suck."

On her Nexopia profile page, JR also posted passages taken from heavy metal songs. Citing it as her favourite goth lyric, she quoted some lines from "A Gothic Romance (Red Roses for the Devil's Whore)," by Cradle of Filth, which contains a reference to Ligeia, a character from an Edgar Allan Poe short story:

> In a pale azured dawn like Ligeia reborn, I tore free of my sleep-
> sepulchre
> On the sea-misted lawn where stone figures, forlorn lamented
> the spectre of Her
> Bewildered and weak, yet with passion replete, I hungered for
> past overtures
> The curse of unrest and her ardent caress, came much more
> than my soul could endure.

JR also posted an image of a CD barcode printed with the words "People = Shit," a song by the band Slipknot.

Membership on social networking sites is free. All have profile pages that allow users to list their "likes" and "dislikes." It is not unusual for users to copy information from the profiles of other users, according to Sergeant Schottner. This apparently irked JR, who wrote that she disliked people who stole from other sites. On Nexopia, she listed her likes as "cream, jumpolines, midgets, tricycles, squirrelmen and killing livestock, dark poetry, loud music." Among the favourite bands she listed were Korn, Cradle of Filth, Children of Bodum, Marilyn Manson, Murder Dolls, and Slipknot.

She continued with an extensive list that showed her in a transition from a little girl's world of "ribbons" and "buttercups" to a more rebellious world of "mosh pits" and "kinky shit." With little regard for spelling and punctuation, she listed her likes as: "pretty guitars, loud music, piercings, tattoes, suspension, safety pins, instant messaengers, eyes, unnatural hair colours, eyeliners, pinstripe, wicca, plastic spoons, japsanse fans, mr. ming master and the overly happy ballroom characters, anime, swimming, fire, candlewax, thunderstorm, boots, buttercups, horror movies, criminal psychology, moonlight, ribbons, alice in wonderland, oversized tryiclues, random questions, mind freak, tim burton, bow ties, toy guns, converse, capes, top hats, oddly coloured contacts, fake eyelashes, duct tape, lions, human anatomy, wings, reiki, tarot cards, penduluma, wookie noises, originality, mosh pits."

Among her "wishes," in her own misspelled words, were: "right eyebrow piecring, horozontal belly surface piercing, centre lip piercing, tongue piercing, sternum piercing, wrist and ankel bars, labret piercing, double web piericing upper arm flesh plating, eye area dermal anchoring, reiki sympbol of power tattow back left thigh, transdermal staples and bars designed between shoulders, cracked and bleeded elaborate broken heart scarification starting lower back stretching north and south, dark for fear of failure."

Her list of dislikes was less extensive: "homophobia, ageism, sexism, hypocrites, public transportation, being dried out, bunnies, llaamas, people who take things from my profiles, chlorine in my hair." She also professed a dislike for "small children."

Although only 12, JR undoubtedly revelled in her online alter ego: a sophisticated, mature, sleek, desirable creature known simultaneously as "x_madness_x," "Runaway Devil," and "killer kitty," the latter like a villainous, lethal sex weapon from a James Bond movie. Eager to shed her little girl image, Runaway Devil would soon be drawn to a charismatic older goth who she saw as exciting, tough, and tender. Through him, all three of her sinister monikers would be fulfilled.

3

PRAIRIE WOLVES

"I might eat you."

Medicine Hat straddles the steep banks of the South Saskatchewan River, where giant cottonwoods shroud the city's river pathway system like a jungle canopy. Trees are a rare commodity on the arid Canadian prairie, but cottonwoods are a determined species. They grow wherever there is water, soaking up the moisture of lakes and riverbanks, making the cottonwood sacred to Plains Indians. For the early Blackfoot people of the region, rivers and lakes held special powers because they were inhabited by the *suyitapis*, the Underwater People, who were the power source for medicine bundles and other sacred items. The spirits of the *suyitapis* flow through the water into the limbs of the cottonwood, which when cut reveal a five-pointed star inside, representing the presence of the Great Spirit.

In the searing heat of summer, the big trees create their own micro-climate. In their shadows grow tall, cool grass and thick willows that are a perfect habitat for deer. Here, too, lurk predators like the prairie coyote, a close relative of the grey wolf.

A hundred years ago wolves were plentiful here, but white hunters shot them for bounty. Hunters also exterminated one of the wolves' primary food sources, the buffalo. Wolf hunters regularly travelled through the area along with whisky traders, giving rise to conflicts with local native tribes and resulting in a legendary massacre in the nearby Cypress Hills, which straddle the Alberta–Saskatchewan boundary just north of the U.S. border. In 1873, a party of American wolf hunters had their horses stolen in the Cypress Hills. Presuming their horses were taken by a party of 200 Nakoda Indians, the wolf hunters attacked the Indian camp after a night of heavy drinking, leaving 30 Nakoda dead. The cries of their spirits, some say, can still be heard in the wind, along with those of the wolves killed and skinned by the wolfers.

Jeremy Allan Steinke, a 23-year-old high school dropout who lived in a Medicine Hat trailer park with his mom, thought he was one with the hunted and tormented wolf. He fantasized about being a werewolf and once wrote that he was part of a "lycan brotherhood" whose empire would one day rise. On one of his personal blogs he posted: "We must meet in the cemetery one hour before the full moon is at its fullest, to speak of a tragedy within the coven! Those who have not overcome the mindless rage need not attend!"

The belief that humans can shape-shift into wild creatures exists in all major world cultures. Psychologists attribute its enduring appeal to the natural predatory instinct that resides in the human psyche. For Jeremy, the thick underbrush of Medicine Hat's treed river valley was his sinister hunting ground – or so he liked to boast to people whenever the moon was on the rise. "Better not go there," he'd say. "I might eat you."

Despite this threatening facade, Jeremy's werewolf fantasy was merely a fanciful alter ego for a boy who was mercilessly bullied in school and, according to his mother, Jacqueline May, abused by an alcoholic father and two subsequent stepfathers. Kids, even some teachers, called him "Stinky" instead of Steinke. "In grade 3, he would leave school and come home because he was teased so badly. I tried to talk to the teachers about it, but nobody wanted to listen," May says.

According to court testimony given by May, Jeremy's natural father came home drunk nearly every day, whipped him with a belt and often dragged him to his room by his ears. May split up with her husband when Jeremy was two. She got back together with him and had another child, a daughter who was four years younger than her brother. The marriage ended after seven years.

"It was not a very solid relationship," Jeremy says of his father. "I'd see him every other summer and every other Christmas."

May's second husband, now deceased, was a "weekend drinker" with three kids of his own. "If one did something wrong and wouldn't tell the truth, he'd line all five up and swat them on their hands with a paint stick until one admitted doing it," May says. When she tried to intervene, she "got yelled at, pushed."

Jeremy says his stepfather was even more brutal than his mother describes. Forcing one of the children to confess to some wrongdoing went far beyond hitting them with paint stir-sticks. "He had a tendency to abuse me and my siblings. Physical abuse, mental abuse. He'd tie us to chairs and make us watch the other children get abused."

May later testified that her third husband once pushed her son into a deep freezer, injuring the boy's head. She says he also once grabbed Jeremy by the neck and gave him "upper cuts to the face and pounded him in the back of the head" when her son tried to defend her during a domestic dispute.

Jeremy says his mother, too, abused alcohol ever since he can remember. May, whose striking, icy blue eyes sometimes appeared puffy and red rimmed, admitted that she was an alcoholic. With skin ashen on a sad face, she often seemed like a portrait of torment. Her shoulder-length red hair often looked slept on. Under this mask of lifelong abuse could be seen the shadow of the beauty that once was: the deep-set almond eyes, prominent cheekbones, and wide lips.

Despite three failed marriages, she continued to make bad choices in men. Alcohol and violence was never far from the surface in the home. Jeremy describes one case of domestic violence where, he says, he successfully stood up for Jackie: "My mom's ex-boyfriend fucking punches her, shatters her cheekbone. A foot and a half taller than me and his arms [were] like the size of my head. I chased him around with a lead pipe and I broke his arm with it, too. I hid around the corner and as he came around the corner I went 'kaboom' and I broke his arm."

Her abusive relationships with men forced the family to constantly move. "I have never been in one place for too long," says Jeremy. "I only had a few friends because I was always moving around so I was never able to make friends very frequently."

He attended grades 1 to 3 in a section of Medicine Hat called South Ridge, a residential development built in the 1970s, and grades 4 to 6 in Crestwood, a 1950s-era community located near the city's Exhibition Grounds. A former elementary schoolmate says Jeremy was volatile: "I remember being in grade 5 with him and he was always late for class. I remember the teacher, finally fed up with him coming in late every morning, confronting him about it, and telling him to set his alarm clock or get his mom to set it for him. That was all it took, and he snapped. I remember him screaming at the teacher in front of all of us, about how he didn't have an alarm clock and how his mom wouldn't buy him one. I remember being scared, he was that angry."

Rhonda, who has known him since grade 1, says Jeremy was "a nice person" in elementary school. Because he was constantly teased, she always expected that he was bound to rebel. "He had a hard time in school. I felt sorry for him."

His longtime friend TeJay Stadelman pitied Jeremy and befriended him in grade 6. "My sister used to pick on him after school. Beat him up," he remembers. As they got older, they "used to go out and party and drink. We were pretty good friends."

As a 12-year-old in grade 7, Jeremy moved with his mom to the Flats, the oldest, industrial part of town near the noisy train marshalling yards, where the thin walls of their small house offered no respite from the incessant clanging of boxcars and idling diesel engines. "It was pretty much the slums of Medicine Hat," he says.

In his early teens, he started using alcohol and marijuana. "I was dating this girl. I was close to 14 and she asked me if I smoked marijuana. I didn't want to sound like a loser so I told her that I had, and she passed me a joint and I started smoking marijuana. Through my teens I was doing ecstasy. At one point I tried acid, then mushrooms."

According to his mother, Jeremy's almost daily pot use made him easier to live with. "It didn't bother me that he was doing marijuana because it made him calm and not so hyper." Her son, she says, has always suffered from attention deficit hyperactivity disorder, or ADHD.

Around this time, Jeremy made a half-hearted effort to hang himself. "He said to me he wished he wasn't alive," says May. "He wished he was dead. He always said he wished he was never born."

He sometimes drank himself into a state of oblivion. The winter he was 15, he got so intoxicated he passed out outdoors and was hospitalized for hypothermia.

Jeremy became a "cutter," a form of self-injury that involves making superficial cuts to the skin, often practised by people suffering from depression. He usually did it alone in his room. "My arms, that's pretty much it," he says. "There's a few times when I stabbed myself in the leg. I never went to the hospital. I don't like seeing doctors. I just wrapped my arms in gauze and wore long-sleeve shirts so people wouldn't see it. I've done it sober but I've also done it high on drugs and drunk."

Cutting is an impulsive form of rebelliousness and attention seeking, and adolescents who cut are rarely attempting serious injury. "People don't usually intend to hurt themselves permanently when they cut. And they don't usually mean to keep cutting once they start. But both can happen," according to D'Arcy Lyness, a Pennsylvania child and adolescent psychologist. "Most people who cut aren't attempting suicide. Cutting is usually a person's attempt at feeling better, not ending it all. Although some people who cut do attempt suicide, it's usually because of the emotional problems and pain that lie behind their desire to self-harm, not the cutting itself."

According to Dr. Charles Goodstein, clinical associate professor of psychiatry at New York University School of Medicine, there is no uniform explanation for why people cut. "Some people say until they cut themselves, they're not sure they're alive. They feel so numb, so out of touch that somehow the slicing sort of validates them. It helps them release overwhelming tension – tension that stems from intense feelings that can't be communicated. The cutting seems to produce a release and there's almost a pleasure in that release. In many cases, cutting correlates with a history of sexual abuse. Cutting is a form of self-punishment by people afflicted by ongoing feelings of guilt who can't cope with it. Cutters learn how rapidly they can gain release and almost look forward to it. Once it becomes this, it's something that's done repeatedly – out of the view of others.

"The statistics are something like one in every 200 adolescent girls between the ages of 13 and 19 regularly cut themselves," says Dr. Goodstein. "Even though it's basically teenage girls, the disorder also affects boys. The disorder can continue through adult life."

As an adult, Jeremy posted a poem called "Eternal Scars" on a public blog:

> There are scars on my arm, they appear every other day,
> The scars on my arm, are with me to stay,
> To serve as a reminder, of the pain I receive,
> Even though the world I live in, is Hell I believe,
> That the world goes on, even after life,
> Know the question is, should I use that knife,
> To end all the pain, to stop all the rain,
> To never know, if there's something to gain,
> Can I set myself free, of all this misery,
> Or shall I remain, drowning in pain,
> No matter which path I choose, Eternal Scars remain!

In grade 10, Jeremy was placed in a course of study for students with learning difficulties, known as the Integrated Occupational Program, or IOP, which the academic students referred to as "Idiots on Patrol." Jeremy studied woodworking and mechanics and joined the Medicine Hat High School Mohawks football team. About five-foot-seven with a medium build, he was not a standout. Nobody gets cut from the team; they either make the starting lineup, play on a secondary squad, or quit. The latter is what became of Jeremy Steinke's ignominious football career, as far as anyone can remember.

Jeremy, who wore No. 43, played corner back and wide receiver. He worked hard during football drills and practices. But in the locker room he was bothersome to other players. Former teammate Spencer Schutte says Jeremy was always obstreperous and trying to pick fights, but the only response he got was ridicule from the other players.

"There's people that are teased in high school and there are people who are asked to be teased because it's an attention getter," says Schutte. "He loved it. He fuelled off it. When we played football he would try to get hit and try to be big and tough but he never really was. He was a pretty small kid. He wanted to cause trouble." He had a reputation as "a runt" who started fights he couldn't finish and would come running to adults for protection, one neighbour says.

Jeremy dropped out three months into grade 10. "I couldn't concentrate in school and my mother was ill. I wanted to help my mom," he explains. Jackie May had been diagnosed with idiopathic pulmonary fibrosis, a scarring of the lungs. Its cause is a medical mystery. She qualified for a provincial medical benefit that paid about $850 a month.

At 16, Jeremy moved in with his natural father, who had taken up residence in Saskatchewan. He followed in his dad's footsteps and went to work in a dusty underground potash mine. After a dispute with his stepmother, he came back to Medicine Hat, moved in with a series of friends in low-rent apartments, and worked at low-paying jobs that he hated – delivering pizza, working at a grocery, a hardware and a sporting goods store, and picking up day jobs from a youth employment agency.

Jeremy eventually made efforts to improve himself, enrolling at Medicine Hat College in 2004 for high school upgrading. He dropped out at Christmas. "I had come back after Christmas holidays to hear the news that my great-grandparents had passed away," he would later say, his voice quavering with emotion at the memory of the only members of his family outside his mom and sister that he felt close to.

In the spring of 2005, Jackie May moved into a mobile home handed down to her by her father at Tower Estates, a trailer park on the edge of town by the airport. Jeremy moved in with his hard-drinking mother. It was a respite from paying rent, but the trailer was cold in winter, utility bills were high, and the water pipes sometimes froze.

The lofty title of Tower Estates belies the unremarkable reality of the mobile home subdivision, where in 2006 the property valuations ranged from $59,000 to $139,000, depending on condition. On the street where Jeremy lived, somebody painted *South Park* cartoon characters on a wooden garbage bin in a quirky beautification effort. Many of the 1970s-era mobile homes were remarkably tidy and well kept, with renovated interiors and land-scaped exteriors lovingly tended to by retirees with pride of ownership. But May's trailer was in its original unimproved condition, with vertical vinyl siding and an attached wooden porch. On a weathered back deck was a col-lection of well-used furnishings – a refrigerator, a stuffed couch, a workout bench, several plastic storage containers, a barbecue, a plastic outdoor chair, a metal-and-vinyl kitchen chair, and other pieces of broken furniture that were arranged haphazardly for use. On the lawn, a stack of paving stones was piled up as part of an unfinished patio project. The backyard was surrounded by a tall wooden fence with no back gate, giving it a fortress-like feel.

Despite its neglected exterior, May did her best to make the inside of the trailer as homey as possible. A cozy couch was lined with pillows and blankets. There was a large-screen TV in the corner. Feminine touches included plants and framed family photographs. Dollar-store treasures lined nearly every surface.

The struggling single mom was especially proud of the portraits of her children that hung on the wall. One showed Jeremy from his high school yearbook as an angelic 16-year-old in grade 10; another showed him even younger, with spiky gelled hair. In her daughter's photo, the pretty girl is elegantly dressed in a formal gown, with beautiful blonde hair.

By her own admission, May admits she could have been a better mother. As she tells the story, she was born into a household of abuse, suffering physical and emotional trauma as early as age four. She moved to Medicine Hat from the family farm in Saskatchewan at age 15 to attend hairdressing school. By her mid-teens, she was living with older men. After her three failed relationships, she embarked on a pattern of destructive, casual relationships with abusive men, many of whom regularly spent the night at the trailer in Tower Estates.

In 2005, she was charged with stabbing Wilfred Yates, her occasional boyfriend. She received a conditional discharge and was sentenced to 12 months probation, which she breached by repeatedly disobeying a no-contact order to stay away from Yates. She was taking counselling to put her life in order so she could focus on her two adult children. According to court documents, her treatment plan "was not going to be successful if she continued to see Yates and didn't try to stop consuming alcohol with prescribed medications."

Jeremy's relationships with women also followed a path of failure. At the age of 20, he dated a 17-year-old girl who says he fathered her child. May disputes this, claiming a paternity test was demanded but never delivered. The teenager was with Jeremy for a little more than a year but couldn't cope with what she says was his Jekyll-and-Hyde personality. "I probably only know 10 percent of him. He can change in a blink of an eye," she says, recalling Jeremy's quick temper and odd behaviour. "He'd sit up in the middle of the night and start talking to himself." Jeremy, she says, could be charming and eager to please – pliable, always agreeing to whatever his friends suggested. Despite rarely working, "he always had 10 or 20 dollars in his pocket. He'd buy gifts and spend every penny he has and try to get close to [a girl's] parents. He was fun. He always wanted to do what you wanted."

After their breakup, Jeremy's ex-girlfriend noticed that his girlfriends were getting younger and younger. Schutte, his former football teammate, says, "I remember him in high school and he was always with quite young girls. He was in grade 11 and going out with grade 9 girls. He was extremely immature. Girls go out with older guys because they're more mature. Not him."

Jeremy worked briefly at the local Tim Hortons doughnut shop, did some roofing, and tried earning various tradesman tickets to work in the oil fields. But, for the most part, he couldn't hold a job. He spent his days drinking, smoking pot, playing electric guitar and writing brooding poetry and lyrics to songs he never finished. "About the age of 20 is when I had my first bump of cocaine," he says.

His small, dishevelled room in his mother's single-wide trailer was lined with rock posters, including one from the American heavy metal band Tool depicting a wrench in the shape of an erect penis. In the corner by a small desk he kept a triple-pickup Fender Stratocaster guitar. A Union Jack was tacked to the ceiling and a flashing amber warning light stolen from a roadway construction project sat on the floor. A pair of dog tags dangled from a wall hook and model cars sat on a desk, where a ball cap rested on a lampshade.

In the cramped living room of the trailer, among the well-intentioned bric-a-brac, was a painted portrait of a baying wolf.

Police officers in town knew Jeremy on sight. He had frequent brushes with the law, but his offences, which included shoplifting from a grocery store, bouncing cheques, and causing a disturbance, were never serious enough to warrant jail time. On the latter charge, Jeremy misled the judge by saying that he was dealing with a divorce and that his bills were piling up. The tactic worked. The judge went easy and granted him an extension to pay the fee.

In the summer of 2005, at the age of 22, Jeremy started to "go goth," according to close friend Grant Bolt, an unemployed pot smoker who took antidepressants to control suicidal thoughts. Grant, small in stature with buggy eyes and a trim beard, had known Jeremy since both were 11. When they got older, they "used to just drive around and smoke weed, go to the mall." He and Jeremy were like brothers. "We had everything in common – music, movies. He just seemed like a good guy. Before he started getting goth-like, we used to hang out all the time. I don't know what happened. He was a lot more aggressive."

Jeremy says he and Grant had both dabbled in the goth lifestyle when they were in their early teens: "Originally, myself and Grant had got into goth around age 13 or 14. We started getting harassed. We were the only two goths in Medicine Hat at the time. Because we were being harassed we decided to put that in the closet."

But that had now changed. Goth culture was more prevalent in the conservative prairie city in 2005, and Jeremy was keen to join. "I realized that the goth culture had become a lot bigger than it used to be and I started associating myself with them and going back to being gothic. I had the same personality. I just changed my appearance" – black jeans, dark T-shirts, leather overcoats. He usually wore his hair spiked. "Sometimes I'd have a shaved head." Jeremy also began wearing eyeliner; "Eye paint or some shit, freaky-deaky," says Cam Barkley, a hard-drinker and cocaine user who knew Jeremy briefly. The black eyeliner made his arresting, translucent grey-blue eyes stand out. The effect was ghostly.

"He started getting into heavy metal-style music, wearing goth makeup, trying to become some crazy guy he wasn't," Grant Bolt recalls. "He wanted a new crowd and they accepted him."

Jeremy started listening to extreme heavy metal bands like Children of Bodom. The band's name is derived from an infamous multiple homicide that took place in Finland in 1960 at Lake Bodom near Espoo, about 22 kilometres west of Helsinki. On the night of June 4, 1960, four teenagers were camping on the shores of the lake when three of them were stabbed to death. Nils Wilhelm Gustafsson, wounded by "a blunt instrument," was the sole survivor. He led a normal life for 44 years, until he became a suspect in the murders in 2004. In October 2005, a district court found Gustafsson not guilty.

Jeremy also liked Slipknot, a nine-member shock-rock band from Des Moines, Iowa, that performs with grotesque theatrical masks and writes songs like "Bomb the Trendies" that are filled with rage, anger, and disdain for "preppies" who slavishly follow the latest fashions and pop culture: "Bomb the fucking trendies – bandwagon jumping/In my eyes they're ripe for a thumping!" In another song, "My Plague," the band angrily writes: "I'll reach in and take a bite out of that shit you call a heart."

Slipknot won a Grammy Award in 2003 for best heavy metal performance for *Vol. 3: The Subliminal Verses*, one of the group's few albums not to feature profanity. Unlike Slipknot's other recordings, it did not carry a parental advisory label. A special edition of the album did carry a parental warning, however, due to songs like "People = Shit" that were recorded live and uncensored.

Jeremy's other favourite band was Cradle of Filth, a symphonic, goth metal band from Suffolk, England, that may have piqued his interest in lycanthropy. One of the more sophisticated of their genre, the band plays music laden with themes heavily influenced by gothic literature, mythology, and horror films, and by lycanthropy and vampirism.

In the song "A Crescendo of Passion Bleeding" from its 1994 album, *The Principle of Evil Made Flesh*, Cradle of Filth writes:

> *Even the moon will not lend thee her light*
> *The darkness serves will to snuff out human life*
> *That I might reclaim the world as my right.*
> *I kill without scruple or silent regret, in haunts of the sinister*
> *   lunar aspect*
> *For I am the pleasure that comes from your pain,*
> *Tiny red miracles falling like rain.*

In 1998, Cradle of Filth put out *Cruelty and the Beast*, a concept album based on the legend of the Hungarian "blood countess" Elizabeth Báthory (1560–1614), an infamous Transylvanian serial killer who allegedly slaughtered over 600 young maidens so that she could bathe in their blood. Ten years later, in the 2009 album *Godspeed on the Devil's Thunder*, Cradle of Filth would unearth another medieval serial killer, a French nobleman named Gilles de Rais, who was executed in 1440 for sorcery and the murder and sexual abuse of countless children.

One song from *Cruelty and the Beast* is titled "Beneath the Howling Stars":

> *Soon in full moon fever they were wed*
> *Lycanthropic in the conjugal bed*
> *Littered with aphrodisiacs to tease dynastic union*
> *And beget them further maniacs*

The song "Lustmord and Wargasm (The Lick of Carnivorous Winds)," also from *Cruelty and the Beast*, hints at a lycan empire:

> *From temptation's peak we will see the world unfurled at last*
> *Now the wolves of time who stalk Mankind shall be as one in*
>   *grim repast*
> *Commemorating sickle moons, the pack are poised to reap*
> *A scythe of white roses in bloom whose twisted thorns will keep.*

The band's lyrics appealed to Jeremy, who emulated that style of music and attempted to write his own death-metal lyrics. Werewolves, he thought, sounded cool, a perfect fit to his goth persona. He and several of his friends embraced lycan mythology, which was creeping into popular culture with the 2003 and 2006 *Underworld* movie series, pitting vampires against werewolves in an immortal battle for supremacy.

"Lycanthropy" comes from the Greek words *lykos*, or wolf, and *anthropos*, or man. "Lycanthropy, a psychosis in which the patient has delusions of being a wild animal (usually a wolf), has been recorded since antiquity," according to psychiatrists Harvey Rostenstock and Kenneth R. Vincent:

> The Book of Daniel describes King Nebuchadnezzar as suffering from depression that deteriorated over a seven-year period into a frank psychosis at which time he imagined himself a wolf. Among the first medical descriptions were those of Paulus Aegineta during the later days of the Roman Empire. In his description of the symptom complex, Aegineta made reference to Greek mythology in which Zeus turned King Lycaon of Arcadia into a raging wolf. Thereafter, references to lycanthropy appeared in the ancient literature. Many medieval theologians envisioned lycanthropy as a consequence of the evil eye.

Rostenstock and Vincent detailed a case of lycanthropy involving a 49-year-old married woman who had delusions of being a wolf and "feeling like an animal with claws." Throughout her 20-year marriage she experienced compulsive urges toward bestiality, lesbianism, and adultery:

> The patient chronically ruminated and dreamed about wolves. One week before her admission, she acted on these ruminations for the first time. At a family gathering, she disrobed, assumed the female sexual posture of a wolf, and offered herself to her mother. This episode lasted for approximately 20 minutes. The following night, after coitus with her husband, the patient suffered a two-hour episode, during which time she growled, scratched, and gnawed at the bed. She stated that the devil came into her body and she became an animal. Simultaneously, she experienced

auditory hallucinations. There was no drug involvement or alcoholic intoxication.

Clinical lycanthropy is a rare phenomenon usually associated with schizophrenia. Jeremy's claims of being a werewolf were never so severe as to require clinical care. They were simply part of his invented, attention-seeking Internet persona and probably sprang from his interest in industrial and death-metal music. He once posted a poem on a website containing lines that reflected his werewolf fantasies: "You're the light when it's dark, you're the moon when I bark."

Werewolves, vampires, and the goth lifestyle suited Jeremy. They were the perfect outlet for an unemployed, bullied high school dropout, and he was quickly embraced by the crowd of younger Medicine Hat Mall goths, who looked up to him. "A lot of people turn to the gothic sub-culture after having a hard time in school, feeling alienated, and looking for a way to express themselves that mirrors those feelings," according to Toronto goths Matt Ardill and Siani Evans, who once wrote an op-ed for the *Toronto Star* titled "Relax, it's just black."

In the goth world, societal misfits often seek, and sometimes find, respect and understanding – a theme prevalent in pop culture depictions of goth society. In *Edward Scissorhands*, a metaphorical 1990 movie about goth culture by filmmaker Tim Burton, the gentle, misunderstood lead character (played by Johnny Depp) is a boy with scissors for hands who wants nothing more than to be accepted by a judgmental world. *Ginger Snaps*, a Canadian movie directed by John Fawcett and released in 2000, depicts a pair of goth outcasts who are despised by classmates in their suburban high school. Ginger and her sister Brigitte likewise disdain everyone and everything in their dull town – much like many members of the younger goth community in Medicine Hat.

The city's goth crowd soaked up anything to do with goth pop culture, like the movies *Underworld* and *The Crow*, starring 28-year-old actor Brandon Lee as a rock musician who comes back from the dead to avenge his own murder. Lee was killed during the final weeks of filming when a dummy bullet, which had become lodged in one of the guns, fired into his abdomen, elevating him to mythical status in goth circles.

"Most goths become goths because they have been spurned by 'normal' society," according to Goth.net, one of about 650 sites listed on the Gothic Web Ring, an Internet compendium of websites dedicated to goth lifestyles. "Because of this rejection from 'normal' society, goths have banded together to associate with other free thinkers. This has a beneficial effect on both the individual and society as a whole. For the individual they have a sense of belonging, and friends they can associate with. For society it removes one more misfit filled with rage from society's streets."

Despite its sometimes threatening facade, goth culture tends to be non-violent, pacifist, and tolerant. Police statistics presented at the National Youth Gang Symposium in Orlando, Florida, in June 2002 indicate that, as a general rule, goths are less likely to be involved in violent crime than the general population. "Basically most goths turn angst into a lifestyle," one of the presenters at the symposium said.

Jeremy, though, had an aggressiveness that could not be tamed by the normal strictures of the goth lifestyle. He wouldn't even be considered a "true goth" by those deeply enmeshed in the subculture. Jeremy and others like him are regarded as simply angry poseurs who "go goth" for shock value, a trend that offends goths like 24-year-old Sarah Manley, who managed a Medicine Hat record store. "I would not consider some of these kids to be real goths," Manley says. "Goth is a lifestyle, not something to do for a few months to make your parents mad. A lot of them don't even know what goth is all about. The community, in general, is non-violent. It's about being yourself and being your own person. I have an alternative lifestyle and I have lived my life like this and I think I am a stronger person for it."

Manley was assaulted because of her appearance in the wake of the Columbine school killings in 1999, where 12 students were killed by two trenchcoat-wearing boys wrongly portrayed by the media as belonging to the goth subculture. "It is an easy subculture to target," she says. "When Columbine happened, I was in high school. High school is not a very easy place to be anyway, and that made it all the more difficult. There was a lot of, I would say, persecution. I was beaten up. It was not a fun time."

Goth plays into middle-class fears of cults and vampire-obsessed kids preoccupied by death and killing, but true goth culture is not about that, says Manley. "Sure, there are people who think like that, but they're losers. Just because you listen to a certain band doesn't mean you are going to go out and kill your friends, no more than you can say all blondes are dumb or all blacks have a certain culture."

Chelsea, an Alberta goth, is typical of many who cringed at media stereotypes about the goth community that were reported in the wake of the Columbine killings. "Most people who become goths endured some form of abuse growing up," she says. "Being goth makes people feel like they can be beautiful in their own way, outside of mainstream society's measurements. Most are respectful and happy people now because they can be who they want without being judged. There are exceptions but that is the same with any subculture. Most goths I know have very benevolent beliefs such as Buddhism."

Jeremy's re-emergence into the goth scene in 2005 occurred at a time when he was searching for acceptance. His relationships had failed, he was living in his mom's trailer, and he was becoming estranged from people his own age: "Me and my friends were kind of drifting apart a little bit. A lot of distance between us." The goth community had few age barriers, which appealed to him: "I've never been able to hang out with my own age people because of the harassment I received through school. In school is when I started hanging out with kids younger than myself." The younger goths adored the hyper Jeremy. With a green 1981 Firebird that he drove despite being unable to afford the insurance, Jeremy had status.

Jeremy's desire to hang out with younger people is common among those with fetal alcohol spectrum disorder (FASD), whose developmental problems often include stunted growth and lower mental and emotional capacities than others in their age group. "They have an overwhelming desire to have friends but, due to their social immaturity and ineptness, are often rejected by their peers," according to experts Julianne Conry and Diane K. Fast. Jeremy was seen as fun-loving and gregarious to the younger goth crowd that hung out at the mall. Many described him as hyperactive, another classic indicator of FASD disabilities.

Hyperactivity is one of the main conditions in attention deficit hyperactivity disorder (ADHD), the term Jackie May uses to describe her son. The condition afflicts about 60 percent of FASD suffers, according to Conroy and Fast: "People with FAS/FAE [fetal alcohol effects] and attention deficit hyperactivity disorder are impulsive and can put themselves into dangerous situations without thinking of the consequences."

May denies using alcohol while pregnant with Jeremy but admits to taking codeine and Demerol, which she says were administered to her in hospital for a tumour on her ovary. "I did not drink with my kids. I was pumped full of Demerol and codeine for the first four months [of Jeremy's pregnancy]." Jeremy was never proven to have FASD; a confirmed diagnosis requires the mother's admission of alcohol use.

With their black hoodies, dark eyeliner, skin piercings and white face makeup, the young goths revelled in the shock value of their appearance and spent most of their free time "doing nothing and going nowhere," according to Morgan, a 14-year-old who also hung out with Jeremy. "Everyone else kicked you out or rejected you. It makes you better friends." Jeremy, she says, was "sweet, caring, loud, and funny." According to Raven: "Everybody thinks we are crazy and deranged, but it's just a look. Inside we are just like everyone else." Jeremy, says Raven, was not "true goth" in his dress or lifestyle. "He wasn't into the look like I am. He wasn't as hardcore as a lot of us."

Jeremy also fancied himself a swashbuckler. He fantasized about being Captain Jack Sparrow after seeing the movie *Pirates of the Caribbean*. Actor Johnny Depp's pirate character – modelled after Rolling Stone Keith Richards, with head scarves, jewellery, kohl eye makeup, and a charmingly wasted drunkenness – was rock star cool. "Jeremy said he wanted to be a pirate because it looked like it would be fun," one friend says.

Morgan says Jeremy "would do anything if it meant someone would love him." She describes him as "one of the most loyal, caring people I know. He's the friend who'll get up at unearthly hours of the night and drive all the way across town just to give you a hug if you are upset and need one. He'll go the extra mile to cheer you up or make you smile."

Sweetness is a term used by many of the girls who knew him. "I remember meeting him when I was 13 or 14," says one former classmate. As an underage teen, she often mooched smokes from Jeremy. "He was a sweet guy, that's why I felt bad for using him. He was by no means popular back then. He gave me the impression that all he wanted was to fit in, and he tried hard to achieve it, but it only made it worse for him. Everyone called him Jeremy Stinky, so I think he was picked on a lot. From what I gathered he was hanging out with the 'loser' crowd and was into drugs such as pot." Kids can be cruel, and she admits she was no different when it came to teasing Jeremy: "In my personal opinion, knowing how kids were at the time, including myself, he had a rough social life."

In the goth community, Jeremy was described as polite, fun, and caring. And it was here that he found acceptance. In the goth world, the kid from the trailer park by the airport escaped the teasing and torment that had dogged him all his life. Since many of his goth friends were underage, and he could buy alcohol and had wheels, he had authority and respect. Jeremy, the swashbuckling "Captain Jack," was put on a pedestal.

As he delved more deeply into the goth lifestyle in the fall of 2005, or at least his interpretation of it, Jeremy's appearance grew more threatening. In addition to what Cam Barkley described as Jeremy's "freaky-deaky" eye paint, the lycan-pirate and aspiring heavy metal musician often sported a black neoprene cold-weather mask. It covered the lower half of his face and his nose, and when worn in combination with his black hoodie revealed only a pair of eyes made demonic-looking by the black eyeliner he wore.

His neoprene mask wouldn't have garnered a second glance in Medicine Hat's sub-zero winters, but when the police spotted him on a temperate fall day looking like a cross between Michael Jackson and a cat burglar, they took a closer look. There being no law against dressing weird, they let him go. But when Jeremy walked into the Medicine Hat Mall dressed as if he could be on his way to a bank holdup, security demanded ID and asked him to leave. He came back, partially hiding his face with a bandana, with the same result. Jeremy was known to regularly mouth off to mall security, and he and his crowd were a steady source of trouble for mall staff.

Despite the adoration of his new goth crowd, Jeremy was looking for something more meaningful. The attention he got for his fierce look and loyalty to friends was not enough. He wanted something deeper, according to the poetry he was writing at the time:

> I live inside an Ice Empire, where my heart is cold & sheltered.
> I wish I could find a queen, who I can trust to melt it,
> Who can light my way, through the darkness of day,
> And save this kingdom from falling!

The queen who would melt his ice empire would be 12-year-old JR, who lived across town on a tidy, suburban street in the middle-class neighbourhood of Ross Glen.

4

TIL DEATH DO WE PART

"I believe in blood . . ."

In a mostly working-class city dominated by pickup-driving oil field workers, ranchers, cowboys, and soldiers from the nearby Canadian Forces Base at Suffield, JR's goblin-like crew of gender-bending mall kids – boys with ghost-white faces, black eyeliner, and black lipstick, and girls with studded collars, chains, and bulky, black hoodies with the logos of death-metal rock bands – were a radical departure from the norm.

As they floated between the food court, record shop, and arcade at the Medicine Hat Mall, this unruly collection of the "undead" easily stood out among the senior citizens who gathered for coffee and cinnamon buns and the young mothers pushing baby strollers with toddlers in tow.

Like shopping centres everywhere, the mall was a giant teenage club-house where suburban kids escaped the ennui of their middle-class lives by mingling freely with troubled, rebellious kids from the wrong side of the tracks whose lives seemed much more exciting. In a town where they felt there was nothing to do, the mall offered a sense of adventure, a place where goth met the Gap in a crossroads of conflicting lifestyles.

The mall's food court, just inside the main doors, took on the role of unofficial goth headquarters. The subculture had about 30 regulars, from baby goths like JR to older people like Raven who were committed to the scene.

"The mall was a meeting place where everyone would always be able to find at least one person of our group," says 14-year-old Morgan. "We'd hang out to talk, plan parties or whatever, smoke, drink occasionally." Some kids, she says, stole for fun. "They would steal stuff and then compare the amount or size of what they've stolen." They often got banned from the premises.

There were actually two groups of teen goths, she says – those who met at the mall regularly and another group that met downtown. "We came to know our different sides as Mall Rats and Downtown Kids. I was a downtown kid, never liking the amount of security always present at the mall. I think we were mainly just a big pain to the people trying to keep the mall safe. Oh, and, of course, there were sometimes fights."

It was here, just minutes away from her parents' suburban home, where JR, a quiet, studious Catholic schoolgirl, had begun spending an increasing amount of time in the summer and fall of 2005. In the virtual anonymity of the Internet, today's teens can pretend to be anyone, as JR did with her Nexopia and VampireFreaks profiles. But the mall was a real-life proving ground where teens could test-drive their new identities, and JR was eager to take her new personality out for a spin.

Her circle of friends was growing. One of those she knew in the mall crowd was Kaylee, a toughened 13-year-old with coloured streaks in her black hair who was a chronic runaway and, like Jeremy, a cutter. Friends describe Kaylee as "wild."

"She did whatever she wanted," says one envious friend. On one social networking website, Kaylee wrote: "I'm a very easy-going person, not difficult to get along with at all. Just don't piss me off or I'll probably find ways to fuck your shit up. I live for my friends, they are the best part of my life." She tersely ended with: "That's all I feel the need to share with you at the moment."

Kaylee and JR were schoolmates who grew closer that fall. Kaylee would quit school in January 2006, but she and JR still kept in touch by telephone and at the mall.

It was Kaylee who had introduced JR to Jeremy, shortly after JR's twelfth birthday. While wandering around the mall one day, Kaylee saw one of her new friends, an adult she knew to be about 22 years old. He had short-cropped blond hair and wore black pants and a black hoodie. His pale blue eyes were rimmed with black eyeliner, his ears were pierced, and he wore jewellery with a skull motif.

"Jeremy!" Kaylee ran up to him and threw her arms around his neck.

Smiling and happy, Jeremy returned the embrace.

"These are my friends," Kaylee said, introducing a few seventh graders, among them two 13-year-old girls, before turning to JR, presenting her last.

JR was impressed with Jeremy. He was popular and had a presence about him. "I thought he was good looking," JR says. "A lot of people thought he was." The group hovered around the food court, drifting into the arcade, some splitting outside to smoke on the benches, and meeting up again inside to cruise around the mall. "We just hung out for the day," JR says. "I wanted to be friends with him. He was really hyper, and the centre of attention. People loved him."

It may have been the first day they learned each other's names, but it wasn't the first time JR and Jeremy had had an encounter. On an earlier occasion, JR and a friend had been in the backseat of his Firebird. There were no formal introductions. He wildly spun doughnuts in the mall parking lot as the girls shrieked in delight. "It was a cool car," JR recalls.

Jeremy says he wasn't interested in JR when he first met her because he thought she was dating Trenchcoat, who was one of his friends. "He was about 20 or 21. I didn't know her true age at the time," he recalls.

In December 2005, JR and Jeremy began casually seeing each other. "I started going to these punk shows and we started hanging out," says Jeremy.

The two soon discovered they had something in common. JR was fighting with her parents over her association with older guys like Raven and Trenchcoat. Jeremy, too, was having relationship troubles of his own. He told JR he was engaged to a girl named Danielle and that the two were drifting apart. "He told me she hadn't talked to him in a while," JR says. They began commiserating over issues of trust in their troubled relationships. "He was really upset. I was worried about him."

By Christmas break, the rebellious 12-year-old was getting into more arguments with her parents about her male friends from the mall. Marc and Debra disapproved of older guys calling the house for their pubescent daughter, but JR and her friends were clever – they outsmarted her parents by passing the phone to the older boys only after one of the girls had spoken to Marc or Debra. "We'd just get somebody else to call her and ask for her," says one friend.

Against her parents' disapproval, JR was also going to all-ages rock shows featuring punk bands at local community halls. "There were punk shows pretty much every weekend. All the alternative crowd would go," she says. Like every generation before her, from that of James Dean in the '50s, to the Beatles in the '60s and Marilyn Manson in the late '90s, JR was an angst-ridden preteen testing the boundaries of young adulthood.

Judith saw a marked contrast in JR when her friend Debra mailed her a family photo taken that Christmas. Taken aback by the sudden change in JR, Judith called from her home in Calgary, asking, "What's happened to your little girl?" Debra laughed. "Yeah, it depicts everybody perfectly, doesn't it?" she groaned lightheartedly.

In the picture, Marc was watching TV, Jacob was wearing a *Star Wars* costume, and Debra had her usual wide grin. Then there was JR. "She's standing there and she's totally 'gothed' out," says Judith. "She's got a black

T-shirt, big black eyeliner, and a collar. She is dead stone-face as she's looking off to the side."

Nathalie Pepin remembers Debra coming to the entrepreneurs' class one day with something weighing on her mind. "She'd had a rough night, problems with her daughter." Debra often shared stories about home life, and of JR's growing rebelliousness. She carried a photograph of JR in her wallet that she often showed to people, saying that her daughter had a "pretty" picture and a "goth" one. Pepin could see for herself: "She not only had the attitude, she had the looks."

"Teenagers, *sigh*," Debra said to Nathalie. "She's 12 going on 20."

Debra was discovering what studies had already shown, that adolescence is the only time in life when people feel older than their age. According to research published in the June 2007 *Journal of Adolescence*, the only decade where people identify with their real age is their twenties. After age 30, the average person feels younger than his or her chronological age. But adolescents have a misplaced sense of maturity that may lead to risky behaviours such as "sexual experience, smoking, alcohol and drug use," says Kelly Arbeau, a University of Alberta researcher and co-author of the study.

Sandra Richard, JR's school guidance counsellor, became more concerned about JR's dress and demeanour. One day, JR came into her office to talk about difficulties she was having at home.

"She was very upset. She wanted to change things. She seemed so adamant. She wanted to be out of the house," Richard says.

With her experience, Richard began probing JR for deeper, perhaps darker, details, but was cautious with her questions, not wanting to put words in JR's mouth. "Why? Is anything else going on?" she asked.

"These rules are too much," JR said.

Richard told her that curfews and the like were not unreasonable for someone her age.

"I hate it there. I hate it there," JR said.

JR told Richard she wanted to go into foster care. As the school counsellor prodded for information, it became obvious to her that JR was not being physically mistreated or abused. "If there had been concern for her safety, I would have started making phone calls."

JR, as it turned out, was simply mad at her parents. "She had no control in what she wanted to do," says Richard. She told JR that foster care was not an option for girls who were simply upset with their parents over things like dating.

One day, JR came into the school office looking for a bandage. Richard noticed a pentagram on JR's hand. To Richard, it was offensive to see a symbol associated with paganism and Satanism at a Catholic school.

"It's not, it's something else," said JR. To her, the pentagram was simply the benign symbol of Wicca, the loosely formed system of nature worship that had piqued her interest.

JR told Richard that she got the pentagram design on her hand from a book at home and that her mother knew about it. "Because we are a Catholic school, I ask you to wash it off out of respect for the school and for me," Richard told her. According to Richard, JR said she'd get the book and bring it to school, but she never did. Wicca's lack of formal structure would have held special appeal for JR, who was seeking similar freedom from what she saw as her parents' rigid rules.

"In Wicca there is no scripture, no dogma," explains Detective Constable Charles Ennis, a Vancouver, British Columbia police dispatcher who is known in the pagan and Wiccan community as Kerr Cuhulain, Grand Master of the Order of Scathach. One of the first police officers to go public, 28 years ago, about his Wiccan beliefs, he is the author of *Law Enforcement Guide to Wicca* and has testified as an expert at trials including the so-called Robin Hood Hill murders in West Memphis, Arkansas in 1993, where one of the accused, a teenager, called himself a witch.

According to Ennis, an October 2008 survey by the Covenant of the Goddess, an international organization of Wiccan congregations, determined that 11 percent of Wiccans were under the age of 17. "Wicca is about empowering yourself, and if you feel powerless it has a natural attraction," he says. Wiccans, Ennis notes, embrace a non-violent creed, known as the Wiccan Rede, which says, in part:

> Bide within the law you must, in perfect love and perfect
>   trust.
> Live you must and let to live, fairly take and fairly give . . .
> Honor the Old Ones in deed and name,
> Let love and light be our guides again.

"Some of our detractors have interpreted this to mean 'Do whatever feels good,' but this is incorrect," Ennis, as Kerr Cuhulain, writes in his book. "The Wiccan Rede is a serious responsibility, as it calls upon the Wicca to examine each and every one of their actions to determine their implications to others. . . . It calls for a high level of self discipline from every Wicca. . . . The Wiccan Rede requires Wiccans to use their heads instead of someone else's list of rules. It requires us to take responsibility for our actions."

While some goths are involved in Wicca, that's the exception rather than the rule, according to Ennis.

Wiccans often refer to their faith as "The Craft" or the "Old Religion," but Jeremy did not see Wicca with the same depth that JR did. He referred to her bluntly as a witch. "She practises all that witchcraft," he would say later. "She's all spiritual and shit."

Feeling misunderstood at school, JR began to seek solace from Jeremy, who was on the rebound. With his relationship with Danielle on the rocks, and with JR split from Devon, the two began hanging out platonically at punk shows and at the mall. "I seen her off and on through about January and then I started seeing her more often," Jeremy says.

In early February 2006, Jeremy told JR that he was no longer engaged to Danielle. He posted online a melancholy poem in response to the breakup that said: "My love left me hanging by a rope."

Jeremy wrote to Grant Bolt about Danielle some weeks later, saying: "Hey man, how's you doin? I wish I could kill Danielle that stupid bitch. God, she's so totally Emo!" He also wrote about the breakup in an exchange of e-mail messages with a friend named Sheliah, who had the online username Morbid Flames. He told her that he and Danielle were squabbling over possessions and arguing because she insisted that Jeremy deliver her things to her. "RAWR I'm so mad at her . . . she was too stubborn to come over," he wrote to Sheliah. "I'm very pissed off now cuz of women's bullshit!" Jeremy, JR, and their friends often wrote the phrase "rawr," mimicking a lion's roar, when they were angry, changing it to RAWR when they even more upset.

In February, around Valentine's Day, Jeremy sent JR an e-mail asking her to be his girlfriend. What he wrote pleased her. "Jeremy gave me this really sweet poem. It was about me. I was flattered," she said later. "A few days later, he asked me out on the phone." Their first date would be at an all-ages punk show at a community hall. "I liked him. He was really sweet and attentive. I really liked him."

JR knew Jeremy was older but was unsure of his age. She went to the punk show with her girlfriends to meet Jeremy, who was standing across the room. Still only 12 and worried that he might think she was just a kid, JR sent one of her friends to ask Jeremy whether he knew her age. Because most of her friends were already 13, she asked her friend to tell Jeremy she was 13, too – at least according to her memory of the event. Jeremy claims he assumed she was much older: "I was under the impression she was 16."

After speaking to JR's emissary at the punk show, Jeremy walked over to JR. He wanted to know her answer to being his girlfriend. "So, what's the verdict?"

JR said yes.

Because she knew her parents would disapprove – they already were not pleased about 16-year-old Devon and the older Raven and Trenchcoat – JR decided it would be best to keep her relationship with

Jeremy a secret. She would deepen her relationship with him through surreptitious late-night phone calls and Internet messages. Because JR's bedroom was down the hall from her parents' room, she would either sneak the cordless phone into her room to talk softly to Jeremy, or go down to the basement, where she couldn't be easily overheard. "We were talking on the phone almost every day," she says.

She once dared to invite Jeremy and one of his friends to her house when she knew her parents would be out for a few hours. Even though Aubrey didn't care for Jeremy, she came over, too. "We listened to music, watched a DVD on a heavy metal band," says Jeremy.

Occasionally, Jeremy picked up JR, Kaylee, and her other friends at school or at the mall and brought them over to his mother's trailer to hang out. Although across town, it took less than 10 minutes to drive from the mall in his mother's grey 1987 Dodge Dakota pickup truck, which Jeremy was forced to use because he could no longer afford the lapsed insurance and repairs to his Firebird. Occasionally Jeremy would pick up JR near her house, always meeting her at a school bus stop down the street from her parents' house. He never phoned her, communicating instead by e-mail and on Nexopia. Jeremy had a computer, but no Internet connection at home, so he sent e-mails though the free computers available at the public library or at a youth employment centre. JR loved the attention of the older Jeremy. Even though their relationship was platonic, sneaking out with him to go to the mall or to his mother's trailer was a thrill.

Tensions at JR's home were increasing over her association with older guys and with her growing irresponsibility. One night, when her parents left her to babysit Jacob, JR and Aubrey took off to the nearby 7-Eleven. When Jacob realized the girls had left him alone in the empty house, he became frightened and called Debra's cellphone. "My brother was scared and upset," JR admits.

Debra got the call while attending a company event with Marc.

"EnCana had a Valentine's get-together in Medicine Hat and you could bring your honey, and my wife and I sat with Marc and Deb," recalls

Marc's co-worker Wayne Chopek. "She got a call on her cellphone and you could see there was some concern in her voice. When Deb got off the phone, she talked to Marc and they'd have a little discussion and Marc would be raising a few eyebrows. They got back into the conversation and the phone would ring again. They probably would have stayed longer but they did take off early."

JR's parents grounded her indefinitely for leaving her brother alone. It was, as JR defined it, the breaking point: "I couldn't take them anymore."

Chopek also says JR appeared irritated with Jacob at an EnCana family open house at the gas plant. He took it as nothing more than a typical pubescent girl's frustration with a little brother. "We actually rode in the van with them that the company had rented. Jacob was always being subdued by Marc because he was a very active child. Marc would say 'Okay, Jacob, settle down, we'll be out there soon,' because it was a 45-minute drive to the plant. The children were told once they get out of the van to stay by the adults because it's a gas storage facility and there are things you can get into. Jacob was just itching and Marc had to grab him by the shoulders and say, 'You're here to visit. You're not here to play.'" JR, he recalls, was quiet.

"It seemed like she was almost embarrassed for her little brother. He'd be bouncing beside her and she'd just sit there with her arms crossed in front of her, you know, like 'why am I doing this?' Like it wasn't her choice to go. You could see the maturity was coming out in her more than her little brother. She was quieter and would sit by her mom and Jacob would jerk her chain a bit."

According to Judith, Jacob was becoming afraid of his older sister. "She was supposed to walk him home from school but he didn't want to go with her." Jeremy says he once saw JR choking her brother. "It freaked me out."

Near the end of February, Jeremy saw on JR's Nexopia page that she was 15, not 16 as he thought. Although their age difference would have been eight years, it meant little to him: "At the time, I really didn't think too much about it." His group of friends ranged in age from 13 to 25. Younger people, mainly girls, were simply accepted as part of the group.

On Nexopia, Jeremy adopted the username Souleater. For his "likes" he listed "fellow lychan brethern." Among his music likes were Cradle of Filth, Dying Fetus, Murder Dolls, Marilyn Manson, Korn, Stoned Sour, Megadeath, Slipknot, and Pantera. His "dislikes" were: "my heart being broken again, homewreckers, hypocrites, lies, the sun, untrustworthy people or unreliable people, backstabbers, cheaters, spiderwebs (not spiders they're kewl), planes, posers, prostitutes." Of prostitutes he wrote: "I like to kill them, play with their insides then eat . . . (didn't your mama tell you not to play with your food)." He also said he disliked "niggers, pigs, cops, godforsaken accordian aahhhh."

Soon Jeremy joined the goth/industrial website VampireFreaks.com, where he adopted the username Souleater52. From her VampireFreaks account, JR accepted Souleater52 as one of her friends. Around the name Souleater52 she typed "<3" indicating a sideways heart, a common short-hand symbol for "love" or "sweetheart." After it she wrote: "We need a small male infant with a harness and a leash and it shall make wookie noises and do my math homework . . . and wear bells."

Like many users on VampireFreaks.com, Jeremy fashioned an alternate identity using dark bravado. "I believe in Blood, Destruction, Guts, Gore & Greed!" he wrote on his profile. Among the likes he listed were "gothic beings, mosh pits, loud music, piercings, tattoos, scarification, pain, kinky fetishes, heavy metal, blood, razor blades, eyeliner, poetry, dark clothing, aggressiveness and nails."

On his profile page, Jeremy posted a photo of himself in a black hoodie and a black ball cap turned backwards, holding a bottle of beer in each hand. His face is blurred in the grainy camera-phone snapshot. It appears deathly white except for two dark eyes highlighted with black eyeliner.

Jeremy also professed a fondness for "the dark, the moon, the stars and biting" and for lycans. Among his dislikes was "the sun." In private messages from his VampireFreaks account, Jeremy professed to be a 300-year-old immortal and said a lycan empire would one day rise. He also had an account on Windows Live Hotmail under the name Death's Spade in which he listed his age as 213.

His profile pages exuded boldness and confidence. At school he had been bullied; at home, beaten. The Internet was different. It allowed Jeremy Allan Steinke, for the first time in his life, to be somebody.

JR's relationship with her parents steadily worsened. "I wanted to keep having fun, disobeying," she says. "We were fighting a lot and I was being grounded on weekends."

JR envied her friend Kaylee's freedom. Her own conventional life was filled with rules and curfews. The defiant Kaylee constantly challenged authority and didn't seem to worry about the consequences. Kaylee did what she wanted. JR began to imagine her own life without parents.

Jeremy offered support. Unable to see each other on weekends at the punk shows she was now forbidden from attending – a punishment for abandoning Jacob – they talked on the phone late at night, met at the mall, or snuck off to his trailer. "We got closer, talking more, most days. We were hanging out and getting a lot closer," JR says. "He would always take my side . . . and make me feel better. Everybody would be asleep and I'd be on the phone. I'd have to sneak it into my room." Jeremy serenaded JR over the phone with songs he wrote just for her. "I felt really flattered and loved. He was really romantic. He told me that he loved me all the time. I was falling in love with him."

Jeremy felt the same way about JR. The two began a series of private messages through Nexopia in March 2006 under their adopted usernames.

March 2, 2006, 4:25 p.m.
To: **Runaway Devil**
From: **Souleater**
Subject: **till death do we part**

So, um, yeah do you truly feel that you have fallen in love with me? I really want to know. If so all you have to do is tell me. You mean so much to me. I don't want anything to ruin what we have so please tell me everything truthfully. Are you going to be able to go to the punk shows on the 9th next week at the Scouts Hall and the 17 not next week the one after? It's at the Moose yet I don't know why. Well I miss you lots. Hope to hear from you soon. xoxo l8r beautiful! :love:

JR, as Runaway Devil, responded to Souleater in a message dated March 8 at 8:56 a.m.

To: **Souleater**
From: **Runaway Devil**
Subject: **re: hello there**

well you see, I fucking love you.

Jeremy, the budding death-metal lyricist, also e-mailed JR a song he wrote titled "Till Death Do We Part." Sent on March 6 at 12:45 p.m., the words read in part:

Your the blood that flows though my veins,
your the sun breaking though the clouds when it rains . . .
my love is for you forever, as we die here together
we'll be together forever, till death do we part.

He signed off his e-mail by saying: "Hope you enjoy, love you tons, l8r cuddlebunny."

JR replied on March 8 at 9 a.m.:

To: **Souleater**
From: **Runaway Devil**
Subject: **re: lyrics**

Ah ha yey you make me feel so loved :hearts: yes I do love you you're wonderful. Kiss

Increasingly concerned about their daughter's older male friends, JR's parents started monitoring her computer pages. She wasn't allowed to accept any more telephone calls from older boys. "They didn't like all these older guys calling. They said I wasn't allowed to talk to guys at all. Jeremy called once and was told not to call again," JR says.

With her calls restricted, JR increasingly turned to the Internet to communicate by e-mail and instant messaging. Her messages with Jeremy and other friends were filled with slang familiar to those who use cellphone text messaging. This truncated shorthand, however, can be cryptic, a form of modern-day Morse Code impenetrable to unwary parents. The list of expressions is evolving constantly and includes "emoticons" – icons used to express emotion – such as the common happy face :-) or sad face :-(with other characters added to express sadness, such as an apostrophe :'-(to show a tear. Facial symbols can also be written with noses as :'-(or :-) A neutral expression can be indicated by ^_^ and ~_~ is often used to show anger. Commonly used phrases include:

omg - Oh My God
gf - girlfriend
l8r - "later," or goodbye
cul8r - see you later

lol - laughing out loud

rofl - rolling on the floor laughing

lmao - laughing my ass off

lmfao - laughing my fucking ass off

ttyl - talk to you later

?4U - I have a question for you

404 - lost or unknown, taken from the HTTP error message for "page not found." Often used when a message is not understood.

IDGAF/D/S - I don't give a/fuck/damn/shit

wtf - what the fuck

jfk - just fucking kidding

n2b - not too bad

^5 - high five

<3 - heart

</3 - broken heart

:D - wide grin

Several websites, such as TeenChatDecoder.com, allow parents to type in acronyms to decipher this "secret language of teens." Parents Centre, a British government website, posts a "chationary" of Internet slang, as do dozens of other parental sites. But many of today's parents are utterly unaware of Internet slang and remain naive even about the Internet itself, according to Dangermouse, the online name of a computer expert who blogs on a Medicine Hat community website.

"In my capacity working in technology, I have had some very disturbing discussions with very naive parents," he has written. "It's not that they are uncaring, unconcerned parents – they just don't get what kind of technology they are dealing with."

In live Internet messaging, where computer users can chat with each other in real time, AITR is used to mean "adult in the room." Often the number 9 will be used to warn that parents may be approaching. The number will be repeated more frequently the closer parents come to the computer.

Still grounded on weekends after abandoning Jacob, and prevented from taking calls from older guys, JR incorporated many of these warnings and symbols in her private messages and e-mails to Jeremy, including one where she signed off with five "9s," possibly signalling the approach of her parents. Separated from JR, Jeremy replied with yearning.

March 8, 2006, 2:36 p.m.
To: **RunawayDevil**
From: **Souleater**
Subject: **Haha!**

God I can't get over not seeing or talking to you, I yearn to hear your soft suttle voice, & long to be held in your arms where ever that might be I don't care but just to share the time we have together with you are t die for and there is not anything that could ever replace the way you make me feel! :hearts: I miss you, I love you & I wish that we could just go somewhere we could jest be alone together for a little while . . . : (or as long as you would like? I think tonight I'm going to write another song to you! :D won't that be fun especially seeing as you shall not read it or hear it till I see you next! tehee :rofl: well I guess I should go or something but I hope to hear from you much sooner than later! ttyl Cuddlebunny *hugz&kissez*

Jeremy's sensitive and romantic e-mails belied a simmering passion for violence that his messages would soon reveal. "I've had twisted thoughts in my heads since I was 13. I'm sadistic-like," Jeremy says. At horror movies, during the most gory scenes, "I stand up and burst out laughing and start cheering 'em on." In 2005 he went to see *Land of the Dead*, the last of writer George Romero's *Night of the Living Dead* zombie movie series. "I started laughing and cheering 'em on. I was like, do it again." Somebody at the front of the theatre told him he was "a sadistic fuck." He says, "I couldn't help but laugh, man."

Jeremy also bragged that he owned an impressive Ninja sword collection and longed to have an authentic katana, the sword of the Japanese samurai renowned for its extraordinary sharpness: "They can cut through a piece of steel like a hot knife through butter." His fondness for knives dated back to the age of 13, when he says he was jumped and beaten up by five people and had to start arming himself.

One of his favourite movies was *Bully*, a film about a group of friends who conspire to murder a school bully by luring him to a swamp and butchering him with knives. But his top favourite was *Natural Born Killers*, the Quentin Tarantino screenplay directed by Oliver Stone in which the murderous lovers Mickey and Mallory go on a cross-country killing spree after slaying her abusive parents. The movie was inspired by the true case of 18-year-old Charles Starkweather and his 14-year-old girlfriend, Caril Ann Fugate, a pair of spree killers who either separately or together, depending on their conflicting testimony and evidence, murdered 11 victims in Nebraska and Wyoming between December 1, 1957 and January 29, 1958.

On March 9, Jeremy posted a poem called "The World" on his public Nexopia blog. It talked of a morbid desire to kill and read, in part:

> The world I live in is dark & cold,
> The things these pitiful souls do seem to never get old,
> I wish for they would all die . . .
> The earth can burn,
> To hear them all scream I yearn,
> Their blood should be spilled,
> For some of them my heart they killed,
> But it is not that for which I wished they'd die,
> But for this planet being filled with hatred, deceit & lies!

Whether he was referring to JR's parents is unknown.

———

Jordan Attfield, a 17-year-old from Saskatchewan with a troubled home life, was living on the street when he met Jeremy at a Medicine Hat punk rock show in March 2006. Jordan had ear and lower-lip piercings, wore hoodies, and sported a black glove and spiked wristband. He and Jeremy both liked the same kind of music, played guitar, and shared an interest in lycan mythology. Jeremy offered Jordan a place to sleep on the couch in his mom's trailer.

"I took it the first chance I got," says Jordan. It was rent-free, and he liked Jeremy.

It was not the first time Jeremy had offered a haven to troubled teens. The trailer was a refuge without rules for wayward kids. Jeremy's mother, Jackie, had a soft spot for them and allowed her son to take kids in like stray pets. Jordan was no different. He and Jeremy hung out together, played guitar, and soon formed an amateur industrial/goth/metal garage band called Project Status Quo, with Jeremy on guitar and lead vocals and Jordan on bass.

"Jeremy was a really hyper kid," says Jordan. "Everybody liked him because he was really funny." But Jeremy could be moody. "He was nice but there were days where he was miserable."

Jordan is reluctant to discuss the depth of their lycan beliefs, saying only, "I believe in that stuff, too." He says Jeremy once deliberately cut his own hand with a knife and lapped up the blood. "He never drank blood out of a glass or anything. I never saw that, but he did when he saw it on himself. He'd lick it up."

Daniel Clark, a clean-cut, 22-year-old oil field worker from Brooks, about an hour west of Medicine Hat, would receive a chilling lesson from Jeremy about the lycan brotherhood that Jeremy fantasized about on his profile pages. Unlike Jeremy and his circle of goth friends, Daniel liked Toby Keith and other country music artists, not the brooding and violent music of the goths. When he was introduced to Jeremy and the local goth crowd through his sister Crimson, Daniel made a point of not wearing his cowboy hat. "I took it off because I wasn't sure about these goths." He didn't want to do anything to provoke the bizarre-looking man with the eye makeup and neoprene face mask. As it turned out, Jeremy had no issue with Daniel's music. Jeremy was "tolerant and friendly," Daniel says. "He was very respectful in me and my girlfriend's home. He never swore at us."

One day, Jeremy told Daniel that he was a 300-year-old lycan. He never took the claim seriously: "I said, 'Yeah, whatever floats your boat.'"

Then, just before a full moon in March 2006, Jeremy cautioned Daniel not to come for a walk with him and a friend along the river.

"I wouldn't suggest it – we'll tear you limb from limb," Jeremy told him.

Daniel was shocked. "Excuse me?"

"Yeah, I'll eat you."

"You come near me and, I swear to God, I have a baseball bat in my shop. I'll beat you up."

Later, Daniel saw Jeremy wearing something strange. He was used to the eye makeup, bandana, black neoprene face mask, fishnet arm stockings and other accoutrements of the goth trade, but this was different. He took a closer look.

Dangling from Jeremy's neck was a small vial of blood.

5

RAWR!

"I have this plan . . ."

Marc and Debra continued monitoring JR's computer use and grew increasingly distressed by their daughter's macabre profile pages. It must have pained them that JR was all about the dark when they were all about the light.

Suspicious that his daughter was continuing to communicate with older men online, Marc rushed the computer to Memory Lane, a local computer store. He was adept at tinkering with computer hardware because of his job and electrical engineering courses, but he needed help. "He was really upset. He asked me how he could hack into his daughter's MSN account," recalls Richard Munro, Memory Lane's corporate sales director. "I told him we couldn't help him, that he should go to the police. He was just a concerned father trying to do what was right for his daughter."

Marc's frantic attempt to view the contents of JR's Internet messages created a ruckus at the computer store. He raised such a commotion that staff came out of the back room, trying to help. They had seen the opposite so many times – parents without a clue about technology, totally unknowledgeable about the dangers of the Internet, purchasing computers for their kids. "We live in a moment of time when, for the first time perhaps in history, there is an information gap between generations," says Dave Martin, a Memory Lane staffer. "I see parents coming in buying their third computer for the kids, and they don't even know how to turn it on."

With the store employees unable to help, Marc and Debra decided to box up their computer. Its removal proved to be no obstacle for the cunning JR. She simply went to the public library, where she could use computers at no charge, away from the prying eyes of adults. Her Nexopia logs show that on March 13 at 7:31 p.m. and on March 14 at 4:56 p.m., JR wrote two messages to friends, alerting them that the heat was on and that her computer had been taken away.

"That fucking sucks. So where are you using the net now?" asked a user named "nc00112." Runaway Devil replied at 1:10 p.m. on March 18: "At the Y and the library." In one message to a friend, JR, with a tone of bored amusement, wrote: "My computer's been taken away – lol."

As her forbidden friendship with Jeremy blossomed, some of JR's friends became increasingly uncomfortable with her infatuation. Jocelyn, a classmate of JR's, was shocked that her 12-year-old friend was getting into a romantic relationship with a grown man. She saw them kissing and admonished JR: "You shouldn't be with him. He's much older than you."

"It's my choice," JR sniped. "Leave us alone."

Jocelyn knew Jeremy to be in his twenties, but JR argued with her: "He is not! He's 17." She later admitted that she never asked Jeremy his age. "I knew he was a lot older but I didn't want to know for sure."

Before Jeremy came along, JR and her girlfriends would spend hours watching television. Now, JR's friends were left to sit and watch TV alone while she talked to Jeremy on the phone. Aubrey felt shunned by JR's attention to Jeremy, and their age difference upset her. "I never really thought of him as dangerous," she says. "I just thought that he was older and really immature for his age. From what she said, she was in love with him. I never really got good feelings about him, especially because of the age difference. I guess I just decided to keep that out of my mind."

Aubrey thought Jeremy was hopelessly immature. He often tried to show off when he was at the mall, which she thought was juvenile. "He'd jump and grab onto the decorative blue bars they have outside of the food court and climb onto the roof," she says. "He would mouth off to the security guards for no reason, and once he got banned."

On one of her profile pages, Aubrey would later write: "I HATE Jeremy Slimeball."

Alyssa, one of JR's grade 7 classmates, tried to reason with her one day in the girls' washroom at school.

"My mother treats me like a little kid. I can't even stand to be in the presence of her anymore," JR told her angrily. "How do I get her to listen to me?"

"Get rid of Jeremy," Alyssa said. "You should co-operate with your mom and do as she says."

"You sound just like my mother," JR said, exasperated.

Even Jeremy's ragtag group of drug-using older friends disapproved of the relationship. When Jeremy confided to Grant Bolt that JR's strict parents didn't want him around her, Grant was less than sympathetic: "Buddy, what are you doing?" Jeremy was 23 years old. His girlfriend was in the seventh grade – end of story.

Daniel Clark, the clean-cut country music fan, also admonished Jeremy: "You're a grown man. You should have a job. You shouldn't be running around with young girls."

To express his frustration about how others viewed his relationship with JR, Jeremy wrote a song he called "The Intervening," which contained these lines:

> We'll never listen to you or your lies, why don't you just go ahead
>   and fucking die . . .
> We all know you are going to burn in hell, they'll all keep
>   asking but we should never tell.

Although officially grounded, JR snuck off with Jeremy whenever she could, meeting him at the bus stop down the street from her house or at the mall. After one of their secret rendezvous in mid-March, Jeremy wrote a private, ominous computer message:

March 13, 2006, 3:08 p.m.
To: **Runaway Devil**
From: **Souleater**
Subject: **hey sexy**

How goes it? You were a sight for soar eyes and I miss you more than killing people. Can we get together and kill people together? I have a poem 4 you and you shall see it when I see you. tee hee. Well I guess I should go, I love you tons :love:

JR responded to her dark mentor four hours later. Killing people, she indicated, sounded like fun: "Ah ha! Yes we shall," she wrote. "I miss you too, a large large amount that cannot be contained in mere words. I wish to see this poem. love you x."

Jeremy expressed his love for JR in a number of sappy poems he wrote to her in March, including:

There's something about your beauty,
That makes life with you feel like a movie,
It's like a dream come true,
The skys' are always blue.
and
When I'm with you I feel alive,
You make me want to take that dive,
I swear to you that I could never lie,
Your soft sweet lips could get me high.

One day, JR asked Jeremy if he thought they could get married. He agreed. They talked of getting tattoo rings, having a goth wedding, and running away to Europe to live in a castle. In mid-March, the morbid, lycan-obsessed Jeremy, with his fondness for violent, sadistic movies and thoughts of killing people, decided to surprise JR with a token of his love and adoration. He gave her a small vial of his own blood, perhaps the same one that Daniel Clark had seen dangling from his neck.

On March 14, Jeremy wrote an e-mail to JR under the heading "Hey Sexy!" asking her how she liked his gift: "I'm glad that you miss me but I wish you didn't have to. :(But I guess the only way that is possible is by us being together indefinitely right? . . . I have a song in the midst of being written for you! I hope you'll like it too! & what of the vile of blood I gave you what are your words on expressing your thought on that item of my love to you??? Yay!"

He also talked once again of killing: "When are we going to go get together & kill some more pitiful souls??? :nuts: well ttyl hopefully you can call or sumthin' & let me know what's up for 2morrow if I'm picking you up again or what's going on??? Take Care my lovely! :date: Love You! XOXOXO :love:

A couple of days later, Jeremy exchanged messages with a friend whose username was Kill My Heart, saying that he and JR were fantasizing about killing Marc, Debra, and Jacob in a copycat scenario of his favourite movie, *Natural Born Killers*.

March 16, 2006, 9:22 p.m.
To: **killmyheart**
From: **Souleater**
Subject: **Re (8): No subject**

The whole point of killing them would be to start a spree across Canada! :rofl: kinda like the legendary Mickey & Mallory love :love: birds! now have you seen that movie? it's called "Natural

Born Killers" it's the best love story of all time I loves it so much
I wanna do it myself!

Judith hadn't seen Debra in months. She drove to Medicine Hat in March, for a visit, and saw the sudden change in JR. "Just talking with JR back then, she would make fun of her mother. It happens, the 12-year-old being sarcastic. Saying things like, 'What do *you* know, mom?' But I was just surprised that Deb was trying to reach out to be a friend. JR clearly was being condescending to her."

Judith could see clearly that JR was annoyed by her parents' rules. JR's friends, too, were watching her become more sullen. "After she met Jeremy she felt like she was being controlled and sheltered too much," says Aubrey. "She told me she was really angry that they weren't respecting her rights."

"I couldn't talk to them anymore," JR says. "I felt like they didn't love me anymore."

In addition to taking the hard-line measures of boxing up the computer and grounding her, Debra and Marc insisted the three go for counselling, which JR surprisingly agreed to without much fuss. The manipulative JR may have seen her willing participation in counselling as a way to achieve more freedom.

After several sessions, Marc and Debra noticed their daughter was being more co-operative and less hostile. With the change in attitude, her parents finally relented to JR's constant desire to go to one of the punk shows to see her friends, but only on the condition that they accompany her. JR agreed, despite the embarrassing chaperone arrangement: "I wanted to see my friends I hadn't seen forever."

The show was Friday, March 17, 2006 at a local community hall with the bands One Shot Left, The Johnsons, and Radio For Help – an all-ages show put on by Show-N-Hell Productions, a Medicine Hat independent production company.

But for JR, the main attraction at the show would be Jeremy, whom she had seen only sporadically over the past several weeks.

During a set break, JR, Aubrey, and some other friends wandered outside. Jeremy was there, standing in a crowd. "He picked me up and swung me around. He was really happy," says JR. The others took a walk around the block. "We were running about like idiots," Aubrey says. "I ran back across the street to get something that fell out of my pocket." When Aubrey returned, JR and Jeremy were gone.

The two had wandered away for some privacy. "We started making out in the alley," JR admits.

They weren't alone for long. Debra and Marc appeared outside, looking for the girls. They approached Aubrey.

"Where's JR?" Debra asked.

"I'm not really sure," Aubrey replied.

Together, Aubrey and Debra walked up and down the block calling JR's name. Debra went into the alley with Aubrey trailing behind. When she came around the corner, Debra saw her daughter in the arms of an older-looking man with eye makeup, short cropped hair, a black hoodie, black lace arm stockings, and a studded wristband. The young couple's pent-up passion had exploded in the alleyway. Following behind his wife, Marc came around the corner and also caught his daughter with an older guy who looked like a goth vampire, both standing there like deer in headlights.

When Jeremy saw JR's angry father, he bolted.

"Jeremy saw us, he turned around and walked away as quickly as possible," says Aubrey. "JR looked really ashamed. And her parents were really angry."

Debra especially was upset at catching her 12-year-old daughter necking with a much older man. All the counselling and agreeing to terms and conditions were for naught. "I can't believe you would do this," she said to her daughter.

Marc stormed off to get the car with his shamed daughter in tow. Aubrey stayed behind, awkwardly trying to calm Debra down by walking with her. "She was really mad," says Aubrey.

Marc returned with JR to get Debra and Aubrey, who climbed in. The tension in the vehicle was palpable. Marc drove Aubrey to her sister's house, dropping her off to spend the night. She was anxious to get out of the car and escape the black mood hanging heavily in the air.

A few minutes later, Marc, Debra, and JR pulled into their driveway. If JR resented being grounded before, the real punishment was just beginning. Her parents told her she was grounded for an entire month and lowered the boom: no phone or computer privileges. JR was banned from listening to the music she liked, including Marilyn Manson and Cradle of Filth. They confiscated her MP3 player. Her beloved eyeliner and hair-straightener were taken away. She was told to go directly to school and right back home. Friends were turned away at the door when they showed up in the morning to walk to the bus stop together. It was mortifying. Trips to the mall with friends, even Aubrey, were out.

JR says she felt like a prisoner in her own home: "I was under quarantine. It was like I was under house arrest. They took everything out of my room except my clothing and my bed. I was really angry." She was especially upset with her mother. "I was close to my mom. I could tell her anything. Now, I felt like she didn't love me anymore."

Bristling under her parents' control, her fury grew. She kept communicating with Jeremy on computers at the library and the local Y. She wasted no time making sure the damaging scene her parents had caused at the punk concert didn't undo her relationship with Jeremy. The day after she was caught in the alley, she typed a short but powerful message she knew would ensnare him.

March 18, 2006, 3:01 p.m.
To: **Souleater**
From: **Runaway Devil**

sex sex sex sex oh and love.

Jeremy replied that night, drawing a frowning face in his return message. JR had added "love" as an afterthought, which bothered him. According to his mom, all he'd ever wanted in life was to be loved and accepted. Despite his threatening facade, werewolf fantasies, and fascination with violence, his syrupy poems showed that he was capable of tenderness. The sensitive Jeremy was in love, but all JR apparently wanted was sex.

March 18 2006, 11:53 p.m.
To: **Runaway Devil**
From: **Souleater**

sex sex sex and love what's that supposed to mean? :(

It took JR two days to get to a computer so she could stealthily message back. The sexualized 12-year-old let her boyfriend know she was in love – and lust.

March 20, 2006, 7:15 p.m.
To: **Souleater**
From: **Runaway Devil**

That I miss you a overwhelmingly large amount and love you. And also that I want to BANG you ah ha ha ha ha ha love.

Her overture to Jeremy wasn't the first time she'd done damage control. At the punk show, Jeremy grew jealous of Raven after he saw him talking with JR, resulting in an e-mail exchange in the following days. From the content of their messages, it is apparent that Raven may have warned Jeremy that JR was lying about something, possibly her age, or that she was flirtatious with other guys.

"RAWR. Raven angers me," JR wrote to Jeremy. "I want you to trust me and Raven has no reason to tell you not to. Stupid bird. Well I want you to know I love you and can't wait to be able to hang out with you, smile and be happy, huggles and kisses."

Jeremy admitted to JR that he was jealous of Raven. "I'm still a little upset with Raven myself," he wrote. "I do trust you just not as much as I want to. But I'm really working on it because I really do love you and I don't want to lose you so please have faith in me, and us, and I'm doing a lot better now. I still have some quarks to get out but soon enough, hopefully by the next time we're able to hang out, I'll get all fixed up. . . . sweet dreams. . . . .what do you think of my singing?"

With JR grounded and their Internet messages growing more intimate, Jeremy made a forbidden call to JR's house, which was intercepted by her parents. He apologized to her later online, saying he'd dialled her number by accident. He ranted about her parents overreacting about their relationship.

March 20, 2006
To: **Runaway Devil**
From: **Souleater**
Subject: **Hey beautiful**

Hey how's it going? I'm okay I guess. But I'm still sorry that you got into trouble. when I tried to call Aubrey I was thinking of you and I think when I went to dial to apologize I accidently dialled your number. so sorry that totally sucks you got grounded for a month. God your parents are so unfair. cussing. My mother was nothing like your parents know why? cause she's been living on her own since she was 15 and she used to hang out with 25 year olds and stuff and she knows what it's like to be us. too bad your parents don't. they should get with the program and realize that times are ever changing and they can't stop it. like what if mankind's lifestyle changes are they going to refuse to change too! Because they won't make it very far then. Well I hope to talk to you sometime soon, i miss you. Singing: I want you, i need you I have you I won't let anybody have you, tee hee slipknot rules. well hope to see you soon or something I love you.

As a result of JR's pleadings, Marc and Debra agreed to uncrate the home computer for her, but only if she removed the older guys from her Nexopia and VampireFreaks friends lists.

"I saw that you took me off your friend list. Normally I wouldn't ask why . . . but maybe I will never know," Raven asked, using his online username, DarkeSeveran.

"Yes, well, nothing personal," JR responded, telling him that all the older boys had been removed. "My parents found pictures of me and I got into all kinds of shit. . . . Not sure how much my dad knows so I'm just being cautious."

"Why did you un-add me?" a friend named MCR-Fan asked.

"Because my parents are checking my Nex but I'll add you back later," JR replied.

Marc and Debra were making strides in curtailing JR's secret online life, but she was growing increasingly angry about her lack of privacy and freedom. She regarded her mother and father as snoopy and untrusting. She hated having her online pages monitored and being treated like the 12-year-old she was. She wasn't getting her way, as she was used to, and it was making her more resentful by the day. Alone in her room, on the bus, sitting in class, she began fantasizing about getting rid of her parents.

"She told me she didn't want to be there anymore," says Jocelyn. "She told me her parents were being mean and they weren't treating her the way she wanted to be treated. They weren't letting her do the things she wanted to do, hang out with her friends or hang out with her boyfriend."

Aubrey agrees: "Things started to go badly after she started to feel like she was being controlled too much and they were being unfair. It made her really angry."

In late March, JR wrote a message to Jeremy that would come back to haunt her.

March 20, 2006, 7:10 p.m.
To: **Souleater**
From: **Runaway Devil**
Subject: **re: hey beautiful**

RAWR I hate them. So I have this plan. it begins with me killing them and ends with me living with you. So we are set. I'm going to try and call you but I really don't know if I'll be able to. They are treating me like shit. I hate them sooo much. But I hope this won't bring us far apart. I hope to talk to you soon and love you with all my heart. love

The next day, Jeremy wrote back to JR about her plot to do away with her parents.

March 21, 2006, 9:51 p.m.
To: **Runaway Devil**
From: **Souleater**
Subject: **hey beautiful**

Well I love your plan but we need to get a little more creative with like details and stuff. I wish they wouldn't treat you that way. grr It angers me to hear that. I dislike them very much. don't worry I love you too my sexy beast. I hope to hear from you soon, too take care my love. You have the key to my heart and soon enough you shall have my heart if I die anyway cause

if I give it to you now I'll die then you won't be able to hear me
say how much I love you.
love xoxoxo

On Friday, March 24, 2006 at 3:26 p.m., Jeremy posted a chilling poem on his Nexopia page:

My girlfriends family are totally unfair,
They say that they really care,
They don't know what is going on, they just assume,
As their greed continues to consume,
She is slowly going insane,
She continues to thank that I came into her life to help her out,
And to stop what they keep trying to shout,
It's all total bullshit,
Their throats I want to slit,
They will regret the shit they have done,
Especially when I see to it that they are gone,
They shall pay for their insulince,
Finally there shall be silence,
Their blood shall be payment!

Being grounded only made JR more determined to seek freedom. One night near the end of March, she snuck out of her house for a rendezvous with Jeremy. The creaking of the back door alerted her parents, who caught her and marched her back inside.

In early April, Runaway Devil tried again. This time, she crawled through a basement window so she wouldn't be heard. The window at the back of the house had a broken lock and no screen. She ran down the back lane and to her nearby school bus stop, their regular rendezvous point, where an eager Jeremy was waiting in his mother's pickup truck. He drove them back to his mother's trailer at Tower Estates. He opened the front door and they walked down a hallway to Jeremy's cramped bedroom, avoiding his mother's boyfriend, who was passed out on the couch. His mother was nowhere to be seen.

They shut his bedroom door and settled on the bed to watch a movie, under the Tool poster of a wrench in the shape of an erect penis. "I want to bang you," JR had written. The two cuddled up on Jeremy's small bed and had sex.

"We made love . . . because I loved him so much," JR said later. "I thought it would bring us closer together. I thought it would make him happy. I knew he wanted to have sex with me."

After their session, Jeremy drove her back home and she slipped into the backyard. In a well-crafted plan, she had left a pair of pajamas on the deck and pulled them on over her pants. The family dog, Julia, started barking. Marc and Debra woke up and came downstairs.

"I made up a story about having a bad dream and that I went out to get air," said the cunning JR. "They weren't sure whether to believe me or not."

6

A BLOOD SHEDDING FIGHT

"I will kill, I will spill the blood for you tonight . . ."

There are several legends as to how the city of Medicine Hat got its name. According to one, the Plains Blackfoot engaged their northern enemy, the Cree, in a battle along the banks of the South Saskatchewan River. During the fight, a Cree medicine man lost his headdress in midstream. The Cree believed the lost "medicine hat" to be a bad omen and fled in retreat, only to be defeated by the Blackfoot.

By early April, 2006, Runaway Devil and Souleater were plotting a massacre of their own.

Jeremy was becoming infuriated with JR's parents, telling one friend that they had "locked her up." As their forbidden Romeo-and-Juliet romance continued to eat away at them, the two began having more late-night phone calls about how to solve the problem of her parents. JR would softly creep out of her bedroom as late as 1 a.m. and use a basement phone to have whispered conversations with Jeremy long into the night, sometimes for hours. They fantasized about escaping to their castle in Europe, but decided running away wouldn't work because her parents would track them down.

If they eliminated her parents, they reasoned, it would be unfair to leave her little brother alone in a world without his mom and dad. In their warped sense of benevolence, the innocent eight-year-old would have to die, too.

They often discussed how to kill her family. "We talked about it so much," JR says. They ran through various scenarios, including shooting, stabbing, knocking them out and setting the house on fire. Kaylee says JR told her that she tried to poison her parents but it didn't work – a claim that was never verified. JR says it was Jeremy who first broached the subject of killing her parents. But according to an e-mail Jeremy wrote on April 4 to a girl with the username Super.Jesus, it was JR who was hatching the murder plot. "Tell her parents to shove it," Super.Jesus wrote to Jeremy when he told her about the problems they were having with Marc and Debra.

He replied: "We were thinking more among the lines of killing them! :rofl: yepperz & the best part is it was her idea! :D"

JR's friends also say she was the one pressuring Jeremy to kill her parents. In several overhead conversations, JR appeared to be the puppet master and Jeremy her marionette.

On one April day just before Easter, some of JR's grade 7 classmates were running merrily in the spring air, innocently chasing each other around the big trees outside the long, low, red-brick building that was their Catholic school, and squealing with delight. Their playful frolicking must have seemed juvenile to the brooding JR, who sat alone on a metal electric utility box nursing more sinister thoughts. As Jocelyn and Alyssa ran around maniacally, burning off pent-up energy from the morning's classes, a spiteful JR dialled Jeremy's number. Grounded, stripped of her computer, makeup, hair straightener, and MP3 player, she was furious.

Jocelyn and Alyssa could tell that JR was spitting mad and it was obvious she was talking to Jeremy. They were shocked at what they overheard: that she hated her parents so much and wished they were dead; she couldn't stand it anymore; they had to die; she *needed* him to do this for her. The hateful talk was too much for Alyssa. "I don't want to hear this," she said, grabbing Jocelyn by the hand. They ran into the school. Amid the rebirth of spring, symbolic of the approach of the holiest of days on the Christian calendar, such talk upset the Catholic girls.

"She asked Jeremy to help her kill her parents," Jocelyn says. "I walked away because I didn't want to hear anything about that."

Jordan Attfield also remembers a phone call in which JR begged Jeremy to kill her parents, a call that would mark the beginning of the end of his relationship with Jeremy.

Jordan was sitting around the trailer that day, and, as usual, was drinking. He polished off a six-pack and says he was "medium drunk" when he wandered to the kitchen and picked up the phone to make a call. Jeremy was on the line in his bedroom, talking to JR.

"Will you kill them?" she asked.

Jeremy was noncommittal. "I'll think about it."

Jordan hung up. Like the girls in the schoolyard, he didn't want to believe what he was hearing.

Jordan was becoming troubled by Jeremy's moodiness. He had spent two months sleeping on a couch in the trailer, and that was fine, for a while. But Jeremy was becoming "weird" because of his thwarted relationship with JR, and Jordan could take it no more. He had been wanting to move out of the trailer, but had nowhere to go. The phone call about killing JR's parents was the last straw. He decided to leave as soon as he could.

In mid-April, Grant Bolt had a disturbing, marijuana-induced conversation with Jeremy. One night in the dark parking lot behind the Medicine Hat Lodge, the two sat in Jeremy's truck and smoked a joint. It was clear that Jeremy had something heavy weighing on his mind, and in the melodramatic fashion of his poetry, he asked: "How far would you go for love?"

"What the hell are you talking about?" asked his glassy-eyed friend.

"JR is pretty much going to break up with me unless I do it soon."

Jeremy, however, didn't have the courage to kill alone. He wanted an accomplice. "I don't think I can do this by myself. I need someone I can trust. Are you in?'

"Go fuck yourself," Grant replied.

A physically small and mentally frail grade 10 dropout, Grant lived at home with his parents and collected social assistance for a variety of problems. He ruminated on the conversation and responded the only way he knew, by giving Jeremy a copy of their favourite film, *Natural Born Killers*, saying, "Here, man, just watch this." In the movie, the murderous Mickey Knox (played by Woody Harrelson) and his girlfriend Mallory (played by Juliette Lewis) kill her abusive father and her mother. The movie, as Grant described it, is a "romance horror flick."

"We both just kind of liked it. It was one of the classics. He wanted ideas on how to do it," Grant says. He denies he was giving Jeremy a how-to video; rather he was attempting to impress on his friend the hopelessness of a situation that could come to no good end: "I thought it would change his perspective."

Jeremy was fascinated by violent movies and seemed unable to distinguish fantasy from reality. He admired how in the movie *Bully*, friends had banded together to help each other do away with the problem bully who was plaguing them. "It shows you what friends do for each other . . . Those are the kind of friends you need," he would say later. But, to Jeremy's chagrin, Grant Bolt had turned him down in his hour of need. This was incomprehensible to Jeremy, who was unswervingly loyal to friends and would do whatever anybody asked of him, to be accepted. He would especially do anything for his beloved JR. *Anything*.

This attitude was frighteningly evident in a poem he posted on Nexopia. Inspired by the death-metal music he listened to, Jeremy was writing increasingly violent poetry and lyrics for his own songs. He called this one "Blood Shedding Fight," and in it he pledged to do JR's bidding:

You feel you're alone but you're not, I will give you everything
that I got
I will prove to you this is true when you see everything that I do.

Chorus: I will kill, I will spill the blood for you tonight, it will be
a blood shedding fight.

You satisfy my hunger, you quench my thirst
You should know you'll always be the first one to come, one to
go, one to always let me know what you think how you feel
And if it's my heart you want to steal you know that I am here
for the year if with me you want to be sincere.

Repeat chorus: I will kill I will spill the blood for you tonight,
it will be a blood shedding fight.

If you want the world than we shall conquer if you promise that
you will stay longer
We'll fight them all and see them fall and watch our shadows
grow tall, they're all doomed and consumed but bloodshed and horror
We'll continue to kill and torture if thy lady desires more of a
blood shedding fight.

As spring arrived in Medicine Hat and the highways cleared of ice and
snow, it became easier for young people in surrounding communities to
come in to the city to attend punk shows.

Mick, a 16-year-old from Leader, Saskatchewan, 200 kilometres
northeast of Medicine Hat, had met Jeremy through his Medicine Hat
girlfriend, Hailey, who was 14. Hailey knew both Jeremy and JR
from hanging out at the mall and from various punk shows. She was
one of the regular mall rats with whom JR spent time, a member of the

motley circle of rebellious adolescents who hung out at the food court.

Mick contacted Jeremy on MSN Instant Messenger and told him he wanted to meet Hailey at a punk show featuring the thrash-metal bands GFK and Mute at the Moose Lodge in Medicine Hat on Friday, April 21. Jeremy offered to drive to Leader and pick up Mick and said he could stay the weekend at his mom's trailer. Mick was thrilled to score a ride.

Mick and Hailey were brooding teens who had both been diagnosed with depression. Each feared the other was suicidal, and they were drawn together out of mutual concern. They were excited that Mick would be staying at Jeremy's trailer – it would allow Hailey to spend some precious time with her boyfriend on the weekend.

Jeremy drove to Leader on Wednesday, April 19. It was a five-hour round-trip journey – an eager gesture typical of Jeremy's obsessive desire to find acceptance and please friends. He arrived in Leader just before midnight Wednesday and stayed in Mick's room.

On Thursday, Mick's mother, Shalene, left for Medicine Hat at about 10:30 a.m. with her husband, who had an appointment with a stop-smoking hypnotist. Mick and Jeremy hung out for the day, listening to music and watching TV. Fearing he would lose JR if he didn't kill her parents and still obsessing about how to do it, Jeremy exchanged messages with Grant Bolt on VampireFreaks.

"Hey man. What are you doing? I enjoy hitting myself and making my face bleed," Grant joked in one post he wrote on Jeremy's page for all to see.

Jeremy carelessly replied with a chilling public admission: "Oh yeah . . . lol hope you enjoy hitting urself . . . i on the other hand would rather do morbid stuff to others! like Jaxz rents [parents] 4 example! which i'm going to do this weekend."

Mick and Jeremy stayed up late and woke mid-morning on Friday. They left for Medicine Hat at about 1 p.m., passing Mick's parents on their way back to Leader. When Jeremy and Mick arrived at Tower Estates around 6 p.m., Jeremy's mother was not at home. She was out on a binge that would last through the weekend, drinking with friends.

Jeremy made some hot dogs and macaroni for himself and Mick, and then got ready for the punk show, donning a fresh pair of black jeans, a dark T-shirt, leather bracelets, fishnet arm stockings, his black neoprene face mask, and a black hoodie. He dropped Mick off at the Moose Lodge but didn't stay. He went to fetch Grant Bolt, picked up a case of beer, and came back about two hours later. Missing was JR, who was still grounded from being caught in the alley with Jeremy the previous weekend.

The local Moose Lodge was an unlikely setting for anti-establishment goth kids with VampireFreaks accounts. Like other fraternal organizations, Medicine Hat's Loyal Order of the Moose, Chapter No. 1073, had seen its membership decline over the years and rented out its facilities to help cover the building's increasing operating costs. Outside the lodge stands a giant statue of a rather thin moose with antlers.

Jeremy sat with Grant in the box of his mom's truck and cracked a beer. During punk shows, the parking lot at the Moose Lodge was a social scene for Jeremy and his friends. They would hang out, boozing and smoking pot under the statue of the giant moose. The incongruity was bizarre: a moose representing a community-minded service organization standing sentinel over a bunch of anti-establishment goth kids who embraced the motto "Fuck the Mainstream" – the name of a goth clothing line sold as an offshoot of VampireFreaks.com.

As Jeremy and Grant sat drinking, a friend came by with a truckload of friends to join the party. After guzzling about six beers, visiting with friends, and occasionally wandering inside to take in the pulsating, jackhammer-like music of GFK with their screaming vocals, Jeremy returned with Mick to the trailer at about 1 a.m.

While Jeremy and his friends were getting ready for the GFK and Mute show Friday night, Marc and Debra took Jacob and JR out for a spin on their motorbikes, a warm-up for a family ride to Ontario they were planning for later that summer.

The next morning, Saturday, April 22, offered a picture of suburban bliss in Ross Glen. Marc, now 42 years old, had taken delivery of his white Dodge Ram pickup, after having its steering box replaced by the dealership. A stickler for mechanical perfection, he had complained to them earlier in the week that the repairs weren't done properly, recalls Sheri-Ann Herman, an employee at the dealership. She was new to the job and Marc had been her first unhappy customer, so she'd been eager to make things right. She and a co-worker promised to deliver the truck personally to the family's home. On Thursday, they got a little lost, but as they rounded the corner in the suburban neighbourhood, Marc was on the front lawn, cheerfully waving them down. He was apologetic for the way he had acted at the dealership.

"I'm really sorry, I've been having a lot of problems at home with my daughter and I was a little upset. I shouldn't have taken it out on you," he told Herman. Marc was very animated and talkative. He test drove the truck and was thrilled with the repairs. The steering was dead on. Marc chatted with Herman on the lawn beside the sparkling white pickup. He seemed to be a completely different person from the stormy customer who had come in four days earlier.

Debra walked into the driveway, effusive and bubbly. The 48-year-old mother of two was dressed in black leather motorcycle chaps and jacket. "I thought she looked pretty smoking hot," says Herman.

Apart from their daughter's rebelliousness, life seemed good for the family. They had come so far. Gone were the days of relying on the food bank and living in a cramped, rented townhouse. Marc and Debra were homeowners and entrepreneurs in charge of their family's destiny. As Saturday unfolded in Ross Glen, Jacob was planning a sleepover with Gareth, his best friend and next-door neighbour. Other than an occasional sprinkle of rain, it was a perfect spring day for a typical suburban family.

On the other side of town, in the trailer park at Tower Estates, Jeremy and Mick got up about 10 a.m. on Saturday and plugged in Jeremy's electric guitar. Mick had shown Jeremy how to read tablature, a form of musical shorthand that uses numbers in lieu of notes to indicate where to put one's fingers on a guitar fretboard. The two traded riffs from their favourite metal songs. Kaylee, the free-spirited runaway, came by, and the three sat around listening to music. Jeremy, longing for JR, perhaps had lyrics from Cradle of Filth going through his head: "All woman, pure predator, wherein conspiracy and impulse dwell like a seething fall from grace . . . Thee I worship."

Hailey arrived at the trailer park, to visit Mick. It was drizzling rain on and off, a good day to stay inside and drink. Jeremy and his friends didn't need weather as an excuse. Any day was a good day to party. About mid-afternoon, the phone rang. It was the police, looking for Kaylee, who, as usual, had been reported as a runaway. Jeremy decided it was safer for her to hide out at Raven's. He needed to buy booze anyway, and hopefully score some pot. Jeremy had big plans for the night. Getting wasted was high on the list.

After dropping Kaylee off at Raven's, Jeremy bought a 12-pack of beer and an eighth-ounce bag of pot for $40. He smoked two "bowls," or small pipefuls, with his supplier and headed back to the trailer. About the time Jacob and Gareth were enjoying their hot dogs in the family's backyard, Jeremy was smoking pot and sharing beers with Mick and Hailey. "We just hung out," Jeremy says. "I planned to get drunk."

Early in the evening, a 14-year-old named Erica showed up with two friends. Jeremy's trailer was a welcome hangout, a place where under-age kids could always count on having a good time. The party continued into the evening. As Erica and her friends floated around the trailer, Jeremy, Mick, and Hailey drank beer and listened to music. The brooding Jeremy no doubt wished JR was there, too.

Jeremy was getting drunk and stoned. After going through the 12 beers he had bought, he raided his mother's beer supply in the refrigerator so that he, Mick, and Hailey could keep drinking. When that was gone, he pulled a bottle of vodka out of the freezer.

Across town, the grounded JR soothed herself with a bubble bath, taking a phone call about 8 p.m. from a girlfriend. Instead of talking on the phone, she told her friend to send her a message online. Away from the prying ears of her parents, it would be much more private.

"Do you want to go swimming or to the mall tomorrow?" her friend asked.

"I can't," JR replied.

"Why not?" her friend messaged back.

There would be no reply. JR had already signed off. Perhaps she had bigger plans.

High on pot and booze, Jeremy left the trailer about 9 p.m. When he returned an hour later, he seemed agitated.

Jeremy, as it turned out, had paid a visit to Jordan Attfield, his former roommate, who by now had moved out of the trailer. Jordan had found himself a place across town, far enough from Jeremy to get away from his mood swings, but not far enough that Jeremy couldn't find him.

On Saturday night, Jordan was watching a movie with his new roommates, Daniel Clark, the rig worker and country music fan, and Daniel's sister, Crimson. With them were Jordan's girlfriend, Stephanie, and another girl, Cassie. They were interrupted by a phone call from Jeremy, wanting to speak to Jordan. According to Stephanie, the phone call upset Jordan, who grew quiet and sullen. About 9 p.m., Jeremy pulled up in his mother's pickup truck, music blaring loudly.

Jordan hid downstairs, hoping to avoid Jeremy. Stephanie let him in. Jeremy had come to plead for help killing JR's family. He walked downstairs and bluntly asked his ex-roommate: "Jordan, will you help me with this?"

"No way. I don't have it in me to kill another human being."

Although Jordan wasn't sure if Jeremy was serious, he was clearly bothered by the conversation. When Jeremy left he locked the door.

93

Fuming, Jeremy returned to the trailer and called Jordan back. Hailey and Mick overheard the conversation. "I heard them arguing," Hailey says. "I heard Jeremy yelling at Jordan. I overheard Jeremy talking to Jordan about killing them."

Jeremy slammed down the receiver, clearly mad. "Somebody is chickening out," he snarled, to no one in particular.

According to Jordan, Jeremy told him during the phone call: "If I ever find out you or anybody else told the police about this, I will kill all of you because I won't know which one is the rat."

Jordan was shocked. "So all these innocent people will have to be killed because of what one person said?"

"Yeah."

Jordan put down the phone and, according to Cassie, became withdrawn. "Jordan just sat there. He looked upset. He didn't want to talk about it." It was about 10 p.m.

Back at the trailer, Jeremy calmed down after the phone call. The group gathered in his bedroom and began watching *Natural Born Killers*. At about 10:30 p.m., as they watched the movie, Jeremy called the Blonde Vampire. Kacy Lancaster, a 19-year-old friend of Jeremy's who had a crush on him, used the name on MySpace.com. He asked whether she could buy him some cigarettes and come to his house. Eager to oblige, she arrived at about 11 p.m. By now, Jeremy had become excited by the movie.

"Have you seen this? Have you seen this?" he asked Kacy.

Oliver Stone's film, an over-the-top depiction of killing and bloodshed, is intended as a damning satire of the pernicious violence in North American culture. In the opening scene, Mickey and Mallory slaughter five people in a New Mexico coffee shop just for the apparent fun of it. The murderous couple go on a killing spree and become a pop culture phenomenon, their exploits chronicled by syndicated TV crime reporter Wayne Gale (Robert Downey Jr.), who recounts how the "Renaissance psychopaths" killed Mallory's brutal, sexually abusing father by drowning him in a fish tank and burned her mother alive in her bed.

"JR doesn't have a fish tank," Jeremy blurted as he, Kacy, Mick, and Hailey watched the movie.

After the vicious murder of the parents, the couple turn to see Mallory's brother, who, it is revealed, is actually her son, the product of a rape by her own father, who is depicted in the movie as a slovenly pig in a sleeveless "wife-beater" T-shirt. Instead of killing the little boy, Mickey and Mallory tell him he's free.

"That's where it's going to be different," Jeremy exclaimed. "JR is going to kill her brother."

Jeremy often talked casually about killing people, but for Hailey the fantasy was becoming frighteningly real. She told Jeremy to stop talking about killing JR's family.

"If you can talk her out of it, I won't do it," Jeremy said.

Hailey walked to the phone and dialled Kaylee's number. She pleaded with her to call JR and talk to her. Hailey can't recall much of the conversation. By now, everyone was fairly drunk. Hailey drank so much that night she vomited twice.

After the movie, Kacy left. At about 1 a.m. Mick walked Hailey back to a nearby convenience store, where she called her mom to come and pick her up. Mick waited out of sight around the corner to make sure Hailey got in the car, then walked back to the trailer, where Jeremy had locked himself in his bedroom. Mick could hear Jeremy talking on the phone. He knocked on the door.

"Jeremy, I need my stuff, man," Mick called out.

There was no answer. Mick could hear a muffled conversation. He knocked again.

"Jeremy!" Still no answer. "Jeremy!"

Mick walked back to the living room. He had no choice but to share the couch with Erica and try to sleep.

Through the bedroom door, Erica overheard part of Jeremy's conversation. It was about 2 a.m.

"Are you sure you want to do this?" she heard him say.

With Mick hogging the couch, Erica curled up on the floor and went to sleep. Mick tossed and turned, falling in and out of a restless sleep. He heard the front door bang and the sound of Jeremy driving away in his mother's pickup truck.

Mick yawned and went back to sleep.

Souleater's night was just about to begin.

7

WHY?

"It's what your daughter wanted . . ."

Jeremy stood inside the tiny lobby of Cam Barkley's apartment building, waiting for the sound of the security buzzer to open the door. He heard the lock click open, pulled on the handle of the glass door, and entered. He bounded up the stairs two at a time to the third-floor apartment, hungry for cocaine. Rebuffed by his friends Grant Bolt and Jordan Attfield as accomplices to help murder JR's parents, Jeremy turned to coke for courage. Cam, he knew, was a good source.

It was nearing 3 a.m. when Cam buzzed Jeremy in. Inside the stale-smelling apartment, Cam was lounging on the couch and watching a movie, an array of empty booze bottles and full ashtrays on the table in front of him. His 15-year-old girlfriend was beside him, smoking a joint. Jenny, a thin, pretty, dark-haired girl, was chronically high. She had dropped out of school and left home to live with Cam, wasting her days doing cocaine and pot. She had no job and had pawned most of her belongings to buy food. She ate when she could.

Cam, a goateed 18-year-old cocaine user, was spending his Saturday night watching the movie *Black Hawk Down* with Jenny and drinking, smoking marijuana, and snorting coke. Nights frequently blurred into days inside the apartment. Every night was party night at Cam's place. When Jeremy showed up in the middle of the night, the trio did the usual thing: "We snorted more cocaine," says Jenny. "Jeremy started to get high Jeremy did a fair amount. He did a bunch of lines, I guess."

Jenny was stoned, too. She can't remember exactly how much pot they smoked or how many lines of cocaine they snorted, but it might have been more than six lines each.

Cocaine is a central nervous system stimulant. Its effects, which can last from 20 minutes to several hours, make the user feel euphoric, energetic, talkative, hyperactive, and restless. It often produces a feeling of invincibility.

The three snorted the coke in the kitchen, came back to the living room, and started drinking vodka and Vampire brand wine straight from the bottle. The California-based Vampire Vineyards markets its wines as "the blood of the vine – the ultimate beverage resource for vampires seeking alternatives to the mundane ways of this world." Its first 500 bottles of Vampire Syrah in 1988 were purchased in their entirety by rocker Alice Cooper. The following year, 672 bottles of Vampire Sangiovese were sold to the Anne Rice Fan Club in New Orleans. The company maintains articles of vampire myth and lore on its website. Jeremy, hardly a sommelier, described Vampire wine, at about $20 a bottle, as "really good stuff. It's not very dry either. It's got a crisp taste to it."

Jenny offered Jeremy some ecstasy, an illegal, amphetamine-based recreational street drug that took root in the rave culture of the 1980s, where its euphoric effects heightened the laser light shows and the heavy beat of techno and electronica music played at the all-night DJ dance parties. After taking the pill, he bought two grams of cocaine from Cam. Jenny thinks Jeremy stayed about an hour.

High on pot, cocaine, ecstasy, beer, vodka and Vampire wine, Jeremy left the apartment and drove to a nearby convenience store for a pack of gum. JR disapproved of the smell of smoke on his breath. He came out, sat alone in his mom's truck, and snorted the two full grams he had bought from Cam. "I was off like a rocket," he recalls.

JR's phone call had aroused in Jeremy all of his fantasies about killing people. Everything coalesced within him: his morbid poetry, his anger, his fondness for the most sadistic scenes in violent movies, his Internet bravado of "blood, destruction, guts gore and greed," the "dark, the moon . . . aggressiveness and biting" and lycans. Yet, if he was the werewolf he boasted about, a member of a "lycan brotherhood" that would one day rise, he wasn't following the Hollywood script. In werewolf mythology, humans shape-shift into lycanthropic beings with the full moon. In the predawn on Sunday, April 23, 2006, the moon was in a waning crescent.

Jeremy drove away from the convenience store toward JR's house, less than a kilometre away. He knew he would be reunited with his precious JR in minutes, just like the murderous Mickey Knox bent on liberating his beloved Mallory from the hellhole of her parents' house. Jeremy, who soaked up violent pop culture like a sponge, perhaps recalled the lyrics from another Cradle of Filth song: "Nothing will keep us apart. We could kill them all if our desire tore free. Our union is one, sweet sinful Eve."

Jeremy crept to the front of JR's house and stood next to the towering pine tree that grew up and past her bedroom window. He knelt down, picked up a pine cone, and pitched it at the glass. JR looked out and down at Jeremy, motioning for him to go to the basement window by the deck in the backyard, the one she regularly used as an escape hatch to sneak out of the house to see him.

Jeremy went to the back of the house, saw that the window was open, and paused. She had come to him through that same window, and now he would go to her. He had never dared to sneak into the house before, but this night would be different. JR had beckoned him with her phone call, perhaps casting the same spell on him that Cradle of Filth had written in a lyric: "She lulled me away from the rich masquerade and together we clung in the bloodletting moonlight. Pearled luna, what spell didst thou cast on me?"

Jeremy summoned his courage and went in. In the pocket of his black hoodie he carried a knife.

Debra heard a noise. Roused from her sleep, she may have suspected that JR was once again trying to sneak out. Dressed in a blue nightgown, she walked down to the basement and turned on the light. In his black clothes, black neoprene face mask, black fishnet arm stockings, leather wristband, neck bandana, and with his eyes lined in black, Jeremy would have been a terrifying figure. Debra, who friends had described as a lioness, would have been no match for Souleater.

The cocaine-fuelled Jeremy slashed at Debra. She screamed and held up her arms and hands in a defensive posture, exposing her torso.

Jeremy lunged and jabbed.

Marc bolted out of bed in his black boxer shorts and flew down the stairs. He saw Debra on the floor and the chilling spectre of a masked figure, all in black, standing over his wife. He reached for a screwdriver that had been left on one of the bottom stairs. For a brief moment, there was a standoff. Then, according to Jeremy, Marc attacked: "He came at me real fast. I was scared shitless. I thought I was going down. I went to back up and I tripped and fell and he jumped on me and attempted to stab me in the chest." Jeremy deflected the blow and knocked the screwdriver out of Marc's hand. "He grabbed my face and shoved his thumbs in my eye."

Jeremy began slashing wildly. He was breathing heavily from his encounter with Debra, and JR's 200-pound father was now on top of him. But Jeremy had the advantage of cocaine and a sharp blade. He does not know how many times he stabbed Marc: "I was freaking out. I lost control . . . He jumped on top of me and that's when I started stabbing him."

Jeremy wiggled out from under Marc and turned to run. Despite his injuries, Marc caught the masked intruder and began choking him. Jeremy started stabbing him again.

JR ran down to the living room and peered down the stairs into the basement, where her dad and her lover were locked in a fight to the death. "I saw my mom at the bottom of the stairs lying there. I saw my dad and Jeremy fighting. . . . I was hearing them yelling things. I ran back upstairs."

Marc began to falter. "Who are you?" he asked.

Jeremy made no reply.

JR's father fell back onto the floor. Bleeding heavily, he looked up at his assailant. "Why?" Marc pleaded.

"Cuz you treat your daughter like shit," Jeremy screamed. "It's what your daughter wanted."

These horrible words would be the last Marc would hear.

Panting and soaked in blood, Jeremy stumbled up the stairs and met JR in the kitchen. "She gave me a hug, kissed me and told me that she loved me . . . She turned around and went back upstairs. I waited for maybe 30 seconds. I don't know how long but I turned to go upstairs to find out what she was doing. I assumed she was grabbing some belongings or something and I heard some kind of conversation. I don't know what was said."

"JR! What's going on?" Jacob asked his big sister, cowering in his bed.

"Shhh. Go to sleep," she told him.

JR cradled Jacob's neck in the crook of her arm and squeezed. Hard. Jacob dug his fingernails into his sister's forearm, leaving a half-moon imprint in her skin.

"What are you doing?"

He broke free of his sister's grip and ran into the hall.

JR heard the sound of Jeremy's heavy breathing as he lumbered up the stairs to the bedroom level, drenched in her parents' blood. "He was staggering up the stairs. There was blood all over him. He was dragging his sleeve on the wall."

Hyperventilating from his death fight with Marc, Jeremy looked at Jacob, and then at JR. "We can't just leave him."

Next door, Phyllis Gehring was awakened by a noise. She thought she heard the sound of a child's cry.

Like his father, Jacob struggled for his life. The blood seen by the four police officers who entered the house after Sarah Penner's 911 call clearly indicated that the little boy fought in his purple bedroom like the Jedi warrior he often pretended to be. It was everywhere, on nearly every surface, including his toys. His blood also soaked the carpet in the hallway outside his bedroom door, where, in the cold parlance of forensics investigators, "a major bloodletting event" occurred.

After her brother died, JR walked down the hall to the upstairs bathroom, rinsed off the knife that was used to kill Jacob, and left it sitting on the counter in a pink puddle. Jeremy turned and staggered down the stairs to the kitchen. He waited for JR, twitching and pacing wildly. JR appeared, and gave him a hug. She grabbed the agitated Jeremy by his arms.

"Wait for me," she commanded. "I need 15 or 20 minutes. I have something to do."

Still stoned, the paranoid Jeremy swivelled his head as he stole nervous glances at the corners of the room and out the window.

"Somebody saw me. I have to go," he said, shaking and trembling.

JR looked at him in disbelief. *You're not making any sense. Stop twitching and jerking. Get a grip.*

"I can't breathe," Jeremy said, gasping. "I'm going outside for some fresh air."

JR was furious that Jeremy appeared ready to abandon her to the bloody scene. "You're just going to leave me here?"

"Hurry up," Jeremy hissed in a loud whisper.

JR ran back upstairs to her room, grabbed her canvas knapsack and stuffed it with a pair of pants, toiletries, and her mother's purse.

Jeremy went outside to the back deck. *What the hell is she doing,* he wondered. He paced nervously. *For fuck's sake, JR. Hurry the fuck up.*

Jeremy waited on the deck for about a minute. Panic set in again. He took off running down the street to his truck.

The next thing he remembers, he was driving back to the trailer park down South Boundary Road, which skirts the southwest part of the city and would have had very little traffic at dawn.

Queasy and nauseous, he slammed on the brakes, tumbled out of the truck, and vomited.

Her things gathered, JR went back downstairs to the kitchen. There was a blood smear on the inside of the back door above the handle.

Her beloved Jeremy was gone.

8

THE PARTY

"I gutted them like fish."

Houses and street lights blurred past in the dark as the taxicab picked up speed. "You work at the golf course?" the cabbie asked, looking at JR in his rearview mirror. She was a good-looking girl, 60-year-old Albert Fleckenstein thought, this brunette with blue eyes and fresh skin. Real sweet looking, probably around 16.

"No," JR replied, clutching her black bag in the back seat.

"It's kind of early," Fleckenstein said.

"I want to get an early start. I just got off being grounded for two weeks and I'm going to see a friend," she said calmly.

After Jeremy had fled the house, JR called the trailer, but got no answer. "I was panicking," she claims. "I was talking to myself. 'Oh my God, what do I do?' I felt sick like I was going to throw up. I had to get out of the house. I grabbed the phone off the kitchen table and went to the deck so I wouldn't have to be in the house."

Outside on the deck, her eyes were drawn to the broken basement window, through which she could see her father's body on the floor. She reached in and closed the blinds, "to block it so I wouldn't look into the room."

She called the trailer again. Still no answer. And again. At about 5:15 a.m., a groggy Mick finally answered the phone. Jeremy wasn't there, he told JR.

"But I need to come over, right away."

"You'll have to take a cab," Mick told her.

JR didn't know the address because Jeremy had always driven her to his trailer. Mick gave her the street number, which JR wrote in blue ink on her palm. She hung up, walked into the living room, found the phone book, and dialled the number for Care Cabs.

Darlene Walls, the dispatcher, logged the call at 5:25 a.m. In a voice Walls described as "whimpering," a young female asked for a cab to pick her up in 20 to 30 minutes.

Realizing she had no money, JR pulled the credit card out of her mother's purse and hurried down the road to a bank machine at the 24-hour 7-Eleven about seven blocks away. "I ran. It made me feel better," she says.

Swiftly, JR entered the convenience store, walked past the clerk to the automated teller located on the back wall between the Slurpee machine and soft drink cooler. She punched in her mother's PIN, and withdrew some cash. She said nothing to the store clerk. Then she ran back home. The cab was already waiting.

Fleckenstein had arrived at the darkened house on time, but saw no one. He called Darlene Walls on his cellphone. Nobody had come out of the house, but there was a black bag sitting by a truck in the driveway, he told her.

He waited in the cab for a few minutes and then called again. Walls was about to give him another trip when he saw a girl running up the street toward him.

JR went to the driveway, picked up the bag, and got in. She was breathing hard from the run, but appeared calm. "I was trying really hard to hold it together and trying to be normal," JR recalls.

It was about a 10-minute drive across town to Tower Estates, a $14 cab fare. JR tipped Fleckenstein $1 and walked up to the trailer.

Fleckenstein, who had been driving a cab for 23 years, kept a protective eye on her. "At that time of day I don't like to leave anyone standing alone," he says. "She looked at me and went in."

Inside, Jeremy greeted her with a big hug.

"I love you," he said. Jeremy was bedraggled and worn out, but other than a cut and rapidly swelling eye, "he was cleaned up," according to JR.

Jeremy had come home not long before JR arrived. "He was breathing really heavily," according to Mick. "He went to the bathroom and turned the shower on." When JR arrived, her hair looked "tangly." She was wearing a black sweatshirt and was carrying a pair of black Converse running shoes.

JR followed Jeremy to his room. "We sat on the bed and he kissed me," she says.

Jeremy began stuffing his bloody clothes into a white plastic grocery bag. Mick recalls Jeremy "cussing under his breath" as he walked between the kitchen and the front door. "He and JR put something in a garbage bag and went out the door."

As they walked away from the trailer, Jeremy gave JR a blanket. They got into his mother's Dodge Dakota pickup truck and drove off. The sun was just beginning to come up.

JR was exhausted. They drove to an apartment building on her side of town, not far from the house where her family lay dead. Jeremy parked behind the building and took some blue latex gloves out of a bag. He told JR to throw them in a dumpster. "He wiped down the inside of the truck. I was spaced out. It was so surreal."

They walked into the apartment building, up three flights of stairs, and knocked on Cam Barkley's door. Only a few hours had passed since Jeremy had left the apartment, and Cam and Jenny had barely gotten to sleep. Jeremy was holding his arm and had a swollen eye. He was, according to Cam, "looking rough."

"I just got fucked up. I just got fucked up," Jeremy told him.

JR stood silently at Jeremy's side. According to Cam: "She was spaced out, wasn't all there. It was like she had seen a ghost."

Jeremy asked Jenny for some ice for his eye. Tired and still half-stoned, she went to the freezer, came back with the ice, and sympathetically offered the wrung-out Jeremy and JR their bedroom while she and Cam slept on the couch.

Taking a seat in the living room and holding the ice to his sticky eye, Jeremy asked Cam a question.

"He spooked me. He asked me how to clean blood off knives. Not knife. *Knives*," Cam says.

According to JR, she and Jeremy went to the bedroom. Jeremy got into bed and took off his shirt. She lay down next to him but couldn't shut her eyes. She got up, paced around outside the bedroom for a few minutes, and came back in. "We were talking and I kinda cuddled up to him. He was trying to make me feel better and comfort me. I was scared. He asked me to rub his back. We started kissing, and he pulled me on top of him and we had sex."

Jeremy put a shirt over his face to block out the light of the rising sun and fell asleep. Despite their post-murder sex, JR could not rest. "I didn't feel like anything was real. I was so out of my mind. I couldn't really process what had happened and I was trying really hard not to think about it."

It was early afternoon when JR and Jeremy woke up. Cam, too, was awake. He reached for his only bottle of liquor and was upset to find it was almost empty.

"I felt really sick, nauseous-like. I had a really bad stomach ache," JR recalls. She nibbled on some dry Cheerios and went to work applying eyeliner. They were going out.

As Jenny slept, Cam, Jeremy, and JR got into Jeremy's truck, went to the liquor store, and drove a short distance to the fourplex apartment on Clelland Crescent where Jenny had lived for two months before moving in with Cam. It was just across the street from the 7-Eleven where JR had run to get some cash with her mother's credit card.

They were barely one kilometre down the road from the house where Gareth was discovering the bloodied bodies of her family.

A well-known party house and crash pad, the apartment on Clelland Crescent had a reputation in the neighbourhood. The constantly revolving tenants were a sketchy lot.

A party was in full swing when Souleater and Runaway Devil arrived. Music blared as dishevelled, glassy-eyed young men drank and smoked on the balcony. It was a sunny, warm spring day. People had been drinking and smoking weed at the filthy fourplex since noon.

Jeremy wore dark sunglasses to cover the bruise that by now had caused his eye to swell shut. He seemed eager to introduce JR to the dozen or so people at the apartment, where his old friend TeJay Stadelman lived with his close buddy Tyler Randlesome and various people who would come and go, crashing on the couch while they hung out to drink and smoke pot. It was, in a macabre way, a coming out party for JR. At long last, she was free. Jeremy was finally able to introduce his pretty girlfriend to many of his friends. She'd been grounded for so long that there hadn't been any recent opportunity for them to meet the girl he was in love with.

"All he really told me was they used to pretty much lock her up like she was in prison," says Grant Bolt, who was meeting JR for the first time.

At the party, the attention-seeking Jeremy lifted his sunglasses to show people his black eye, grinning with pride and bursting to tell someone his war story from the previous night. Injuries from fights and drunken scuffles were not unusual for Jeremy and his rough circle of friends, who wore their wounds like medals of bravery.

Everybody was drinking. JR lied to TeJay that it was her birthday. "I gave her a couple of drinks," TeJay says. He poured her some cherry whiskey. The sweet liquor would be her toast to a new life. It was Sunday afternoon, but there would be no school for her tomorrow. Just freedom.

TeJay, a hard drinker in frequent trouble with the law, had spent the previous night in the police drunk tank. As soon as he got out of jail that morning, he went back to the apartment, showered, and promptly went out to buy more booze.

Belinda Hope, who had just turned 17 in March, introduced herself to JR, who was sitting on the couch in the living room of the apartment with Jeremy. Belinda held her three-month-old daughter, Angel, cradled in her arms: "I didn't want to lay her down because people were drinking."

Belinda and her mother had arrived in the morning with a vacuum as an olive branch – Angel's father was Tyler Randlesome, whom Belinda had recently left. Belinda and Tyler had started dating again and, in a show of affection, Belinda had offered to help clean the dirty, neglected apartment. But now that the party was in full swing, Belinda gave up on her housework. Her mother left when Jeremy showed up. According to Belinda, "She said she didn't feel right."

JR was smiling and asking Belinda questions about the baby. The two dark-haired girls chatted easily. "I just thought she was a really nice girl. She seemed really happy," Belinda remembers.

As Belinda sat in the living room trying to coax a burp out of sweet baby Angel, Jeremy and JR started "going for it" on the couch in front of everybody. "They were lying on the couch facing each other, whispering in each other's ears and giggling. They were kissing too much and it made me uncomfortable," says Belinda, who left the room. The couple's display of passion was hard to ignore." They seemed pretty happy. They weren't upset at all. They were kissing and hugging and laughing and whispering." Cam Barkley, too, saw the couple nuzzling. "JR was straddling Jeremy on the couch and they were face to face the whole time," Cam says, depicting JR as the amorous aggressor. "JR was rubbing up on Jeremy on the couch."

Tyler was drinking heavily at the party and admits everything about that day is "vague," but he, too, distinctly recalls JR and Jeremy on the couch at about 2:30 p.m.: "Their hands are all rubbing each other."

If JR was largely innocent of the murders, as she claims, how could she be so callous as to be making out and giggling and laughing with her

killer boyfriend at a party just down the street, only an hour after police
had found the bodies of her family? "I was really trying to hold it together
and be normal and laugh when everybody else laughed," she said later.
Jeremy, she said, was being "weird": "He seemed distant and closed off. He
had never been that way around me before. I needed to make sure he still
loved me. I was kissing him. I had to make sure he was still there. He was
the only person who still loved me. He'd take care of me . . . It made me
scared. I needed to make sure he still loved me. I was, like, clinging to
him to make sure he was still there."

As Runaway Devil and Souleater engaged in their passionate embrace,
Sergeant Secondiak was leading the police's second sweep inside the gory
death house.

Police walkie-talkies crackled with news of the nightmare unfolding
at the crime scene. "What came back on the radio is that, yes, truly there
are people dead," Norm Boucher, the former police chief, recalls. "There's
blood all over the place. I kept on listening." Within about five minutes,
Boucher got on his cellphone to an inspector to discuss the situation. He
then turned on his AM/FM radio to monitor newscasts. Nothing was yet
being reported. He called the inspector.

"It's truly a scene. It looks like a mass murder situation," Boucher
was told.

Jenny woke up at Cam's apartment in the afternoon with a headache and
an unquenchable desire for more weed. Alone in the empty apartment,
she showered and smoked the last remaining pot from the night before.
She called Kacy Lancaster, the Blonde Vampire. "We were quite close. We
were good friends." Jenny wanted to pawn a keyboard and some DVDs
but, at 14, was too young to legally sign the consignment form. Kacy
would oblige. Together they went to a downtown pawn shop in Kacy's
red Mazda pickup and got $62 for Jenny's things. They went to McDonald's,
ate some fast food, and then picked up Grant Bolt and bought some pot.

At about 3 p.m. Kacy, Grant, and Jenny arrived at the Clelland Crescent party house. JR and Jeremy were just stepping outside.

"Jeremy wasn't quite normal," Grant says. "He was there, but he was empty."

He was also hungry.

"We were all standing around. Jeremy asked me to take him and JR to Burger King," Kacy says. She recalls Cam Barkley running around, smashing bottles. He had drunk nearly a case of beer and a 26-ounce bottle of Hpnotiq, a sticky-sweet vodka-based liqueur blended with fruit juices and cognac.

Kacy, with her crush on Jeremy, was always eager to help him, so she drove him and JR to the nearby Burger King drive-through. When they came back to the party house, Jeremy and JR sat outside on the lawn eating burgers and fries.

As the two killers munched on fast food in the sunlight, more investigators descended on the crime scene. Constable Darcy Brandt, a dog handler, arrived with Rocky, a German shepherd, to search for evidence within a half-kilometre radius of the house. Another half-kilometre and the search area would have included the party pad where JR and Jeremy were enjoying themselves on the front lawn. "We snooped in anything we could find," says Constable Brandt – garbage cans, backyards, alleys. Two other dog units were also involved in the search. Rocky and Brandt were assigned to the east and southeast quadrants of the search area. None of the dog teams turned up any evidence. (Rocky performed well despite an injury suffered two and a half years earlier while apprehending a drug suspect. Impaled by a tree branch in the chest, the dog required five surgeries to remove wood fragments that spread throughout his body. In 15 months, Brandt's dog would die from a piece of wood lodged in his pancreas, the thirty-third police dog in Canada to die in the line of duty.)

———

James Whalley, a good friend of Jeremy's, arrived at the apartment, but not to party. Unlike most of those at the fourplex, the 22-year-old had a job. He had been staying at the apartment with Tyler, TeJay, and "various people who would crash on our couch all the time," but had become fed up with the living arrangements. "I was sick of paying all the bills." James had gotten his bedroom furniture out the day before and was there to pick up his TV, washer, and dryer. Moving the big items was difficult. "There was people everywhere."

James bumped into Jeremy eating fast food on the lawn. Clowning, he grabbed Jeremy's hand and took a quick bite out of his friend's hamburger. "Jeremy had a fat black eye. He wanted to talk to me," James says. He followed his friend back inside and into a downstairs bedroom. The two had been very close friends and Jeremy felt he could confide in James. JR followed them into the room and sat on the bed.

James was a bit impatient. He had to meet someone about moving into his new place and wanted to leave. "I was busy. I had stuff to do."

As soon as they entered the bedroom, Jeremy blurted out: "We killed my girlfriend's family last night. I gutted them like a fish."

The young man looked at them in disbelief. It was eerie hearing the words coming from his friend. "His tone of voice was completely mellow, like we were having an everyday conversation."

Immediately, JR confirmed Jeremy's shocking admission. "My little brother gargled," she said.

The entire conversation lasted maybe 30 seconds.

"You guys are crazy," James said, and walked away.

"Who would believe their best friend did something like that?" he said later. "I didn't want to see that house again. I didn't want to be anywhere near that house."

Before James drove off in his truck, he ducked his head in through the basement bedroom window to yell a quick goodbye to Jeremy, accidentally knocking down a mirror that had been propped up on the window ledge. The mirror shattered, showering JR and Jeremy in shards of broken glass. Seven years of bad luck – and counting.

Kacy, Jenny, and Grant left the party and drove toward downtown. They crossed the river to Police Point Park, where they smoked two bowls of marijuana. Missing her wallet and wanting cigarettes, Kacy drove back to the party, arriving about 4:30 p.m. Jeremy and JR were again cuddling on the couch.

Jeremy led Kacy into a bathroom and asked her, as he often did, for another favour. This one was much bigger than bringing cigarettes to his trailer or driving him to Burger King. He needed her to wipe down his mom's truck and hide it. "He said there was some stuff there he didn't want his mom to see. He said he wanted the seats clean when he returned it to his mom," says Kacy.

Kacy obliged, enlisting the help of the stoned Jenny. Through her drug haze, Jenny heard parts of a conversation that JR and Jeremy were having with Kacy. "They were saying something about moving a truck," Jenny recalls. "Kacy came out and asked me to drive her truck. I was stoned and not driving well. She was driving the grey truck, I was following. We went towards the Flats."

Kacy led Jenny to a treed area in the Flats. It was a site familiar to her. She and Jeremy used to go there to smoke weed. She parked Jeremy's truck behind some bushes – not to hide it, she claims, but because "I didn't want anyone breaking into it." Kacy handed Jenny some disposable wipes and together they started cleaning "palm-sized splotches" out of Jeremy's pickup. It had "a couple of stains on the seat. It really didn't look that bad," says Kacy.

Jenny was so stoned she says she didn't know what they were cleaning or why. "I was tired. I had snorted a lot of cocaine. I was very stoned. I thought it was rust." Jenny wiped down the passenger side, including the armrest and the door lock. "Kacy just started wiping things down . . . I started wiping down my side. I was very stoned. I wasn't asking questions." Kacy says she also removed some garbage from the truck – receipts, empty pop bottles – "just to be nice."

Kacy was happy with the job they had done and with her motherly attention to detail. Jeremy would be pleased. She and Jenny drove back to the party in Kacy's Mazda truck. When they arrived, they found an agitated Jeremy. News of the murders was being reported on TV and radio. The paranoia that Souleater had felt in the moments after the murders had begun to set in again.

9

CRIME SCENE

"Everything was soaked in blood . . ."

Constable Gerald Sadlemyer was at the police gunnery range for firearms training when his pager went off at 1:50 p.m. on Sunday, April 23, with a message to phone Sergeant Brent Secondiak, the head of the patrol unit who was the first to respond to the call at the house in Ross Glen. An eight-year member of the Medicine Hat Police Service, Sadlemyer had been on the forensics identification unit for only 15 months. By 2:20 p.m. he was in a briefing at police headquarters. Three bodies had been found inside a house. Sadlemyer was to gather his gear, including a still camera, and meet other investigators at the scene.

Constable Mike Storozuk, an eight-year member of the MHPS with three years on the forensics team, was on his day off when he got a call at 2 p.m. to report for duty. Forensics specialist Sergeant David Hacking, a 20-year veteran officer, was also off duty, as was Sergeant David Brandrith, a 27-year veteran assigned to the major crimes unit. The three officers met Sadlemyer outside the death house just before 4 p.m.

Crime scene investigation is not at all like its depiction in the TV series *CSI*, where crimes are solved by beautiful people in tight-fitting

T-shirts and tank tops. Crime scenes are investigated by people – some beautiful, most not – wearing bulky white protective coveralls, known as "bunny suits," to prevent contaminating the sites with dirt, hair, and skin. Collecting crime scene evidence is a slow, methodical, and laborious process. What takes minutes on TV takes hours, even days. Processing it takes weeks and months.

Made of a disposable paper-plastic material, bunny suits are worn to minimize what is known in forensic science as Locard's Principle of Exchange. Developed in he early 1900s by pioneering French criminologist Edmond Locard, the concept states that whenever there is contact between two items, there will be an exchange of material. Locard's Principle has been the bane of criminals ever since. "Wherever he steps, whatever he touches, whatever he leaves, even unconsciously, will serve as a silent witness against him," Locard wrote.

> Not only his fingerprints or his footprints, but his hair, the fibers from his clothes, the glass he breaks, the tool mark he leaves, the paint he scratches, the blood or semen he deposits or collects. All of these and more, bear mute witness against him. This is evidence that does not forget. It is not confused by the excitement of the moment. It is not absent because human witnesses are. It is factual evidence. Physical evidence cannot be wrong, it cannot perjure itself, it cannot be wholly absent. Only human failure to find it, study and understand it, can diminish its value.

Sadlemyer, Storozuk, Hacking and Brandrith pulled the hoods of their bunny suits over their heads and elastic slippers over their shoes, donned face masks, protective glasses, and latex gloves, and slowly entered the split-level bungalow in Ross Glen. It was 4:10 p.m. The street was now swarming with dog teams, onlookers, reporters, and photographers. Inside the house, all was deadly silent and still. Less than one kilometre away, JR and Jeremy were making out on a couch at a party that was in full swing.

With Storozuk using a video camera and Sadlemyer taking photos, the officers began recording a grisly scene.

They walked to their right, into the front living room, where nothing seemed out of the ordinary: a small plant on an end table, a couch, chair and a dream catcher hanging on one wall. In the kitchen they found the everyday things of family life. On a light oak-coloured table were a glass bowl, a roll of tape, a pair of black-handled scissors, and a pink recipe file box. On the white countertop sat a white microwave oven, a white coffee maker, a jar, and a clutter of children's craft supplies. The drawers and doors on the light-oak cabinets were all closed; the white dishwasher showed no signs of telltale fingerprints and the light-coloured linoleum floor showed no drips of blood. On the side of the refrigerator was a child's drawing. On the back door, however, something unusual caught their eye – a "red substance" that Sadlemyer photographed.

The stairwell leading up to the bedroom level was a different story. A blood smear on the left wall started above the furnace thermostat and ended at the landing at the top of the stairs. A blood smear on the right wall was at a similar shoulder height. Both swept up each wall, as if painted with a brush.

The officers photographed the knife in the diluted red pool on the bathroom counter and the carpet outside of Jacob's room, still wet with his blood. Inside his room, blood was everywhere. "It was quite a mess," says Brandrith. They saw the dead boy. According to Sadlemyer: "There was a lot of blood all over the walls and the boy. There was blood on the floor. The sheets, everything was soaked in blood. The boy was covered with blood from head to toe, all over the boy's body. There was blood on the walls and a large wound to his neck."

They entered JR's bedroom and recorded the scene. As they turned to leave the room, video camera rolling, they saw blood on the light switch next to the door.

The men went back downstairs, to the main level, and began following the blood trail to the basement, including the right stairway wall smeared with blood.

At the foot of the stairs was the body of Debra. "She was covered with a lot of blood from head to toe," says Sadlemyer. To her left, in another part of the room, was the body of Marc, his arms reaching up and his hands clenched in what Brandrith described as "a pugilistic manner." His black boxer shorts had a bloodstain in the crotch area where they had been ripped open by a cut. The investigators looked up. Blood was also spattered on the ceiling. The investigators knew that this had been a death battle. "There was blood spread from one end of the room to the other — the ceiling, the floor, all over the place," Brandrith says.

Given the nature of the crime scene, one thing was obvious to the officers. This was clearly an act of rage.

As they were going through the basement, they encountered a little black dog that, according to Hacking, appeared to be "very afraid." Brandrith tried to catch it but it ran away.

Brandrith and Hacking had seen this sort of scene before. In 2001, they investigated another triple homicide involving a 22-year-old man suffering from paranoid schizophrenia who shot his father, mother, and 21-year-old brother. He was found not criminally responsible for the murders. Now, less than 10 years later, they had a second triple homicide – unusual in a small city with a violent crime rate 17 percent below the national average.

The four officers finished their walk-through of the crime scene at 5:07 p.m. They could not begin collecting any evidence without a warrant, so Brandrith ordered the scene sealed and posted officers around the perimeter of the property. As they were leaving, Brandrith ordered Sadlemyer to take a photo of the family portrait that Sergeant Secondiak and the other first responders had seen. Because the girl was still missing, Brandrith decided they might need to release her picture to the media for their help in locating what police feared was a possible kidnap victim.

"We were concerned for her safety," recalls Brandrith.

———

Sandra Richard, JR's school counsellor, was driving through Ross Glen at 2:30 in the afternoon when she encountered a police roadblock. As she started to take a detour, her cellphone rang. It was the police, asking for information about JR. They needed to contact her. Richard thought hard and gave the officer the names of a few girls she knew to be friends of JR. It was urgent, the officer said. They needed phone numbers and school photos. She agreed to go to the school and meet Constable Gordon Stull, the Medicine Hat Police Service school resource officer.

Stull had been assigned to school liaison for only two weeks. He, too, was at the gunnery range when he got a call to report to Sergeant Robert Cole, the officer assigned to gather all leads on the whereabouts of JR. Stull's assignment was to meet Richard and the school's vice principal to get any information he could on the missing girl.

Shortly after 3:30, the three were in the school office. Stull informed them that JR's family's had died and that the police were desperate to locate her. Stull knew it was a homicide – "I was told it was a horrific scene" – but did not go into details with the school administrators. JR was officially a missing person, possibly abducted, possibly at a sleepover with a friend. The last thing the police wanted was for a little girl to come home unexpectedly and walk into the middle of a tragedy involving her family.

Richard knew JR was involved with a local swim club, but wasn't sure which one. She told Stull it was possible that she might be away at a swim meet. Stull asked for JR's school photo, which Richard retrieved from a computer. Stull e-mailed it to Cole. Richard began going through records to retrieve phone numbers of JR's friends. She told Stull that students some-times keep friends' phone numbers taped inside their locker doors or in notebooks. Although Stull could not legally order a locker search, Richard did have the authority to enter student lockers. She looked up JR's locker number and combination in a record book and walked down the hall while Stull waited in the office.

Richard reached inside the locker and began flipping through a binder. A loose page fell out. It was a hand-drawn, 12-panel cartoon strip depicting a family of three stick figures being burned alive while two others watched, laughing. In the cartoon, one stick figure is happily running toward a vehicle labelled "Jeremy's truck."

In the first panel, labelled "let's go for a walk," two adult stick figures are walking with a child while another larger child stands to one side with a frown on her face and X's for eyes, depicting an angry expression. In another panel, the angry stick figure pours gasoline into a water sprinkler and says, "Mwa-ha-ha." In the following panel, the little stick figure happily plays on a swing while the adults watch from a picnic table. "Oh no, we're covered in gasoline," the next panel reads, followed by panels showing the family burning and screaming: "Ahh, I'm being burned alive," "Help, Help. My flesh is being burned off," and another with a caption reading: "The unimaginable pain." In the last panel, two stick figures are seen laughing and saying: "Aha, your burning alive."

Richard also found a note, written in neat, tight script:

> May the hatred and anger built of blazing infernos fill you
> and overcome you. May the pains of a thousand torchered
> souls come upon you like scalding blade and eclips all other
> nobel feeling. May your hopes, dreams and happiness fall
> into the swirling pit of despair never to return. May your
> peace of mind and safety be gone to you to be forever afraid
> and ailled. May the black overcome you and the pain never
> ending. May all you love be stolen and destroyed just out
> of reach, to never again feel such joys. amen xx.

Later, a classmate would identify the handwriting as JR's.

Richard knew what the stick-figure drawing meant. "Jeremy's truck," in her mind, meant Jeremy Steinke's grey pickup truck. She had seen the 23-year-old, whom she had mistaken for a Medicine Hat high school student, hanging around the Catholic junior high in his pickup on several occasions.

Richard hurried back to the office and showed the drawing and chilling note to Stull. He examined them and quickly made his own conclusion. The girl was no longer just missing, she was a murder suspect. Up to now, the police were concerned for JR's safety. They never imagined a 12-year-old honour student and swim club member could be implicated in the possible murder of her entire family. He immediately reached for the phone and called Sergeant Cole.

Stull told Richard to return the papers to JR's locker. He ordered it to be sealed and its lock changed until he could get a warrant. He recorded the time as 5:43 p.m.

By 6 p.m., all of the investigating officers from the crime scene were at police headquarters. The scene was frenetic. Tips were coming in, leads were being sorted from interviews with neighbours, and next of kin were being sought. Staff Sergeant Glen Motz, a 26-year veteran in charge of the criminal investigation division, was the file commander responsible for the overall assignment of tasks. He called a team briefing for 7:15 p.m. By now, JR had been identified as the girlfriend of Jeremy Steinke. The damning evidence in her locker was leading police to believe she was a suspect.

The police had already released her photo as a possible missing person and asked the media's and the public's assistance in locating her. Her picture was flashed several times on that night's local TV broadcast of the Medicine Hat Tigers Junior A conference final playoff hockey game, which everybody in town was watching. Rumours spread that she had met the killer online and that he had abducted her.

James Whalley was at a friend's house watching television and drinking beer when JR's picture was broadcast. The phone rang. It was a friend "in mid-freakout," says James. He told her he had seen JR and Jeremy just hours before at the party.

"You have to go to the cops," she told him.

An admitted "pothead," James was more worried about what the police would do to him: there was a warrant out for his arrest for failing to make a court appearance on one of the many minor charges that he regularly collected. "I was frantic, freaking," he recalls.

Despite his own precarious legal situation, James did the right thing – he decided to go to the police. He was not the only person tormented by the murders. An emotionally rattled Jordan Attfield showed up at the station to give a statement, sobbing as he did so. James, though, provided the most damning and crucial information: that Jeremy admitted to him that he "gutted them like a fish" and that JR said her little brother "gargled" as he was dying.

With the stick-figure drawing and the interview with James, the police officially elevated JR to a suspect in the deaths of her family.

Sergeant Secondiak found it hard to believe that Jeremy Steinke could be part of such a heinous act. He had stopped Jeremy dozens of times for minor driving offences and knew him well. "He never had a driver's licence. I wrote him multiple tickets. I talked to him a hundred times and never thought he'd be capable of something like this."

The release of JR's identity would prove to be a complicated legal dilemma for the media. It prompted one man to post a comment some days later on a Medicine Hat community website that had revealed her identity. Canadian law bans the publication of the names of young offenders, but the release of her name as a missing person launched her into the public realm.

"We can't unring that bell and now," the man wrote. "We all know who the 12-year-old is. In this day and age of the Internet, this means anybody can figure it out, too, by looking on blogs such as this. Now, of course, the [*Youth Criminal Justice Act*] prohibits the media from publishing her name . . . But what laws are there governing websites, newsgroups and blogs? Is there any precedent on this? I am just curious because I think again we are seeing where technology is moving faster than the law and perhaps such publication bans will become impossible to enforce."

————

With evening beginning to fall and newscasts reporting the murders, Jeremy and JR grew nervous as the party wore on. Around 7 p.m., Kacy got a phone call from Kaylee. She, too, was scared, saying the cops were looking for her because she had been reported as a runaway. Kaylee was calling from Raven's, asking if Kacy could drive Mick back home to Leader. Kaylee was hoping to go along, too, and hide out at Mick's place, as she had done once before. She passed the phone to Mick, who begged Kacy for a lift and offered her $30 for gas. Although she had only met Mick twice, Kacy felt she couldn't turn him down. Like Jeremy, the Blonde Vampire was always willing to help anyone even peripherally associated with their group.

Kacy asked the increasingly edgy Jeremy and JR if they wanted to come along for the ride. She claims she was unaware that the police were hunting for the couple: "I thought JR and Jeremy were just running away, and Jeremy wanted to keep a low profile." As they got into her truck, Kacy told Jeremy and JR to stay down and out of sight.

Kacy, Jenny, Jeremy, and JR drove back to Cam Barkley's apartment, where Kacy thought she might had left her wallet after picking up Jenny. She and Jenny went in, grabbed some pillows and blankets, came back to the truck, and drove downtown to meet Mick and Kaylee. With not enough room for everyone in the cab, Jeremy put blankets and a pillow in the back of Kacy's truck, under the canopy that covered the box. He also tossed in a sleeping bag and his and JR's backpacks. The now-hunted couple hid under the blankets. They had also brought the white plastic grocery bag that Mick had seen Jeremy take with him from the trailer. It was stuffed with Jeremy's blood-soaked clothing.

Jenny was worried about what was unfolding: "We talked and decided to get out of town. I knew something had happened but I didn't think it was as bad as it was."

Jenny had only met Kaylee once before, at the mall a week earlier, and had never met Mick, but she willingly went along for the ride with her friend Kacy. As they pulled out of Medicine Hat, it was about 8:30 p.m. and nearly dark. With Kacy driving, Jenny on the passenger side, Mick and Kaylee in the back seat, and Jeremy and JR under the canopy in the back bed of the truck, they hit the highway and drove into the night, heading east for some strange town in Saskatchewan.

"I didn't even know there was a place called Leader," Jenny says.

Belinda returned to the party house to retrieve a forgotten diaper bag. The house she had so fastidiously cleaned earlier in the day was a disaster. Someone had thrown up on the doorstep and beer cans littered the lawn. Empties were also scattered throughout the apartment, along with bottles and bongs. Hammers had been thrown into walls and a dishwasher had been heaved over a balcony.

JR, Jeremy, and most of the others were gone, leaving only the very drunk Tyler and a few other stragglers. Tyler was so intoxicated that he was rolling on the floor, yelling and throwing things off the balcony. Belinda's relationship with him had been tempestuous. She wanted to get back together with Angel's father, but realized now it was no use. As he hurled abuse at her, she ran with friends across the street to the 7-Eleven. Tyler gave chase. He was so drunk that he bounced off a passing car. Police arrived and started asking questions.

"That's the guy who did the murders," a bystander yelled, pointing at Tyler. "There were all kinds of rumours going around," Belinda says.

Their interest piqued, police started making inquiries about where the two had been. Belinda told them about the party and began listing names of people who had been inside Tyler's apartment. When she mentioned Jeremy, the officer looked up at her.

"When I said JR, he started talking on his walkie-talkie," Belinda says.

The party ended abruptly. Undercover police entered the fourplex, pretending to be potheads looking to score some drugs. TeJay Stadelman was so baked that he fell for the bait and tried selling weed to an undercover officer. "He didn't look like a cop," he says.

For the second time in 24 hours, he was arrested and detained. Tyler, who had been drinking since noon, was also arrested. Cam was passed out cold on the couch when the cops arrived. He awoke to a police Glock pistol in his face and was handcuffed on the spot. Everybody else at the party had left.

The police had taken into custody three extremely drunk young men, but had just missed nabbing the real quarry they so desperately sought.

The forensics team returned to the house in Ross Glen that night with a warrant to collect evidence. Storozuk began working outside at the back of the house making cast impressions of footprints that Sadlemyer had photographed earlier. It was crucial that these not be lost to weather, which up until now had worked in their favour. Light rain the day before had made the ground wet at the time the intruder arrived, leaving "impact" footwear impressions in the backyard consistent with somebody jumping over the white picket fence. One of the investigators rushed home to get his wife's hairspray, which he sprayed into the foot marks to preserve them.

There were nine more footwear impressions by the ground-level back deck near a basement window, which was broken. Storozuk would later spend 12 hours meticulously reassembling the glass in an effort to determine an impact pattern that would tell him if the glass had broken from the outside or the inside, and the type of implement, if any, that was used to smash it.

The other members worked inside until 12:20 a.m., collecting and bagging evidence, including the two knives that were the suspected murder weapons. The blade of the knife found near Marc's body was bent in the middle and at the tip, indicating it had hit bone.

There was so much blood evidence to collect that Hacking called Serge Larocque, an RCMP bloodstain pattern expert based in Edmonton, to help them process the crime scene. Larocque would not be able to begin his investigation until the next day, so the investigators decided not to move bodies until Larocque examined the scene. Patrols were assigned to guard the house overnight.

Due to the grisly nature of the massacre, Boucher was concerned for his men. "I phoned our senior officers to make sure our people were okay. I asked if we had a chaplain, because this is out of the norm for our people. It was a shocking environment. Seeing blood is always tough for anybody. It was a really messy area. The officers, I think, they put a lot of their own feelings aside so they could keep moving ahead and really pursue the investigation." The chaplain arrived that night for one of the debriefings at police headquarters. "Everyone had a good attitude. Not losing focus," Boucher says.

The investigation, involving 20 of the force's 99 officers, was moving rapidly. In addition to James Whalley's statement and JR's stick-figure drawing and note about never-ending pain and blazing infernos, police were obtaining information from the Nexopia and VampireFreaks profiles kept by kids in the community, including Jeremy and JR.

"Things were falling into place fairly quickly," Boucher recalls. "Nobody was spinning their wheels about potential avenues, just getting information on what happened and where it is going."

Boucher also made sure someone was assigned to handle media and discussed a division of duties with Glen Motz. Motz, the senior officer, picked 35-year-old Sergeant Chris Sheehan, a member of the major crimes unit for five months, to be the primary investigator. Sheehan was away on a course at the Canadian Police College in Ottawa when he got the call.

"I thought it was a joke," Sheehan says. "I was the most junior sergeant in the department then." But Sheehan, who had worked in the drug unit and had extensive experience with juveniles and teens, would be familiar with many of the players who were emerging as witnesses and suspects. "He would be very patient, very determined, very aggressive to solve it. He had proven that before, so did Secondiak, so did

Motz," says Boucher. "You try to pick your best people who had been in other situations. We had a lot of good players." Sheehan booked a flight home for the next morning.

Paulette, Marc's sister, was in a deep sleep when the phone rang at her home in Ontario at 1:30 a.m. on Monday, April 24. It was Sergeant Glen Motz calling with the news that her brother, sister-in-law, and nephew had been slain. "I was in shock and disbelief. I couldn't go to work for two weeks, " Paulette recalls.

Debra's brother, Peter Doolan, was numb when he got a call from Motz a short time later. "There is no easy way of telling you this," Sergeant Motz said. "They are dead."

"I thought they had the wrong people," Peter said later in one of his only interviews, with the *Okotoks Western Wheel*, a small-town Alberta weekly paper. "How could a whole family go at once?" Peter thought of his sister, a motorcycle enthusiast like her husband, who would drive all night on her bike and show up at his house at 6 a.m. "We'd rub our eyes and ask how she could be so full of life after a long drive so early in the morning," he wrote in a victim impact statement.

Her answer to that question was so typical of Debra, who engaged everyone she met with her sunny personality and who had inspired others to make positive changes in their lives, the way she and Marc had done.

"It's life, bro," she had told Peter. "It's awesome."

10

THE GETAWAY

"Tell my mom she can have my TV."

Leader, Saskatchewan, population 1,000, is one of the sunniest places in North America. As befitting its 2,350 annual hours of sunshine, it is one of three municipalities in the aptly named rural district of Happyland. Located near the Great Sand Hills, an impressive formation of dunes, the area has been used by movie makers to duplicate Saudi Arabia. Leader also boasts that it is home to the world's largest barn.

Constable Aaron Ewert, a fresh-faced rookie barely out of the RCMP training depot in Regina and on his first posting in Leader, had seen a bulletin put out on Sunday evening, April 23, by the Medicine Hat Police to be on the lookout for suspects wanted in a triple homicide who might be heading his way. Friends and acquaintances of Jeremy and JR told the Medicine Hat Police that Leader was their likely destination. The gossipy, loose-lipped teens could not resist blabbing about what they knew. The police had learned that the group was probably driving Mick back home to Leader. Jordan Attfield also told them of an abandoned barn near Leader where local kids went to party, and police speculated that the suspects might hole up there for the night.

Ewert drove around town in his own vehicle most of Sunday night, cruising several times past the "Welcome to Leader" sign, which is shaped like a tree trunk with a giant woodpecker on one branch, topped by a big owl. The town also boasts a statue of five burrowing owls, indicative of Leader's reputation as an ornithological hotbed, home to at least 13 rare species, including the burrowing owl, which is endangered in Canada.

In an ironic twist unknown to Ewert, Leader is also the birthplace of Elliott Leyton, a social anthropologist who is one of the world's most widely consulted experts on children who murder their families.

About 2 a.m. on Monday, after making sweeps of the town and finding Leader its usual quiet self, Constable Ewert headed home for a few hours' sleep. Assuming the suspects might need gas, he decided to wake up at 5:30 a.m., before the main Esso station in town opened for the day. Armed with descriptions of Kacy Lancaster's Mazda and of the suspects, Ewert parked at a corner that gave him a clear view of the gas station, which has two service bays and an attached convenience store.

The rookie's hunch proved right. A small pickup truck with Alberta plates matching the description of the suspect vehicle pulled up to one of the pumps about 7 a.m. Three teenage girls, one wearing a black hoodie, spilled out of the front seat of the cab and hurried inside.

Kacy Lancaster had left Medicine Hat about 8:30 p.m. on Sunday with Jeremy Steinke and the now aptly named Runaway Devil in the unheated back of her Mazda pickup. JR shivered for the entire two and a half hours. "It was absolutely freezing. I was really cold and shaking a lot. I thought it was fear or something," she says.

In the front seat next to Kacy sat Jenny, who had brought with her the pot that they had scored earlier in the day. In the backseat were Mick and Kaylee, who was hoping to stay at Mick's place. When they arrived in Leader, at about 11 p.m., Mick's mother, Shalene, was upset: "He was in trouble with me. He missed curfew and he pulled up in a vehicle I didn't recognize. It was a Mazda truck with a topper on the back, driven by a blonde girl," she later said.

Shalene did, however, recognize Kaylee and wanted nothing to do with the runaway. Kaylee had been to see Mick a month earlier. When Mick told his mom that Kaylee was 13, she knew somebody would be looking for her. Shalene called the RCMP, who promptly delivered Kaylee back to Medicine Hat.

Mick went inside after his mother turned Kaylee away, leaving the group with no place to go, low on gas, hungry and with only a bag of pot to help them pass the night.

With no service stations open, Kacy drove five minutes out of town and found a place to pull over. "We parked, smoked pot, and went to sleep," she says. It was not a comfortable night. They were so low on gas Kacy could not keep the engine running for heat. Shivering in the cold, early spring of a Saskatchewan prairie morning, Kacy woke up from a fitful few hours of sleep. "It was freezing cold and I wanted to go home," she recalls. Jenny, too, was uncomfortable: "It was cold in the truck. I didn't sleep."

Kacy drove to the gas station and the three girls went inside to use the bathroom, leaving Jeremy and JR curled up under blankets in the back, under the topper. The two murder suspects asked their friends to bring them back a bottle of water.

As the three girls lined up for the bathroom, they saw a copy of the *Medicine Hat News* with the blaring front-page headline: "Couple, boy found dead." There were two pictures of police, one showing a uniformed officer with yellow crime-scene tape in the background, the other showing two officers in white protective suits at the front door of JR's house. Kacy knew the house well – she lived across the alley from JR on the next street over.

Also on the front page was JR's school photo, the one of her wearing Aubrey's studded collar and see-through mesh top. Kaylee, seeing the paper, was about to blurt something out when Kacy shushed her.

JR posing with a replica handgun in her profile photo on a social networking website

Jeremy Steinke as he appeared shortly before the murders, in a photo sent anonymously to the authors. He was found wearing the same sweatshirt when he was arrested. In the background is Medicine Hat Mall, where he and JR often hung out with their friends.

Raven, a goth friend of JR and Jeremy, dressed theatrically, wore black makeup, and painted his fingernails black.

Calgary Herald

Jeremy tried to recruit his long-time friend Grant Bolt to help him with the murders. "Go fuck yourself," Grant replied.

Calgary Herald

Jordan Attfield lived with Jeremy in his trailer for two months. Jeremy tried to recruit Jordan to help him kill JR's parents. Jordan refused.

Calgary Herald

An old couch and other furniture sits on the weathered back deck at Jeremy's trailer.

Sandra Richard, JR's school counsellor, found this drawing in the girl's locker. Reprinted here for the first time, it led police to consider her a suspect rather than a missing person.

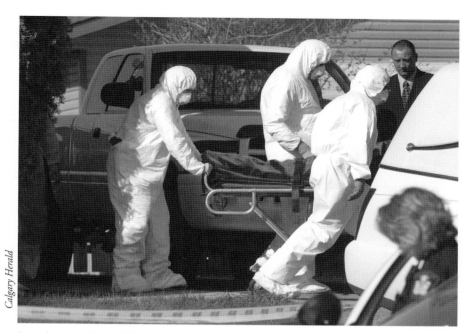

Calgary Herald

It took more than 24 hours for police to process the crime scene before the bodies of JR's family were removed from the house on April 24, 2006.

Calgary Herald

Police guard the taped-off crime scene outside JR's house, where her mother, father, and brother were found dead. Jeremy Steinke pitched a pine cone at her upstairs bedroom window, pictured, to get her attention on the night of the murders.

Sergeant Chris Sheehan was the primary investigator on the murder case. His interviews with Jeremy and JR after they were arrested were never admitted as evidence.

JR wrote to Jeremy that they were "ledgends" [sic] in this jailhouse note from April 26, 2006, three days after the murders.

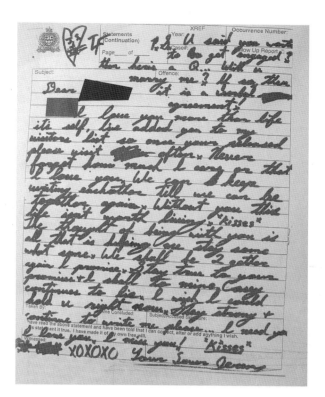

Jeremy asked JR "Will u marry me?" in this letter on April 28, 2006, while the two were in custody. The full text is reprinted on page 173.

Calgary Herald

A girl comforts a friend of JR and Jeremy outside the Medicine Hat courthouse after their arrest.

Jeremy's mother, Jacqueline May, suffered from a
terminal lung disease and needed oxygen by the
time her son went on trial in November 2008.

"I didn't quite know what to make of it," Kacy says. "I was utterly shocked. I didn't know what to think. I didn't know if somebody had broken in and killed her parents. I bought the paper, some water, and Jenny got food."

Kaylee went to the back of the truck and knocked on the canopy, and showed Jeremy and JR the newspaper.

JR giggled.

"That doesn't look anything like you," Jeremy teased, looking at her picture. The couple began pouring over the story intently.

"If it were my family, I would have totally freaked out," Kacy says. "But there was no reaction whatsoever."

"Holy shit, we got to get you out of here," one of the girls said.

Before long, Jeremy and JR grew increasingly nervous, says Kacy. "They were pretty shaky and asked where they could go." Somebody made the improbable claim that Cam Barkley had a plane.

Ewert, watching the scene intently, was suddenly interrupted by a local who ambled up to his squad car and asked the constable if he was keeping an eye on the kids who had pulled into the gas station. "He stopped to talk. I asked him to please continue on. He was a friend. It's small-town Saskatchewan."

The local man had taken notice of the strangers and told Ewert that one of the girls wasn't wearing any shoes. This would indeed be odd at 7 a.m. in Leader, a farming community located off the beaten track at the junction of two secondary highways north of Maple Creek.

With Ewert following at a distance, Kacy pulled away from the gas station and drove to the parking lot of Leader Composite High School, where they stopped. The group began wondering what to do next.

Jenny mentioned that her grandparents had a cabin at Pine Lake in central Alberta. "Jeremy asked if I'd take him there and I said yes," Kacy says.

According to Kacy, a panicky JR cooked up an alibi. "She told us to tell the cops that Jeremy had picked her up at 11 p.m. the night before to stay at Cam's, and that Jeremy and Cam got into a fight because they were drinking." The fake story would account for their whereabouts and provide an explanation for Jeremy's black eye, which was now swollen shut and crusted red with dried blood.

"I was scared," says Kacy. She was beginning to think that Jeremy and JR had something to do with the murders.

Ewert parked a block away from the school, keeping Kacy's Mazda in view. He called for backup from Constable André Gallant, another rookie on his first posting. Ewert, driving the detachment's new police cruiser, with only 15,000 kilometres on the odometer, waited patiently for Gallant. Gallant got into the detachment's four-wheel-drive truck, designated Alpha 3, and met Ewert at 7:25 a.m. with the detachment corporal. The police officers discussed a plan of action and moved in.

Gallant and the corporal approached the front of the truck, one on each side of the cab. Inside they saw Kacy, Jenny, and Kaylee. Ewert went to the back of the pickup truck, where Jeremy and JR had spent the night sleeping. He opened the canopy and noticed a blanket rising and falling as if someone was breathing under it.

Ewert drew his sidearm and pulled back the blanket. As he did, some purple bath beads fell onto the ground.

Under the blanket were Jeremy and JR, minus her pants.

Ewert alerted Gallant that he had two people in the back of the truck. Gallant drew his sidearm and hustled to Ewert's side. They ordered Jeremy and JR out of the truck.

Literally caught with her pants down, JR was handcuffed and put in the back of Ewert's vehicle with the three other girls.

Jeremy was put in the back of Alpha 3. "Tell my mom she can have my TV and that I love her," he yelled out to Kacy, who would dutifully deliver the message to Jackie days later. The police recorded the time as 7:51 a.m.

Bill Clary, Leader Composite's 48-year-old custodian, came to work early that day because he wanted to install a clock in the gymnasium before students arrived for classes at nine. He pulled into the parking lot in his van and was startled by what he saw. The RCMP had surrounded a small pickup truck. Three girls were face down on the pavement, another was being put inside a police cruiser. Small purple bath beads were rolling around on the asphalt.

"Nothing like that happens in Leader," Clary says. "When I saw it, I thought it was maybe just a drug bust." He had heard nothing about the murders in Medicine Hat. The group offered no resistance. "They just looked like normal teenagers."

The police were now in an awkward situation. They had two murder suspects and three possible accomplices in custody in a schoolyard where children between kindergarten and grade 12 would be arriving at any minute, and only one holding cell back at Leader's small RCMP detachment.

As they were being driven to the station, Kacy, Jenny, Kaylee, and JR worried that Jeremy might be charged with raping an underage girl. According to Kacy: "JR had her pants off and the cops wouldn't let her put them back on." One of the girls told JR to claim that the cops raped her. They joked that they might be subject to an orifice search. According to Kacy, JR said: "It wouldn't be sexy even it was a hot cop because I still like Jeremy."

The police put JR into the cell and kept the other girls waiting in Ewert's car. The girls were laughing. Jeremy, meanwhile, was lying in the back of the Alpha 3, apparently trying to sleep. When Ewert looked through the window to see if the young man was okay, Jeremy lunged at him like a caged wolf.

With JR safely in the only holding cell and Jeremy in the back of Alpha 3, the police took the remaining three girls into the station office. Jenny had kicked in the Plexiglas divider to the police car's front seat. "Fuck off. Fuck you," they yelled at the officers. Tired, ornery, hungry, and arrested at gunpoint, the unruly hellions lied that they were on a two-day camping trip.

Inside the tiny police station, while the officers dealt with JR and Jeremy, the girls made unauthorized phone calls. With their actions being video recorded, Kaylee called Hailey, Jenny called Cam Barkley, and Kaylee stole notepads and pens out of a drawer, shoving them down her pants and up her shirt. An officer forced her down onto the floor and handcuffed her.

"Kaylee was making phone calls we weren't supposed to. I was trying to give myself a Breathalyzer. Jenny was taking pictures of herself and trying to get out the window," Kacy admits. "We were all very scared. I was acting on adrenalin, fear, and shock that day."

"We were all pretty scared," says Jenny. "I was scared. I was not a very nice person at all. I was provoking the police, laughing at them, calling them names. I was mad. I was in a police shop and they were saying I was arrested for murder."

At the same time the RCMP in Leader were making the arrests, bloodstain expert Sergeant Serge Larocque arrived at Medicine Hat police headquarters for an 8 a.m. briefing with Sadlemyer, Storozuk, and Hacking. The four drove to Ross Glen and entered the death house an hour later. Larocque began a detailed analysis of the horrific scene.

Bloodstains are categorized in three main groups and 15 subgroups. In examining the house, Larocque would identify two main types: projected stains (caused by blood flying off an object like a knife) and transfer stains, such as those left on a surface by a bloody hand. Most of these would be carefully photographed by Constable Sadlemyer, who would take a total of 1,500 photos at the crime scene.

Outside Jacob's bedroom, Larocque identified "100 plus" projected stains on the carpet. In the boy's bedroom he found "75 plus" projected stains on the floor and transfer stains at the foot of the bed, all consistent with a "bloodletting event from a source moving around the room." There was a heavy contact stain on the boy's bedroom door, a stain at the foot of his bed, and transfer stains on his forearms and legs. There were bloodstains on the walls and chair next to his bed and on a knotty pine dresser, all of which were "in close proximity to liquid blood in flight."

The upstairs bathroom had a transfer stain on the door and diluted stains in the sink and on a Wiltshire Staysharp brand knife, consistent with its being washed off with water. He noted the swipes of blood in the stairwells "consistent with a blood source coming into contact with the walls," and a transfer stain above the deadbolt on the inside of the back door in the kitchen.

Above the body of Marc, on the basement ceiling, were "30 plus" cast-off splatters from a "bloody moving object," such as a knife. Under Debra's body was a large bloodstain in the carpet.

Larocque concluded that Jacob was attacked in the hallway outside his room. Jacob then moved back into the bedroom where, after "a fair amount of activity," he died in his bed. Debra, Larocque concluded, did not move significantly from where she was found.

Sergeant Sheehan arrived on a flight from Ottawa and immediately went to police headquarters for a briefing by Sergeant Motz. "I'm a day late and a dollar short," Sheehan said as he walked into the meeting. After getting the rundown from Motz on the investigation, Sheehan drove to the house, donned a bunny suit, and walked into hell's basement. "This is a big one, Chris," he thought to himself.

"I'm an ex-military guy," he said later. "I'd seen some bad stuff before. It was the worst crime scene I had ever been in."

Looking at Marc's body, Sheehan tried to imagine what the struggle had been like. "You could tell dad was a warrior. Dad fought to his last breath. Right to the end. You could calculate how long the death fight took by looking at the scene."

Sheehan, a father of a six-year-old daughter, walked upstairs to the boy's room. "The most touching thing was the light sabre. I suspect he grabbed it and tried to use it, with the blood all over it." It was one of the many things that haunted investigators. "Little things touched everyone."

From his experience and training, Sheehan could easily surmise what had occurred – the point of entry, which victim was attacked first, the blood smear on the back door handle indicating that it was the point of exit. He knew exactly how the attacker had moved about the house: the blood streaks on the stairwell walls were in an upward direction – wider at the bottom and narrower at the top.

Upstairs, he noticed the small blood smear on the light switch in JR's bedroom. Thieves and home invaders, Sheehan's experience told him, do not turn off lights. That is done only by people who live in the house. He also knew that the murder of three people by knife is not easy, especially when one is a big, solid man in a pitched battle with an attacker, and intent on protecting his home and the family he loves.

These murders, Sheehan knew, were the work of at least two people.

Alerted to the arrests, sergeants Robert Cole and David Brandrith beat a quick path to Leader, arriving in separate vehicles.

It was mid-morning and getting warm when Cole approached Jeremy, still in the back of Alpha 3. Souleater complained that it was stuffy and requested a drink of water. Cole noticed the suspect's badly swollen left eye. In his notebook he recorded that Jeremy was dressed in grey socks, black sweats, and a black hoodie, and had five earrings in his left ear.

Cole and Brandrith drove Jeremy and JR in separate vehicles to the nearby community of Swift Current for a required court hearing to transfer the suspects back to the jurisdiction of Alberta.

After the Medicine Hat officers left with the suspects, Ewert checked the back seat of his almost new patrol car, where the four girls had been sitting. In addition to the broken Plexiglas, the back seat had been slashed.

The court hearing in Swift Current was held at 3 p.m. When it was finished, Brandrith, a friendly man with smiling eyes, and almost boyish-looking despite a head of thick white hair, bought JR an iced tea and a chocolate bar.

Handcuffed, she was put in the back seat of his cruiser, on the passenger's side.

"Where's the little things?" she said, wondering why there were no door handles.

"Well, we remove them so people can't get out," Brandrith replied.

"Can I ask you a question?"

"Sure."

"Where are my friends?"

"They're still being talked to."

As they drove to Medicine Hat she said little, muttering at one point, "I can't believe this is happening to me."

Brandrith felt the need to be frank with her. "Get your head wrapped around it, you're in for a long ride," he said.

"Yeah. I know."

She showed no emotion except when she dribbled some of her iced tea onto the seat of the cruiser. "I'm sorry," she told the sergeant.

Brandrith outlined her rights and other legal details, explaining that she would be taken to a bail hearing.

"What's a bail hearing?" she asked.

JR was mellow and quiet for most of the drive to Medicine Hat, dozing as the tires droned monotonously on the pavement. As they entered the city, she became agitated.

By 6 p.m. on Monday, April 24, less than 30 hours after the bloody bodies of Marc, Debra, and Jacob were found stabbed to death, Souleater and Runaway Devil were back in Medicine Hat, in custody and each charged with three counts of first-degree murder.

For JR, it would be one for the record books. At 12 years and six months of age, she became the youngest person charged with multiple homicide in Canada. Her arrest immediately began drawing headlines, catapulting her into the rarified ranks of young killers like Mary Flora Bell, an English girl who was a mere 10 when she strangled two boys in 1968.

––––––

News of the murders had the city in shock and on edge. Rumours were rife that a gang of goth killers was on the loose, or that 12-year-old JR had been lured away by an adult online predator who used the evil-sounding VampireFreaks to claim his victim.

Dangermouse, the computer expert who ran a local community website, sat at his keyboard and began to post on his blog: "My Medicine Hat brain has troubles digesting a triple homicide in our community. It just doesn't seem like that news fits here."

Locals were flocking to his website looking for information and sharing their concerns.

"This really creeps me out," wrote someone with the user name 1987 who once lived in JR's neighbourhood. "When I was 13, 14, 15, I would take those paths during the night cuz I felt safe where I was living. Well, not any more. I don't want my kids to grow up here!"

One person signed in using the nickname "Scared" and wrote: "I am now so scared this is going to start becoming a common story only with different people and children . . . The sad thing is it just isn't shocking anymore now. You just read that and think wow I can't believe that happened again."

A person named Mo replied: "I don't think it is cause for panic. This was a specific incident. I live a couple blocks away and although I did lock my doors last night, I was not any more scared."

A comment posted by Vicki, who lived three blocks from the scene, read: "I am so sad and scared because my son is the same age as the boy who was murdered. I never thought this would ever happen in this town. I moved here from B.C. to get away from all this stuff. What has this world come to? . . . I am so very upset and feel for the family. My heart goes out to them."

The murders of JR's family in the middle of the night unnerved many people. Sandee Anderson, the owner of Tumbleweeds, one of the city's better restaurants, was so afraid to be in her own home that she slept in her restaurant.

At the gas plant where Marc worked, employees were numb. "The reality of it set in on Monday morning on the drive to work," says Wayne Chopek, the EnCana mechanic who had sat with Marc and Debra at the company Valentine's Day party. "We were listening to the radio and when we arrived at work the pieces all converged together. Everyone was asking each other, 'Is it true? Is it true? Is it true?' It was confirmed it was true. Marc's immediate supervisor came in and confirmed it. He had to identify family pictures and that.

"Our superintendent of the facility showed up that morning. EnCana had grief counsellors there that afternoon and we each got to sit with them one on one. This is a huge trauma to any community, let alone a place where he worked. Everybody at work was very impressed that EnCana felt the need to do that for us. We all felt we were living a dream."

A similar scene was playing out Jacob's elementary school, where students held hands on Monday morning and prayed for their classmate. In an effort to help students understand and cope with the tragedy, the Catholic school board made grief counsellors available to any student who wanted to talk. The flag was lowered to half-mast.

Gawkers and a horde of media gathered Monday outside the murder scene. Sadlemyer, Storozuk, Hacking, and Larocque began removing the bodies from the house at 4:05 p.m. The forensics team had taken hair samples from the three victims and taped plastic bags around their hands to preserve evidence for their autopsies. The bodies of Marc and Debra were placed in body bags and wheeled out on gurneys. No gurney was needed for little Jacob, who was carried out in his body bag by two officers. His was the last body to be removed, at 5:45 p.m.

On her quiet street, which was under siege from reporters and investigators, the enormity of what had happened began to sink in for next-door neighbour Phyllis Gehring.

"You wonder why this family? A kid's life taken away from him, for what? All I know is that they're gone. It's going to be very, very different around here."

In Okotoks, as word spread of the family's slaughter, the news brought their former neighbour Bob Grodin to his knees. He composed himself, sat on his front step, where he and Jacob had chatted together many times, and told *Calgary Herald* reporter Deb Tetley: "My God. They don't have a category for stuff like this."

11

PEACE IN THE SUMMERLAND

"My loverdly parental units . . ."

A prison guard led JR into a small police interview room at 10:30 a.m. on Tuesday, April 25, and left her alone to wait for her interrogators. She sat with her head drooping, dark hair shielding her face, swallowed up inside an oversized blue prison jumpsuit. As she sat motionless in front of a rectangular metal table, Sergeant Sheehan and Sergeant Cole watched her from a nearby room on a black-and-white surveillance screen. Inside the soundproof interrogation room, a camera inside a plastic bubble was mounted on a cinder block wall. A microphone inside a plastic case sat in the middle of the table.

All morning, the men had been setting the stage to get Jeremy and JR to open up and start talking about the murders. They hand-delivered bags of McDonald's breakfast sandwiches to their cells, partly to curry their favour and partly out of the knowledge that bellies full of familiar food would better the chances of co-operation. If they were lucky, the suspects would each confess. If not, they had to catch their untruths and challenge them at every turn. Sheehan and Cole wanted to take advantage of every minute they could before lawyers became involved.

Interrogating underage children is an inherently tricky business for police. Canada's *Youth Criminal Justice Act* provides enhanced rights and protections for children. Under it, police must read a special youth waiver and caution form – known as Form 9.1 – to underage suspects and have them sign it every time they speak with them. In 1990, the Supreme Court of Canada wrote about the importance of this principle in dealing with youths:

> A young person is usually far more easily impressed and influenced by authoritarian figures. No matter what the bravado and braggadocio that young people may display, it is unlikely that they will appreciate their legal rights in a general sense or the consequences of oral statements made to persons in authority; certainly they would not appreciate the nature of their rights to the same extent as would most adults. Teenagers may also be more susceptible to subtle threats arising from their surroundings and the presence of persons in authority. A young person may be more inclined to make a statement, even though it is false, in order to please an authoritarian figure. It was no doubt in recognition of the additional pressures and problems faced by young people that led Parliament to enact this code of procedure.

Form 9.1 was developed because judges were frequently concerned about whether police officers had clearly explained these rights to young people in language "appropriate to the age and understanding of the young person being arrested." It sets out 15 steps that police must follow in reading young persons their rights. Police skip to various sections of the form depending on what answers a young suspect gives. In each section, there are instructions to police officers on how to proceed.

The main portion of the form says:

The law requires that you be told about your rights before I can ask you if you want to make a statement. That is what is going to happen now. I will explain your rights to you and ask to make sure you understand what I have said. If you do not understand a word or something that I have said, tell me and I will explain it to you. It is important that you understand what I am saying. If you do not understand something, stop me at any time and ask. Do you understand?

You do not have to make a statement. This means that you do not have to say anything to me. But, if you make a statement, anything that you say, write or do can be used against you as evidence in court or in other proceedings. Do you understand?

Even if you have already talked to the police or someone else, you do not have to make a statement now. Do you understand?

You should not make a statement because of a favour given or a promise made to you. You should not make a statement because you hope for something in return. Do you understand?

You should not make a statement because you feel threatened or afraid that someone will hurt you or anyone else.

After each "Do you understand?" there is a box where the officer must record the suspect's answer.

Despite the carefully and specifically worded legal form that both Cole and Sheehan walked JR through, her requests for a lawyer and her request to speak to an adult would go unheeded.

The key to unlocking the story from a subject is to establish a rapport. Cole, an experienced polygraph operator, was regarded as a solid interrogator. Sheehan, a former drug unit detective, had a proven talent for gaining trust and prying information out of troubled teenagers and young adults. They decided that the best interrogation tactic to use on JR was that of the "father figure" and the "cool guy," a technique more sophisticated than "good-cop/bad-cop."

"Those traditionally, in its simplest form, work the best with kids," Sheehan explains. "It's like playing chess. If you try the father and it doesn't work, you try the cool, hip cop angle."

Cole, a 19-year police veteran with a greying moustache and neatly cropped hair, tried first, using the fatherly technique. He opened the door to the interview room, warmly reintroducing himself. JR was hanging her head, and her hair was falling forward, hiding her face like curtains. She was crying softly.

"Everybody says how pretty you are," Cole said brightly. "How come you're crying?"

Her response, in a soft voice, is inaudible on the police video of the interview.

He asked her about her dog, but Cole's fatherly concern just made JR cry harder. "I didn't kill anybody," she told him.

"I don't know anything about that stuff. I'm a police officer but want to make sure your rights are protected," he said.

JR swiped at her runny nose with the oversized sleeve of her blue prison jumpsuit.

Cole began going through the caution and waiver. JR asked to contact a lawyer and Cole offered to get her a phone book. He never did. Asked if she wanted to talk to an adult, JR mentioned her school guidance counsellor, Sandra Richard. Later, she asked for Raven, but didn't know his last name. Cole knew that Raven, a 19-year-old whose real name is Tyler Deveau, was part of the mall goth crowd and was on police radar as a friend of the young suspected killers. Police by now had copies of JR's text messages to Raven and had labelled him "a person of interest."

"I'm not saying you can't [talk to Raven], but the police are still investigating," Cole told her.

Cole continued asking JR questions without a lawyer for half an hour. He told her, falsely, that if she was found guilty, she could receive the adult sentence of life in prison unless her lawyer could convince the judge otherwise. Because she was under 14, JR could not be tried or sentenced as an adult.

Cole's efforts proved fruitless. The harder he tried to establish rapport, the more JR whimpered.

Shortly after 11:30 a.m., Cole and Sheehan decided to trade off. Sheehan, a handsome 35-year-old with dark hair and blue eyes, was wearing a pair of trendy glasses. Exuding an air of urban hipness, and as the younger of the two officers, Sheehan was a natural in the "cool guy" role. He introduced himself by his first name, Chris, and began by remarking on the letter *S* in JR's handwriting.

"Your *S*'s are weird. They're upside down," he said. "They are!"

After some more small talk, it was obvious JR was hooked. "I like you," she told Sheehan. "You smell good."

Sheehan decided he would try to connect with JR through music. He said later, "It's all about fishing for that common ground. If movies didn't work, I wouldn't care if it was stamp collecting, I would try to find a personal story that would have to do with stamp collecting. You gotta find something."

"Do you like Marilyn Manson?" he asked.

"Yes," she said.

"What's your favourite group?"

Cradle of Filth, she replied. He'd never heard of the band, but from his time working the drug unit he faked his way through by dropping names like Rob Zombie, founder of the metal band White Zombie, and mentioning the bands Korn and Slipknot. Sheehan asked if Cradle of Filth was more hardcore than Slipknot and admitted he couldn't understand much of what heavy metal bands were saying in their lyrics.

JR boasted that she could understand the words others couldn't discern, which prompted Sheehan to ask how she got into such heavy music.

"Two years ago when I moved here I was all 'I need to fit in' because I didn't have any friends and everybody called me weird all the time. I didn't want to be in the box and wanted to be my own person."

As they chatted, JR told Sheehan: "I feel like I shouldn't be here. Everybody has told me to only talk when there's a lawyer here."

Sheehan inched his chair closer. "If you get upset, that's okay, you can cry on me. It's okay. I don't mind. You probably need someone to cry on right now," he said.

JR protested coyly, "I smell. I smell like I haven't had a shower in two years." She laughed.

"Yeah, you do," he teased back. "But that's okay."

The interview was going well. Sheehan promised to get JR an MP3 player loaded with some of her favourite music, and said he would see to it that she was able to shower and have some toiletries. JR had complained to Cole and now to Sheehan that she had a stomach ache. Arrested, alone, and dressed in a baggy prison jumpsuit, the 12-year-old had to cope with another indignity in a place notorious for lack of privacy. She needed tampons.

Sheehan escorted JR from the interrogation room. "Let's get you a lawyer," he claims he told her. Because they were no longer in the inter-view room, the conversation was not recorded. As he was leading the girl down a hallway to the telephone room, he says, she changed her mind and said she wanted to tell him what happened.

By 3:20 that afternoon, they were back in the interrogation room. Sheehan began taking her statement. But getting the truth out of Runaway Devil was a long way off.

"We hadn't been getting along, me and my family," she explained. "I was thinking about death solidly for two months."

JR told Sheehan that she wanted to finish school and that she cared about her future. "I had a lot of problems in my family but I didn't want them to die."

On the night of the murders, she said she'd called Jeremy after her parents went to bed. "I wasn't allowed to talk to boys, let alone date them.

I was talking to him and really upset." She told Sheehan that she snuck out of the house through the basement window and went drinking with Jeremy, Kacy Lancaster, Cam Barkley, and Jenny – in keeping with the alibi that was cooked up just before her arrest. "We were joking and partying; I was really upset," she said.

JR told Sheehan she was unhappy with her home life. She wanted to run away.

After drinking with Jeremy and her friends, she claimed, she returned to her house early in the morning and found the back door open. "I could see through the window. There was blood. I kinda didn't want to look around. I wanted to leave but I didn't have any money."

"Who dropped you off at your house?" Sheehan asked.

"Jeremy."

"You walked in? He didn't hint to you about anything? He just brought you there?"

She nodded.

"So you went into the house and the back door was open and you could see some blood on the wall. You have to tell me the truth," Sheehan said.

"I kind of knew what was happening but I refused to believe it. I stopped trying, to pretend like I wasn't there."

Sheehan interrupted her. "The worst thing you can do is tell me half-truths. Do it all the way." He put his hand on her shoulder. "Honey," he said. "Tell me all the truth, okay? Please. I believe Jeremy loves you and you love him, but you can't tell me half- truths. Do it all the way."

She paused, and began to tell how they wanted to run away. "Jeremy had to drop me off because we're not allowed to be together. I needed to get stuff. That's why I went there and I got, like, sensitive at the sight of that stuff."

"You open the back door but Jeremy didn't give you a hint of what you might see? Tell me the truth," Sheehan said.

"I don't remember the small talk," JR replied. "He told me to hurry up."

"Did he prepare you for anything before he dropped you off?" Sheehan asked. He placed his hand on the girl's shoulder.

"I knew something was wrong because I saw blood on the stairway," JR continued. "My family would have been up. I went inside and looked down the stairwell." JR said she saw her mother lying on the ground by the couch in her "blue nightie thing."

"I just got a terrible, terrible stomach ache. I got kind of upset and numb. I turned away right away. I had to get out of there. I knew I was going to be charged or something. Then I went upstairs, saw my little brother in the bed, lying there," JR said. She started to cry. "There was blood on his chest and stuff. I grabbed a backpack and I just wanted to get out. I went to the deck and called Jeremy. I was totally freaking out."

"No half-truths, honey," Sheehan said. "Did you tell him what you saw?"

She nodded yes. "I just grabbed him and I hugged him and stood there in the door."

Throughout the taped interview, JR's voice is low, soft and halting, as if searching for the right thing to say.

"You are not showing any emotion at all. That's strange, isn't it?" Sheehan asked.

"All day yesterday I didn't cry," she replied. "Am I a terrible person for not feeling this? And then last night I started crying. I don't know how I'm not crying now."

Sheehan pressed on, telling her that the police had found Jeremy's bloodstained truck and that Kacy Lancaster claimed that JR had ordered her to ditch it. "Can you explain that to me? If there's half-truths, you're going to get caught in them."

JR told Sheehan it was Jeremy who told Kacy to hide the truck, not her.

Sheehan continued to press. "Did Kacy know something had happened with your parents?"

"She knew we were running."

When Sheehan asked about her home life, JR said, "My parents didn't physically beat me or anything, but I was so unhappy there all the time."

From what had already been gleaned from witnesses, Sheehan believed that she was not abused but doubted the rest of her story. It didn't seem plausible that JR simply happened to find her parents dead on the very night that she and Jeremy were running away. He asked JR if she was telling the truth. She said yes.

"Swear," he said. "Swear."

JR paused, and then in a low voice said: "Fuck."

Remarkably, Sheehan somehow kept from breaking out in gales of laughter. JR had misunderstood his command to tell the truth and thought he was ordering her to use a profanity.

"I've been very respectful to you. I've respected all your wishes but you're not telling me all the truth," he said. "You can't protect him. Tell me the story and include the parts you're leaving out to protect him. Please. You know there's way more to it. You know I know a lot about what happened."

"I know he did it but I don't hate him for it," she said.

"So how do you know he did it?"

"I kind of pieced it together and thought it was kind of obvious. He said he and Cam were fighting because they were drinking."

"Tell me what he did. Truth. We're getting there but we're not quite there. I know you're trying to protect him but don't do that. Just tell me the truth. Half-truths are just like lies. Please tell me the story."

"We were drinking –"

"From the top, please."

"I talked to Jeremy on the phone. I snuck out. We were drinking a lot and we were with Cam and Kacy and Jenny. We were just really talking about my parents. And everyone was, like, 'screw your parents' . . . My friends were worrying about me coming to school shaking and crying, a conversation like that. I was so upset. I said okay, I'm gonna run away.

I had thought about it so many times before. I had to go back and get my stuff. . . . I guess the shock of it. . . . I think it was mixed feelings that got to me. I didn't want to look at them or feel them. I was almost afraid. The first thing I felt was shock. And the second thing was freedom. I didn't want to be that person who doesn't care, but I did care."

Sheehan knew her cover was a lie. She and Jeremy didn't just happen to stumble upon her dead family the very night they decided to run away. It didn't wash.

"Something's missing," Sheehan said. "You were drinking, talking about how you hate your parents. Then what? Did you plan on going over there? Was the plan to go over there and kill your parents? You have to tell me the truth."

"We were drinking. I didn't get the opportunity to drink much [before]. People kept getting me more alcohol and we were talking . . . Me and Jeremy left because everyone was passing out."

"You swear to God you weren't in the house when he killed your family? Can you do that?" Sheehan asked. "We've talked to a lot of people. People that you told of this sound that your brother made. The truth shall set you free. You can't tell me half-truths anymore," he said. "All anyone is going to see is a girl without any remorse and [who] is unwilling to accept responsibility for her actions. You're smart enough to see through all of that. So please tell me the whole truth. We've talked to everyone. Please."

Sheehan put his hand on her shoulder and adopted a sympathetic tone: "Honey, honey. I know you don't want to go to jail for the rest of your life. So please tell me the truth. I've treated you perfectly since we first met. Don't lie to me. I know you're scared for Jeremy. I will let you write him a note when you're done talking to me. Please. Tell me the whole story from the top. I won't judge you."

JR took his hand and Sheehan wrapped both of his hands around hers.

"We were drinking beer, for sure. And we went back to the side alley. And we went inside, and I had to get stuff. I was upstairs."

"Tell me. Who were you with?"

"Jeremy."

"And who else?"

"No one. Just me and Jeremy . . . We got in and I went upstairs. My mom was coming downstairs. Jeremy was moving around downstairs and then my dad came downstairs so I bolted up to my room. I grabbed my stuff. I didn't want my brother to see because I know how fragile he is. He's so sensitive," she said.

"My mom was screaming and it was happening. I couldn't stop this from happening. I stated this is what I wanted but it isn't what I wanted . . . I kept my brother upstairs and Jeremy came upstairs. We couldn't just leave him there. He was so sensitive and he got so scared."

"What did Jeremy do to your brother?"

"He stabbed him in the chest and in the throat."

"Why did you let him do that?"

"Because we talked about that. Because of the kind of person he was and he needed that support, I guess, or love, and we couldn't just do that to him."

"Did you and Jeremy decide that's what would happen to your brother? Did you hold your brother for Jeremy?"

"No."

"Where were you? Did you know he was going to kill your brother?"

"I thought he's not going to do that at the time."

She said Jeremy used knives he had brought from his truck.

"Why did he come into your house with two knives?"

"Because we needed to get away and he didn't really care what happened. We talked about my parents, that, 'I don't want to have to kill them but if I run they're not going to stop until they find me.' I really want them dead but I didn't seriously talk about it. It'd just be like stupid, half-humorous, half not talk."

"How long did the fight go on between your dad and Jeremy?"

"Not too long."

"Did you stab your mother, your father, or your brother?"

"No."

"Did you hold any of them [while Jeremy stabbed them]?"

"No."

"Why did Jeremy come into the house with you if you were just going to get some stuff?"

Then JR suddenly switched her story, saying she did, indeed, hold Jacob.

"I didn't want him to have to suffer," she said, referring to her brother. "I was just going to strangle him until he passed out so he wouldn't have to feel pain."

"Did you know your mom and dad were dead?"

"I didn't want to walk down because I knew there'd be blood."

"How did you know?"

"I knew there was going to be something there. I assumed there was going to be blood."

Sheehan began stroking her hair, resting his hand on the back of her neck. JR started talking about her little brother.

"I went in his bedroom. I was trying to calm him down. Jeremy came upstairs and he began to say, 'We need to kill him. You just can't leave him.' I had a knife and, like, I was having a really hard time. He was really, like, pressuring me. I stabbed him in the chest. I slipped or something and I couldn't do it. And I was trying to wash it off of me."

"And Jeremy did Jacob because you couldn't?" Sheehan asked.

JR nodded yes.

"You stabbed him once in the side of the chest and got blood on you?"

"Yes. He was still moving around."

"He was crying?"

"He said, 'I'm too young to die.' He said that a whole bunch of times."

"Where did the knife come from?"

"One from the kitchen was in my bedroom from before. I took it into my brother's bedroom. I didn't know what I was going to do but I didn't want my brother to suffer. I knew he couldn't go through life without his parents. He's already so scared about other stuff."

Jeremy, she said, "did it out of love for me."

Sheehan stood to leave the room and JR began sobbing. When he returned, he put his arm around her. "Are you alright?" he asked. "I've brought you a pen and a piece of paper. Would you like to write a nice apology to your mom and dad and brother to apologize for what happened?"

"What are you going to do with it?" she asked.

"I'm going to keep it," he said, adding that it would help her get it all out.

Sheehan left her alone in the room with a soft felt pen and pad of paper. JR began writing:

> Dear my loverldly parental units. I am writing in response to the events of Sunday morning. A terrible thing happened, something I feel was all my fault. You must know I love you all dearly and are in my prayers. I wish peace upon your souls in the summerland. To my little brother I apologize for letting you hear what had happened, also for causing you any pain and for frightening you so much. To my parents I hope you know that through all that has happened I loved you the whole while. I wish I could take everything back, I wish it hadn't happened. I wish you were with me right now. Because now I have no one. I pray you can forgive me, and Jeremy to, because he was under the influence of mind altering substance and did it out of love for me. He is most possibly the kindest person I've ever met, his wish being for my happiness. Through all the fights and hatred exchanged, I still loved you. I am sorry my sarcasim was taken to heart. I never ment to harm you. I pray you can be at peace somehow.

When Cole arrived to collect the letter, JR asked him again what would happen with it. "Sergeant Sheehan is going to take it. I won't read it," he said. He told JR he would take care of her, that he would be her "guardian angel."

JR had referred to Marc and Debra as her "parental units." It was a cold phrase, an odd choice of words for a mom and dad who had done everything to protect the daughter they loved. *Parental units.* Even in death, she was mocking them.

JR had also wished them peace in "the summerland," an expression she got from her interest in Wicca. In the Wiccan belief system, the summerland is the afterlife. It is envisioned as a resting place between incarnations that contains pastoral fields of rolling green hills and lush grass. In the summerland, no judgment is passed. It is a place where one "can reflect on what light or darkness they might have brought into their life just lived," with an opportunity to try again.

12

LOVE LETTERS

"In due time we shall have our castle . . ."

After he finished interrogating JR and obtained her "apology letter" to her family, Sergeant Sheehan took the girl to her cell and gave her a notebook to use as a diary. "I know how much you like to write," he said, handing her a Sharpie marker. Its soft tip would not allow her to wound herself.

Sheehan knew JR was in her school's fine arts program, liked to draw, and had a creative mind. From her Nexopia and VampireFreaks pages, Sheehan could see that she was expressive. On VampireFreaks, Runaway Devil stated a fondness for "dark poetry," examples of which she posted on her blog. Most of these were likely copied from other sources, including one entry a month before the murders titled "For The Whore, by me." It was too sophisticated to have been written by JR; the spelling and punctuation were too perfect. JR and the crowd she hung with were, to say the least, not exactly spelling bee finalists. On Nexopia, Runaway Devil said she liked songwriting, but mostly she pasted lyrics from Cradle of Filth into her entries, including a verse from their song "Lord Abortion":

Rainbows that My razors wrung
Midst Her screams and seams undone
Sung at the top of punctured lungs
I bite My spiteful tongue

Sheehan told JR that if she wanted to exchange notes with Jeremy, he would deliver them personally, thinking that might be a way to gain information from the co-accused killers. Maybe it would yield something, maybe not. If nothing else, it was another way to gain her trust. "It was off the cuff," Sheehan said later. "I've never even heard of it done before. Sometimes we'll ask people if they want to write a letter of apology to their victims and we'll use it as evidence."

According to Chief Boucher, successfully facilitating an exchange of notes between two accused murderers was groundbreaking territory. "In my experience in Canadian policing, I think this is the first time it was used involving murders. Most people clam down once a murder charge is on them."

That day, Tuesday, April 25, Runaway Devil wrote the first of several revealing jailhouse love letters that Sheehan passed between her and Jeremy. It read: "I love you with all my heart and no matter what happens please don't forget that people are lying, including Casey [Kacy Lancaster]. I feel very alone. Stay strong. God I can't seem to write what I feel but I love you eternally. Try to hope, there is only so much bonds of flesh can do to the soul. kisses"

As JR was penning her love note to Jeremy, her parents lay on metal tables at the medical examiner's office in Calgary, where forensic pathologist Dr. Craig Litwin was performing their autopsies in the presence of police photographer Sergeant Dave Hacking, who had also photographed and helped videotape the crime scene. Each autopsy took two hours, Marc's from 9:30 a.m. to 11:30 a.m. and Debra's from 2 p.m. to 4 p.m. Jacob's would follow the next day.

One of the first things pathologists look for is lividity, a post-mortem condition in which gravity causes blood to pool in the lowest extremities of the body. The settled blood causes purplish blotches on the skin that enable medical examiners to tell body position at time of death. Lividity was not evident during the autopsies, for one simple reason – most of the blood had already flowed out of the bodies before they were brought in for post-mortem examination.

In Jacob's case, most of the blood loss came from a large wound to his throat that severed his thyroid gland, jugular vein, and larynx. The jugular, says Dr. Litwin, carries blood from the brain to the heart and does not "spurt" blood, like the carotid arteries that carry blood in reverse direction, from the heart to the brain. Rather, there is a "constant, steady flow of blood" from the jugular. "There would have been a lot of blood flowing out in a gentle fashion," Dr. Litwin says.

There was, however, nothing gentle in the way Jacob died. The four-foot-four-inch, 68-pound boy had four other stab wounds, two to the right side of his face, each slightly more than 2.5 centimetres deep, and two shallower stab wounds to the left side of his chest, neither of which penetrated his chest cavity. Jacob also had conjunctival petechial hemorrhages on the insides of his eyelids and mouth – tiny, pinpoint bleeding indicative of strangulation. The pathologist could not conclude definitively that Jacob had been choked – the wound to his neck was so large that it obliterated any supporting evidence, such as abrasions to the skin or other strangulation marks.

Dr. Litwin found 24 stab wounds on Marc, which he recorded and identified by a letter of the alphabet. Wound J, to Marc's right abdomen, was 11 centimetres deep and caused 300 millilitres of blood, slightly more than one cup, to enter his abdominal cavity. Wound W, to his right lower back, entered his right lung and caused 600 ml to enter his chest cavity – "a significant amount of blood to accumulate in a body cavity." Marc, the doctor determined, was five-foot-ten and weighed 207 pounds.

Debra's 12 stab wounds were also identified by letters of the alphabet. The most significant was wound A, which punctured her aorta. Wounds C, D, F, and G punctured her lungs. Wound E penetrated her stomach. At the time of her death, she was five-foot-three and weighed 143 pounds.

Marc and Debra had numerous defensive knife cuts on their hands and arms. Both victims, Dr. Litwin concluded, would have had "several moments of purposeful activity" after suffering their most severe wounds. Although Marc was stabbed 24 times, no single wound resulted in death. Rather, the cause of death was massive blood loss from his collective injuries, according to results of his autopsy.

Debra's fatal wound, he concluded, would have been the one to her heart.

Armed with JR's note to Jeremy, Sheehan now had something to offer him as a gesture of goodwill. At 1:05 p.m. on April 25, after he had done his first interview with JR, Sheehan entered Jeremy's cell to see what cooperation he could obtain. They made small talk for 15 minutes before Jeremy asked for a lawyer. Sheehan got a phone book, and Jeremy pointed to the name of a local attorney, who was called. The lawyer was not interested in taking the case. Jeremy pointed to another lawyer, apparently picking names at random: "Okay, try him."

Sheehan would later testify that as he dialled Jeremy said, "Wait. Fuck, don't bother. I'll get one down the road."

"Are you sure?" Sheehan asked.

"Yeah, yeah." Sheehan says he then read Jeremy a warning regarding his right to a lawyer. "No, I don't want one, for fuck's sake," Jeremy allegedly said.

None of these crucial conversations was recorded on tape. The only record of Jeremy waiving his right to counsel is contained in Sheehan's notes.

Sheehan was eager to do an interview that day, but Jeremy was due in court for his first scheduled appearance to hear the charges against him.

He was transferred into sheriff's custody and taken away to the courthouse, where he appeared before Provincial Court Judge Darwin Greaves. The judge informed Jeremy that he was charged with three counts of first-degree murder. The accused did not look into the gallery. If he had, he would have recognized dozens of familiar faces: sniffling teenage girls and stunned boys dressed in black hoodies packed the courtroom. Clusters of young people had clogged the courtroom lobby. Sheriffs tried to manage the crowd, letting in family and reporters first. Jeremy had not seen a lawyer, so he entered no plea and his appearance was adjourned for a week, to May 2.

JR also made her first appearance April 25 in a separately convened youth court, also before Judge Greaves. Sheriffs flanked her as she was brought into the prisoner's box shackled, her slender arms barely visible in the adult-sized blue prison jumpsuit. Her hair was uncombed, hanging in her face. Her head swivelled as she glanced around the public gallery. When Judge Greaves asked her to confirm her identity, she answered "Yes," in a barely audible voice. Because she had not seen a lawyer, her appearance was adjourned and she was swiftly taken back to her holding cell.

As JR and Jeremy made their first court appearances on April 25, relatives of Marc and Debra gathered in Okotoks to make plans for a Saturday funeral service. Too distraught to comment to reporters, they asked to be left alone. "How do we respond to this?" asked Debra's brother Peter Doolan, who had flown in from Ontario. "We don't even know how to respond. We have a lot of things we want to say, but we're just not ready."

Dave Townsend, a Medicine Hat police sergeant in charge of media liaison, held a brief press conference that day at the Medicine Hat police station. After it finished, reporters jokingly told him that the case would have been solved by now on the popular TV show *CSI*. "*CSI* has something we don't – a script," Townsend said.

TV makes getting a confession look simple. A couple of detectives put a suspect in a room, tell him his fingerprints are all over the murder weapon and, before the next commercial, the guy is singing like a lark. But getting someone to confess to a crime is not easy. The Canadian Police College online library lists 23 books on forensic interviewing. Among them is the widely used manual *Criminal Interrogation and Confessions,* which contains the Reid Technique, nine steps of psychological manipulation used by interrogators. The Reid Technique was developed by John E. Reid, who established a private polygraph firm in 1947 in Chicago. Over the course of his career, Reid noticed that subjects displayed physical signs that consistently coincided with polygraph readings indicating untruthfulness, such as eyeballs shifting to the right when searching for a correct answer. Reid eventually developed a system of interrogation that is commonly used throughout North America. Because there is no such thing as a typical interrogation, the Reid system is basically a blueprint for interrogators.

The first of the nine steps is "confrontation" – presenting the facts of the case and informing the suspect of the evidence against him. An overwhelming amount of evidence typically increases the stress level of the suspect. During the interview, the interrogator may move closer to the suspect to further increase his discomfort.

Step 5 of the Reid Technique shows interrogators how to act as the suspect's ally. At the point of the interview where the suspect may appear frustrated and looking for a way out of his predicament, the interrogator tries to capitalize on the subject's insecurity by pretending to be a friend. Offering physical gestures of camaraderie, such as touching the suspect's shoulder or patting his back, reinforces this feeling of trust, as Sheehan did with JR (which would later outrage observers as inappropriate).

In Step 6, the interrogator looks for body language indicating that the suspect is losing his resolve and is willing to capitulate. The suspect may put his head in his hands or hunch over the interrogation table, allowing the interrogator to seize the opportunity for a confession.

Criminal Interrogation and Confessions also suggests a physical layout for an interrogation room. It should be designed to maximize a suspect's discomfort and sense of powerlessness. The classic interrogation room is small and soundproof with only a table or desk and an uncomfortable chair for the suspect. There should be no controls like light switches, door handles or thermostats, heightening the suspect's feeling of isolation. Nothing should be on the walls, except for perhaps a one-way mirror, which increases the suspect's anxiety. Lighting is typically harsh. In this stark environment, the subject's feelings are simple: "Get me out of here."

On Wednesday, April 26 at 8:40 a.m., Sheehan entered such an interview room to continue his interrogation of Jeremy Steinke, which had been interrupted by his court appearance the previous day. It was the same setting that was used to interrogate JR. Surrounded by cinder block walls and dressed in blue jail-issue clothing, Jeremy appeared agitated.

"Legal Aid, they said to keep my mouth shut until I got a lawyer," Jeremy said. Sheehan ignored his request. He pressed ahead with Step 1 of the Reid Technique, telling the suspect that 12 police were assigned to the case and that the evidence against him was insurmountable.

"JR confessed yesterday afternoon," Sheehan said. "We recovered bloody clothes in a bag in the truck. In a white plastic bag."

Sheehan told Jeremy they'd found blood in his trailer and in his bedroom. He also told him that they'd found his cleaned-up truck. "Armor All [a cleaning product] doesn't remove blood or DNA. It smears it and makes it shiny," Sheehan said.

Jeremy said nothing.

"You know this is a big thing. It's all over the papers, all over the country. It's a big thing," Sheehan said. The next day, the *Calgary Herald* would report the sensational details of Jeremy's werewolf fantasy, which quickly spread on newswires and the Internet. Sheehan did not know the story was about to hit, but managed to ask a question that in hindsight seemed prophetic.

"The media is portraying you as a monster," Sheehan told him. "Everybody thinks you manipulated her."

Jeremy shook his head no.

"She cried for hours. I almost cried when she told her story," Sheehan said, referring to JR's confession. He played the monster angle once more. "The only question I have for you Jeremy is 'Are you a monster?'"

Jeremy, his head down with one hand on his forehead, again shook his head.

Sheehan said that police had obtained his Internet chat logs, including the note Jeremy had written three days before the murders to Grant Bolt saying, "I on the other hand would rather do morbid stuff to others. like Jaxz rents 4 example! which i'm going to do this weekend."

Jeremy had told the police he got his bruised eye in a fight with Cam Barkley, but Sheehan called him on it. "Your story of a fight with Cam doesn't check out."

Jeremy still wouldn't talk.

"You're the only person left that can explain what happened," Sheehan pleaded, hoping to evoke a sense of remorse. "There are only two people who were there who are still alive."

Jeremy, in an anguished voice, almost crying, finally began to crack. "You're putting all this on me. You're saying it's all my fault. She told me, she said she wanted it."

"But how did it happen? That's what I need to know," Sheehan said. He now started to be Jeremy's ally, just as in Step 5 of the Reid Technique. "I know you're scared, Jeremy. It's okay to be scared. But you're not a monster. Or maybe you are. I hope you're not because I've never met one. I never met a real monster. All have remorse. All are sorry for what happened."

Jeremy grew emotional. "Do you think I didn't try to talk her out of it? I did. When I did she got upset with me. You can ask anyone who knows me. Ask my mom," he said, his voice loud and agitated.

"Your mom was in my arms crying," Sheehan told him.

The young man leaned over the metal table and buried his head in his arms. He began to mutter. He was displaying the classic Step 6 body language, the point of the interview where Reid says to move in for the confession.

"Can't hear you, dude," Sheehan said.

"Things just kept escalating. They got out of control. I would do anything for JR. I tried to talk her out of it but she wanted it bad," Jeremy said, burying his head again.

"Jeremy, come back, man."

"I'll let you know, I wasn't in the right state of mind. I was drunk. I was high on narcotics. Cam gave me some coke."

"Powder or rock?"

"Powder."

Unlike JR, who was emotionless throughout her police interview, Jeremy was a near basket case, on the verge of tears. "You all say love is blind. Sergeant Cole told me love is blind. I would do anything for that girl."

Sheehan put his hand on Jeremy's arm.

"I love her more than anything," Jeremy sobbed.

"I know you love that girl but tell me how it happened."

"What an amazing girl," Jeremy wailed, folding his arms and burying his head.

"I need to hear your version. I need to know what happened," said Sheehan, putting his hand on Jeremy's shoulder. "Try to keep it together for me, dude."

"I just wanted us to run away. As soon as I got in that house, I wanted to get out, and then her mom showed up and screamed and I freaked." Jeremy was agitated, his voice growing louder with emotion.

"Did she scare you?"

"Yes," he said, his voice quavering. "She came around the corner. I freaked. Then her dad came downstairs. He came at me."

"Were you defending yourself?"

"I just stabbed him. I didn't want to. What do you think an animal is going to do when in a predicament with another animal? What are you going to do?"

"Stabbed him where?"

"I don't know. I was high on drugs. It was just a big blur. It felt like forever."

Sheehan asked if JR's dad said anything to him.

"He asked me, 'Why?' I told him, cuz that's what his daughter wanted."

Without prodding, Jeremy then placed the blame on JR for the murder of her little brother. "I went upstairs. I watched [her] cut her own brother's throat."

"Why did she do that?"

"Because she knew it had to be done. I didn't touch him. I was pacing. Then she came over and gave me a hug. I had to go for fresh air. I couldn't take it anymore. After I got out of the shower she showed up in a cab. I said, 'We have to get out of here. We have to leave.'"

It was at the party house the next day that they "found out everything was blown out of the water," Jeremy said. "I asked Kacy to clean up the truck and park it. We got in the back of Kacy's truck and drove to Saskatchewan and that's that."

That's that. It may have seemed to Jeremy that those two words would end the interview. The feelings of hopelessness and despair, of desperately wanting out of that interview room, were now evident. But the interview did not end. Sheehan kept pressing for more details.

Jeremy admitted to asking Jordan Attfield for help with the murders and confirmed Attfield's version of events. "I asked him. At first he said yes and then he changed his mind. He didn't think he could do it."

"How many times did you stab JR's mom?" Sheehan asked.

"I don't know."

"More than once?"

"Probably. I don't know. I don't know how many times I stabbed her dad. It felt like it went on forever."

Sheehan now had a confession. Jeremy had admitted that he killed JR's parents. But their stories on who killed Jacob were conflicting.

"She said that she stabbed her brother but couldn't go through with it. She said she stabbed him but couldn't go on," Sheehan prodded.

"I said we couldn't leave him."

"Now you cut his throat?"

"She cut his throat! She cut his throat!" Jeremy shouted loudly. "I swear to God, she cut his throat. I didn't want to kill anyone." He began hitting the concrete block wall of the interview room with his hand. He said he was shocked at JR's reaction to the murders. "She wasn't crying. She didn't look very upset."

"Did you like her brother?" Sheehan asked.

"Yes."

"How old is he?"

"I don't know. The week before this happened her brother was harassing her and she started choking him. I was shocked."

"Did the two of you have sex?"

"Sex has nothing to do with how I feel about JR!" Jeremy protested. He seemed well aware that by admitting to having sex with a minor, he could face further charges.

The interview was being recorded on video, but Sheehan also wanted to get the confession on paper. He told Jeremy he would give him some paper and a pen to write an apology to JR's mom, dad, and brother.

"How's that going to help? Everybody hates me."

Remembering the footprint police had found in the mud outside the broken basement window, Sheehan asked what size feet Jeremy had.

"Size 10."

"What kind of shoes were you wearing?"

"What does it matter? You got everything you need. I'm going away for life."

Sheehan left the room to get a notepad, leaving Jeremy in the room alone and emotionally exhausted. He dropped his forehead to the table, wrapped his arm around his ears, and sobbed. As the hopelessness of his predicament hit him, he repeatedly smashed his head on the cold metal table.

"I hope everybody is fucking happy now," he said aloud, to no one.

"Fuck," he said, banging his head three times. "I fucking hate myself."

He hit his head on the table four more times.

The door to the interview room clanked open. It was Sheehan.

"Calm yourself or I can't leave you in here. You can't be banging your head."

Sheehan left Jeremy alone with a notepad and a soft-tipped marker.

"How do you expect me . . . I can't write with this," he said aloud, frustrated.

Several minutes went by, with Jeremy attempting to compose an apology, before Sheehan re-entered the room. He asked Jeremy how he was being treated.

"I had a problem with one of the guards. Other than that, every-thing's been okay."

"Why are you telling me this?"

"I've been having nightmares. I told you, I never wanted it to happen in the first place."

Jeremy was taken back to his cell, where Sheehan again gave him paper and a felt-tip pen, plus the note that JR had written the previous day. He wrote to JR, opening by quoting back to her a line she had written to him:

> There is only so much the bonds of flesh can do to the soul!
> Dear Jaxz, *kisses*
> Im sorry, Im so very sorry, i love you with all my heart, and
> that will never change. [section whited out] I broke, I con-
> fessed. Im sorry! I love you, I truly do . . . and I hope that
> one day I may be able to gaze into your eyez once again . . .
> I slept with your note in my hand every night, the only
> thing pushing me through this is the thought of you. I wish
> we could just go back in time and run . . . run far away and

never look back. Never forget how much you mean to me
or how much I love you! Without you I feel so empty and
wish I could just die . . . no matter what Im with you in
mind and spirit, once this time comes, I hope to be with
you in body too . . . keep this note close 2 your heart if I
can write again I shall

    Kisses, Jeremy

    JR replied later that day – the same day as Jacob's autopsy – with
tenderness to the man who had killed her family three days earlier.

April 26

Dear my loverly Bastante,

Please don't be sorry, I'm the one who needs to be begging
your forgiveness. If only we ran, yes, but don't obsess on
what could have been. In due time we shall have our castle.
I am not whole without you. I love you with everything I
am. I'll never stop and my promises shall be kept. However
desolate it seems and shall become take it one day at a
time. It can only get so bad before it gets better. I will be
with you in spirit. I hope your doing alright, however large
a task, please don't stress out to much. Having your sanity
might be helpful. More than anything I wish to be with
you and hold you again. But until that time comes, know
I love you.

    xoxox

    (In joy and sorrow my sweet 666)

    Jaxz

As the pair poured their hearts out in passionate love letters declaring their
desire to be together, Jeremy's distraught mother, Jackie May, had still not
heard a word from her jailed son. And she was worried.

With gale force, crime scene investigators had turned May's trailer upside down. Over the course of two days, police had dismantled all the plumbing from the trailer's tiny bathroom and pipes under the kitchen sink looking for hairs and traces of blood evidence. They seized the computer and ripped Jeremy's cell-sized bedroom apart. Investigators sprayed the handle of the bedroom door, plus his room, bathroom, and shower with Luminol, a chemical used to detect trace amounts of blood left at a crime scene. The iron present in blood catalyzes in a chemical reaction, resulting in a luminescent glow that can be seen under blue light for about 30 seconds.

May, who had been located by police in a bar and informed of her son's arrest, sat in a state of shock inside her trashed mobile trailer, next to a shrine she assembled to her son in the living room. Set up on a table, it had a photo of Jeremy as a boy, with gelled, spiky hair and a nice sweater, the picture of innocence. "He's not the man everybody thinks he is," she said. The sickening stench of rotting meat hung in the air. Frozen food had been taken out to thaw in the sink days before when police arrived with a warrant.

The ravaged wood-panelled trailer was May's only refuge. In a few short days, the divorced 43-year-old mother of two had become a prisoner in her own home. Her blue eyes red and puffy, her red hair untamed, she was in a fragile state, hounded by reporters and scorned by town gossips. "I can't even go to the grocery store," she said. When police had turned her out of her home to search for evidence against her only son on Monday and Tuesday, she headed to a local motel. As she waited in the lobby to check in, she was forced to endure painful gossip about her supposed werewolf son, the suspect in the gruesome murders. Some were calling her son a pedophile. The words stung.

The day after her son's first court appearance, May was back inside the old trailer in the mobile home park near the Medicine Hat airport.

A trusted family friend, a gruff but protective white-haired man in overalls, was hard at work under the sink, trying to restore order to her dismantled home. It would be hours before she could flush a toilet or fill the sink. May was a wreck. She was vibrating with shock, partly from not eating, partly from being worried sick for her boy, partly from her latest drinking binge, which began before Jeremy had left for Leader to get Mick. Her health was already poor from her terminal lung disease, and there was so much to clean up in the aftermath of the police search that she didn't know where to start.

A knock on the trailer door snapped May out of her stunned silence. Reporters were camped outside, staking out the trailer, hoping to wear her down by taking turns asking her for interviews. But this time, the visitors to the trailer were Jeremy's friends Kacy Lancaster and TeJay Stadelman. Both had been crying. They took turns hugging Jackie.

"I thought we were going camping, then the cops showed up and arrested us," Kacy told her. "Now they've got my truck ripped apart and they won't give it back," she complained, cursing the police for impounding her pickup. Seeing her son's friends was a small comfort to May. She was glad to have young people around her, grateful to have someone she could talk to.

"I know it's not important right now," Kacy said, squaring herself face to face with May and gripping her arms, "but he told me to tell you he loves you and that he wants you to have his TV." As Kacy comforted her, TeJay, wearing a hoodie and a baseball cap, slunk down the hallway into Jeremy's ransacked bedroom. He sniffled as he quietly sorted through his friend's things.

Because May had been out drinking with friends and hadn't come home, she hadn't spoken with her son in more than a week. She knew that some of his friends had stayed at the trailer the night of the murders. They were always welcome in her home. She had a soft spot for troubled kids who had been kicked out or had no place to go. She wanted them to feel safe. Since Jeremy's boyhood, his mother had been his protector. When classmates and even teachers had picked on Jeremy, calling him "Stinky" instead of Steinke, she had marched into the principal's office and demanded they stop, but they wouldn't. Mother and son may have grown to lead separate lives, but their bond remained close.

"He has a heart of gold. We may not be rich, but we have a lot of love," says May.

She may not have been a good mother in the conventional sense, but she says she had a close and loving relationship with her children, and that they could tell each other anything.

"If we ever disagreed, he would always apologize after. We were like that."

Why, then, hadn't Jeremy called her, she wondered? He was too busy, apparently, writing love notes to JR.

On April 28, Jeremy Steinke was brought into the interview room again, this time wearing what police refer to as "baby dolls" – a white robe with no sleeves, no zipper, no strings – nothing that could be used to harm himself. Baby doll clothing is given to prisoners on suicide watch.

"You look like a *Star Wars* dude," Sheehan said.

Jeremy did not laugh at the attempted humour. He had slept "shitty" and had had only three hours of sleep. He had been given a visitor list form but complained that he couldn't put his beloved JR on it, or any of his other friends. "I don't know what the fuck to do."

Over the next six days, Sheehan kept delivering notes back and forth between Jeremy and JR. In one, Jeremy wrote:

Dear Cuddlebunny,
Im sure that you are right, whats done is done. You need not ask for my forgiveness. Indeed, in due time our Empire shall be complete. Before you I was half and now that I am whole, I cant go back to being half. Your the one that I breathe, youre my moon when it breaks through the clouds at night, your all that I need. I long to feel your soft skin, I yearn for your kisses, for they could get me high. I hope

that you stay true to your words. My entire faith has been bestowed unto you. With your words I shall remain strong, for you. Sometimes I have troubles sleeping at night, but Im sure the thought of you before we get through the nights.

In due time we shall be together once again . . . but until that day arrives, stay strong, keep hope & have faith! I love you with all my heart and soul! Never forget that okay my love.

Til we speak again,

xoxoxo

Jeremy

Calgary criminal defence lawyer Tim Foster had read about the murders in the newspaper on April 24 and 25. "I wonder if that's going to come our way," he thought. Foster, a lawyer well known for defending persons charged with impaired driving, spent his first decade practising in youth court, had a strong background in youth issues, and had murder trial experience. In 1993, he defended a 15-year-old lovelorn girl charged with fatally shooting her boyfriend after he threatened to jilt her. Foster got her second-degree murder charge reduced to manslaughter after arguing that his client accidentally pulled the trigger, shooting her 18-year-old boyfriend in the forehead with his own gun.

After several lawyers in Medicine Hat declined JR's case, Foster indeed got the call. When he arrived in Medicine Hat, he was appalled at what he found. The 12-year-old suspect was being held in the local Remand Centre, a facility where people who might be innocent mingle with hardened criminals awaiting court appearances. Due to her age, JR was kept separate, but that only exacerbated the situation, according to Foster: "They were holding her in remand, downstairs in a cell, a police cell accessible by the police station. It was like a dungeon. She was the only one in there."

Later, JR would be assigned two windowless cells, one for her and another so that a case worker from the Calgary Young Offenders Centre could stay with her. According to Foster, the worker went home at the end of the day, leaving JR alone. A mirror in JR's cell was removed as a precaution. Broken glass can be used as either an offensive or a suicidal weapon. For a preteen girl used to primping, preening, and applying eyeliner as teardrops, the absence of a mirror would have been tragic.

Foster introduced himself to Sergeant Sheehan, who had already interrogated his new client. Because her parents were deceased, government case workers had also become involved, including a female child welfare worker and her supervisor, a man, who had gone to speak to JR before Foster arrived.

To Foster's surprise, the supervisor insisted that they were not willing to let JR talk alone with her lawyer. The child welfare worker had to be present at all times. Foster protested, claiming this stipulation contravened lawyer-client privilege. The supervisor still refused.

When Foster met JR, he asked the soft-spoken girl in the oversized blue jumpsuit if she wanted to talk to him alone or with the others.

"I want to talk to just you," JR said meekly. The case workers waited outside.

"I'd never encountered that situation before," Foster says. The nervousness of the child welfare people was palpable. The story was front-page news.

Foster would later learn of JR and Jeremy's incriminating love notes and her apology letter to her "parental units." But when he first met her, he was unaware that she was communicating with Jeremy.

In one of her notes, JR responded to Jeremy by referring to themselves as legends in the vein of the infamous Mickey and Mallory of *Natural Born Killers*, or Bonnie and Clyde: "Never has a person affected me so much. Always will there be something missing without you with me. My lawyer tells me were ledgends. Ha, close to immortality it would seem. Monday Im being moved to Calgary sadness. I need to stay in contact."

Her lover wrote back the next day with a proposal of marriage. He embossed the top left-hand corner of his love note like a teenage girl would: JS + JR, followed by the entwined letters TLF: true love forever. During their romance, JR had asked Jeremy if he thought they could one day get married. Now, in jail, the lovelorn Jeremy popped the question. He opened with a "P.S." at the top of the note, probably placed there because he had run out of room on the page:

p.s. U said you want to get engaged? Then heres a Q . . .
Will u marry me? If so, then it is a verbal agreement.
Dear Jaxz,

I love you more than life, its self. Ive added you to my visitors list so once your released please visit after. Never forget
how much I care or that I love you. We can keep visiting
each other til we can be together again. Without you this
life isnt worth living. *kisses* The thought of being with
you is all that is helping me stay some what sane. We shall
be 2 gether again I promise. Stay true to your promises and
I shall to mine. Casey [Kacy] continues to lie. I wish I could
hold u right now. Stay strong and continue to write me
please . . . I need you. I love you, I miss you! *kisses* xoxoxo
          your lover Jeremy

JR was thrilled that the man who had slaughtered her parents had asked her to marry him. She wrote back the same day:

May my heart become cold to all others.
Dear Jeremy,

Ahahaha! I never thought I'd find myself hysterically laughing in a holding cell in these kind of circumstances . . . or
ever really. But still! Ahaha you make me so happy! Yes! Yes!

I will I would love to. Of course I'll come visit you I'll have to find where youre being held. Ahaha god Im so happy I must be happily insane then. Either way apparently I get a phyciatrist. Interesting information I came across. Anything you say to anyone including a phyciatrist, unless issued by a lawyer can be used against you for fucks sake. Rawr. The world really is against us. Do you have a lawyer yet? Do you know where your going in the near future? Oh I wish I could hold you and make you feel better! Argh I love you so much. I'm going crazy. Have you been in jail before? Ha Ive counted and at times during the day a guard will come to see if Im okay every 90 to 120 seconds lol

Oh did Casey happen to be in love with you?

We've been in the papers everyday apparently. I haven't seen them but hopefully can Monday. Everything related to me knows that I am in jail and what not, but dont know anything other than the charges and seemingly doesnt believe because my aunty says they still love me. Although it was as if I wasn't alive before. Oh remember that gift I had for you? It was a charm bag I had made for your well-being and such. You may think its stupid but I put a unusually large amount of effort into it. I believe the planetary alignment and everything else that takes months to explain was correct so it's still helpful I suppose. I'll pray and reiki you. You will have no choice in the matter.

In the note, she also informed Jeremy that she wasn't pregnant from their night of apparently unprotected sex:

In regards to the first time I snuck out, we're safe. I want to be able to talk to you soo bad I have far to much free time alone, mixed with my fear of isolation. Well you're the only thing keeping me strong XOX

I have so much to say and contemplait but I'm going on here.

xox

Dreams filled with visions of us help us through.

Unable to talk with JR, Jeremy took comfort in the voice of another. From inside jail, he called Morgan, a 14-year-old girl from the mall scene who adored him. Hearing from Jeremy would please her immensely.

13

SWOONING FOR SVENGALI

"We're going to mosh for you, Jeremy"

The Medicine Hat Remand Centre, where Jeremy was being housed, is located on the second floor of the police station, with windows looking out onto the street. In the days after his arrest, Morgan stood vigil outside the red building, gazing upon the impregnable fortress where he was now being held, hoping he would look out and see her devotion. She had always been enamoured of Jeremy and was so infatuated that she sometimes recorded their telephone conversations so she could listen again and again to his voice. When he called from jail, she recorded those conversations, too. "I don't want to forget his voice. What if he calls one day and I don't recognize it and go, 'Who's this?'" she asks herself.

In the earlier calls before his arrest, Jeremy's voice is bright and happy. From jail, he is mumbly, depressed. "It's sad, the difference in his voice," she says. She played his messages repeatedly, swooning. Because she was under 18, Morgan was too young to visit Jeremy in jail and her parents refused to sign their permission for her to register on his visitors list. The only way she could cling to him was through her recordings. She cherished them.

To Morgan, and to many of his other close friends, Jeremy was dashing and loveable. He was the swashbuckling Captain Jack Sparrow, not Souleater, the self-styled werewolf and freakish goth king portrayed in the media. In the days after the murders, many of Jeremy's young followers showed up for his court appearances. JR's friends also turned out to support her, but not with the same disciple-like devotion that seemed to mark the girls who came to support Jeremy. Barred from entering the courthouse because they were underage or on witness lists, they stood outside hugging and crying. As the television cameras rolled, one girl collapsed to her knees, sobbing into her hands.

Many locals found their reactions disgraceful. A woman calling herself Liberal Minded Mom was so disturbed by the scene that she wrote on the community website maintained by Dangermouse:

> Something that really disturbed me was the picture on the front of the *Medicine Hat News* yesterday, the one of all the young girls crying and hugging outside of the courthouse. I cannot believe this sick freak has a 'fan club' now! Most of these girls looked to be about junior high age and one of them had a *Finding Nemo* back pack for crying out loud! What is inside these girls' heads that is drawing them to feel sorry for a triple murderer? (Sorry I guess he isn't convicted yet). Where are these girls' parents? Shouldn't these kids be in school? If I had a daughter that was down at the courthouse crying over such a person I think that maybe there might be something wrong with her.

A user named Anonymous agreed:

> This display outside the court room of all these young girls makes me sick. They are crying for this man and not even thinking about the poor family that just lost their lives. All the

girls outside the courtroom looked like they should have been in school. Where are their parents? Why are they allowing them to attend a murder trial hearing in support of a murderer? Have these girls no remorse for the family?

Jeremy's supporters also put up posters at Medicine Hat High School, which were ripped down by other students. "There are tons of little goths who love him," Travis Paulter, a disgusted grade 12 student and football player, told the *Medicine Hat News*. "My buddy's little sister is obsessed with him and she's only in grade 8."

Jeremy's female admirers would not be silenced. On Nexopia, another young female friend, nicknamed Squishy, wrote to him:

I love you. Fuck what everyone else says. I know what you did. I still love you more than anything ever. You're an amazing friend. I miss you so much, all the memories, everything. Nothing will ever be the same without you. The shows. Moshing. Drinking. Slipknot. The mall. Pot. Talking. The list goes on, baby. Nothing will ever be the same. I love you so much. Jeremy Allan Steinke, you are my best friend. Thank you for all the times you've helped me with everything. And now it's the time where we need to help you. I support you one hundred and fifty percent, sweetheart. Not what you did, but as a friend and best friend. I love and miss you more than anything.

In a posting directed at outsiders, 14-year-old Squishy wrote: "You don't know him like we do. All you see is evil. We see him as loving, caring, kind. You see him as a danger, a threat. We see him as a brother, a friend. Nothing can change what went wrong. Nothing can change what we feel. Nothing can change our hearts. Nothing can change our people."

A friend of Jeremy who called herself Satanic Rose wrote: "It's okay

Jeremy, We're all rooting for you . . . We all love you and although not many people understand, we're still behind you 100%."

Another devotee wrote on one of the websites: "We're going to mosh for you Jeremy. We're going to have a mosh for you every week."

And mosh they did. At punk shows, they were eager to line the front of the community hall stage, thrashing and slamming into one another to the band's music in the mosh pits they formed for their Jeremy. A group of his supporters showed up at a punk show with the number 43 – Jeremy's high school football jersey number – on their faces, which upset other kids at the show.

"Stupid motherfucking goths at shows. WHY THE FUCK did you all have '43' on your faces?" BrokenWings, a 15-year-old girl, wrote on her Nexopia page afterwards. "To show you support what that sick creep Jeremy Steinke did? What the fuck is your problem? I hope you burn in hell. And don't come to our shows anymore with that shit on your face. You will get beaten down."

Corazon, another Nexopia user, responded in agreement: "I am fucking backing you up on the whole 43 on their faces . . . we should kick their asses."

JR, too, had her supporters. Mikki, a friend of JR's, wrote on a community website on April 28:

> She's one of my friends and the news is making her sound like a cold-blooded murderer. SHES NOT!!! I bet she was brainwashed by that freaking freak! I hate him. I want him to . . . never mind. She was pressured into doing it. Last year she was the nicest, happiest person ever. I honestly cannot believe that she did it [kill them]. She talked about hating her little brother but I mean @ 13 who doesn't? None of us took her seriously and that was bad. She is a very nice person and I have come to the conclusion that she was raped, drugged and brainwashed and was forced to do such an awful thing.

Stop accusing her before u know. U have no idea what it is like to be a 13-year-old goth.

A user named Fat Elvis replied to Mikki on April 30: "There is no way Jeremy brainwashed your friend. He would lose a battle of wits with a squirrel . . ."

Another poster wrote about JR: "She was a great girl one day all clean-cut n pretty and I must say I agree."

SadisutoNightmares, claiming to be one of Jeremy's close friends, wrote: "It was her who planned it, her who convinced him to do it, her who convinced him to help her and it was pretty much all her. I think he still deserves what he gets for the wrongs he's done, and as a fact it was her who killed her brother."

"She talked him into it," wrote another of Jeremy's friends, who used the name Broken. "She had been planning this for about three years now."

Several more of Jeremy's friends turned on JR, writing posts saying they had cached pages of her Nexopia profile in which she listed one of her likes as "my dead family under my bed."

On VampireFreaks, a user named "MansonsWhore 666xX" put the two killers on a pedestal. "Forever will we remember you. Forever will you be missed. Jeremy and JR forever in our hearts!"

But the overwhelming reaction from the goth community on VampireFeaks and other sites was disgust. Bloggers filled the public comments section of JR's pages with vitriol:

"No real wiccan would ever kill another, least of all their f—cking parents. You'll get yours as will your pedophile boyfriend."
– *Godsmack Goddess*

"They're both fucked in the head." – *Rapid*

"Congrats. You're a monster." – *Iniquitous*

"May he/she rot in hell. Slimy murderer." – *Foxglovefairy*

"1 Question, WHY? 1 word, DIE!" – *Ghost Princess*

"Did your parents drop you on your head as a child? If only Canada was more like Texas . . . mmm. Death penalty." – *MortifiedHate*

"Sick, Sick, Sick, you freak." – *Babyfcuk*

"How could you do something like that you fucking sick wanker. I hope you rot in hell." – *Loonsvill*

Another goth wrote:

"You fucking creep. Why the fuck would you kill her family? Fucking then run off . . . I mean, come on, she fucking has a life to live still. That's fucking SICK ASS. You're like however old and she's fucking 12. Fucking pedophile. GO FUCKING KILL YOURSELF."

One young goth pleaded with the media to stop covering the story. "Perfectly well-educated, kind wonderful people are getting threatened and beaten because of the stereotypes," she said in a leaflet handed out to reporters. "Forget the big scoop." She claimed that a 13-year-old goth girl was approached at the mall and berated by a young man who said, "Why don't you go kill your parents?"

As young goths in the community began to feel the backlash, a man who signed on to one site as Hatter Citizen came to their defence:

I happen to know several, they attend youth functions I help supervise. A lot of them are A students, full of love and laughter and have a personality unique to them. They dress that way to · draw attention to themselves that sometimes they aren't getting from home, or sometimes just from other kids. Some are making

a bold statement; others are "outsiders" who just want to fit in.
Please don't judge them by how they dress. Take the time to get
to know them as a person instead of judging them by what you
feel are 'normal standards.' . . . These kids are our future, like it or
not. Cut them some slack and don't rush to judge when you
haven't taken the time to find out what makes them tick.

As the circus unfolded in Medicine Hat, relatives of Marc, Debra, and
Jacob in Ontario and Alberta were beginning to unravel emotionally.
The trail of victims left by JR and Jeremy extended far beyond the three
they had killed. Several family members were too afraid to walk outside
or to sleep with their back to the bedroom door, imagining they, too,
might be slaughtered.

On Saturday, April 29, more than 200 distraught family members
and friends packed into St. Peter's Anglican Church in Okotoks for a one-
hour memorial service. "What happened was evil. What happened was
horrible beyond our imagination," Reverend Paul Orritt, who had chris-
tened Jacob, told the mourners.

"If you ever wanted to know what a real hug felt like, all you had to
do was hug Debbie," her cousin Dan Doolan said at the service. He
recalled how a young Debra taught him how to dance while on vacation
at the family's cottage in Ontario. Doolan broke down in tears when he
spoke of Jacob.

Family friend Diane Bob read a letter written by Jacob's grade 3
teacher recalling how Jacob brought her a gift when he learned she was
pregnant. Mourners wiped away tears as they listened to the service and
looked at photos of the smiling family in the church foyer. A single casket,
containing Marc's body, and two urns with the ashes of Debra and Jacob
sat at the front of the church, surrounded by flowers. (Before the crema-
tion, an employee of the funeral home handling the arrangements had
bought a pair of pyjamas for Jacob so that relatives wanting to view the
body wouldn't see him naked.)

After the service, family members thanked the Medicine Hat Police Service for their handling of the case and pleaded for privacy in the face of intense interest in the slayings. "Please allow our family time to grieve and give us the space we need to deal with this terrible tragedy," Peter Doolan, Debra's brother, told reporters. He explained that another service would be held in Sudbury and that some of Debra's and Jacob's ashes would be buried with Marc.

Wayne Chopek, Marc's EnCana co-worker, attended the service: "EnCana was able to provide flights for the family to come to Okotoks for that service and we all thought this was a great thing." Like all of Marc's co-workers, Chopek could not comprehend the slaying of an entire family in Medicine Hat. "Why did it have to happen here? Why did it have to happen at all?"

As people wept, grieving Medicine Hat residents who had set up a memorial at the crime scene kept stopping by JR's now empty family home, which was still sealed off with yellow police tape. A collection of bouquets, teddy bears, and framed handwritten poems was piling up on the front lawn. One visitor to the makeshift memorial was Jacob's baby-sitter. The young woman crouched and buried her face in her hands, weeping. The toys were later donated to the police department's victim assistance unit and would be handed out to children affected by crime and other traumatic events: a source of comfort that came from an unthinkable tragedy.

Relatives of Marc and Debra were inconsolable. Several suffered nightmares in which they imagined that they, too, might be stabbed.

Morgan had no such fears. Despite the serious charges of first-degree murder against Jeremy, she longed for him. Their last meeting had been at the punk show the Friday before the murders.

"He just gave me a hug and said 'see you later.' I'm going to hold him to the see you later part," she said solemnly after one of his first court appearances. Like other young friends, Morgan failed to comprehend the gravity of Jeremy's fate. In their minds, it was as if he'd simply have to go to court a few more times and then be placed on probation.

Morgan became an archivist of Jeremy's press clippings, carefully chronicling in four large binders the coverage of his court appearances. Like the girl who pleaded with the media to stop covering the story, she said that she, too, felt ostracized. "You feel like you are walking around with a sign on your head that says 'Steinke supporter.' You've got this constant extra voice in your head. It is saying: 'They all hate you. They all hate you.'" She labelled her four scrapbooks "Hell," volumes 1 through 4. "You don't just want to put a stack of papers in a shoebox."

Although she didn't condone what Jeremy did, her devotion was unwavering. Morgan and other young teens looked up to Jeremy as the unofficial head of a gothic punk posse of mall rats who didn't fit in elsewhere. "He is sweet, caring, loud and funny. He's a good songwriter and a guitar player," she said.

Because Morgan's name was included on the Crown's potential witness list, Jeremy had a court order forbidding him from contacting her. When it was discovered that he was calling her from jail, he was formally charged with breaching the order.

Her loyalty and willingness to stand in the wings for the Svengali-like Jeremy are mind-boggling. She insists she wants a future with him: "I don't even care how long it is; as long as he gets out some day. I'll be here."

14

THE CONFESSION

"Me and my girlfriend are freaks"

On May 2, relatives of the victims attended another memorial service. This one, in Sudbury, was a Roman Catholic funeral mass during which family friend Diane Bob was called upon for the second time in a week to deliver a eulogy similar to the one she delivered in Okotoks on April 29.

JR's mom, she said, was "an angel here on Earth. When Debra hugged you, you knew her God was shining through." Marc, she said, "was an honest man, sincere, tolerant, humble, generous, kind and soft with words, believed in harmony, and the most important thing was his family." Eight-year-old Jacob "was a beautiful young soul, full of energy and a heart of gold."

Marc's family asked for donations to the Rockhaven treatment facility Marc had attended. The obituary and funeral notice they placed quoted, in French, the Serenity Prayer used by Alcoholics Anonymous and other 12-step programs: "God, grant me the serenity to accept the things I cannot change, the courage to change the things I can, and the wisdom to know the difference." Debra's family asked for donations to the Canadian Liver Foundation.

Back in Medicine Hat that day, many of Jeremy's young goth friends came to the courthouse for one of his court appearances. Kids in black hoodies, elaborate makeup, and nose and lip piercings were eager to show the flag for their beloved friend.

As Jeremy's supporters hugged outside after court, security sheriffs Steven Durk and Sean McGuigan loaded him and several other prisoners into security van No. 255 for the six-block ride back to the city lockup. When they heard Jeremy talking to another inmate, their jaws dropped. "Yeah, she did the eight-year-old and I did her parents. It was all her idea but when someone you love asks you to do something, you do it," he was saying. "I tell you straight up, man. Her dad came at me with a screwdriver and stabbed me in my eye. The eight-year-old will be with me the rest of my life. She's fucked up in the head and wanted them dead anyway."

Durk and McGuigan wheeled into the Remand Centre, unloaded the prisoners, and promptly pulled out their notepads, writing down as much of the conversation as they could remember.

The next day, May 3, in another jailhouse letter to JR, Jeremy expressed his gratitude that she had accepted his offer of marriage: "I'm glad to hear that you accepted my proposal. And you make me incredibly happy as well. I too am going for psychiatric assessment. I'm not sure where I'll be yet, but I'll let you know. The world may be against us, but remember that nothing beats love."

It would be his final note to JR. The two had revealed so much in their scribblings to each other that Sergeant Sheehan felt he needed no more information. He was tired of playing messenger. Jeremy's last billet-doux was never delivered to JR.

Jeremy was scheduled to be transferred by police van from Medicine Hat to Calgary for a psychiatric assessment the following morning. Sheehan saw the transfer as a perfect opportunity to plant an undercover officer in the van with the loose-lipped inmate. For the job of posing as a prisoner for the two-and-a-half-hour hour drive to the city, he chose the seemingly unlikely Cory Both, a young constable who had once taken a five-day undercover training course in cellmate operations – infiltrating a prisoner's cell to gain information from a suspect.

Constable Both was a church-going family man who would need to convince Jeremy that he was a foul-mouthed criminal in order to gain his trust and get him talking about the murders. A hidden microphone wired into the roof of the van would record their conversation, which needed to be artfully managed. If Both asked any leading questions, the taped conversation would be ruled inadmissible in court. If, however, Jeremy spoke freely on his own while being engaged in so-called "passive conversation," the recording could go in as evidence.

Sheehan, who had previous undercover experience and was knowledgeable in case law, coached Both on what needed to be done. Constable Both was to ask Jeremy no direct questions about the murders. The tape would be turned over to Vonda Moreau, a police service clerk, for transcribing. Sheehan warned Both: "If it comes back with a single question mark, I'll kill ya."

Both was nervous but game. Sheehan and some police staff sat Both in a chair, put a cape around his neck, brought out a pair of clippers, and shaved his hair into a mohawk. With the goatee and handlebar moustache he already wore for undercover work, Both's transformation was complete. A pair of dirty jeans and a T-shirt, and he looked like one badass dude – much to the chagrin of his wife.

Sheehan equipped Both with the information he had gleaned from Jeremy during his interrogation the week before. One more piece of corroboration couldn't hurt, especially since Sheehan did not record Jeremy waiving his right to a lawyer. In the police van, talking to someone Jeremy assumed to be another prisoner, no waiver would be needed. Both stayed up all night studying case law to ensure he wouldn't blow it.

Getting the van prepped and wired wasn't easy. Sheehan had been seeking approval from his superiors for days about doing a cellmate operation. When they agreed, Sheehan had to find an unused van from the government surplus yard, fill out paperwork, get insurance, and retrofit it with a microphone.

On May 4, Jeremy was loaded into a cage in the back of the van at the Remand Centre. The driver stopped at the courthouse at 9:15 a.m. to pick up Both in a prearranged stop to make it appear as if Both had just made a court appearance. The officer was placed in an adjoining cage. The metal dividing wall that normally separates prisoners from each other's view had been removed, to foster a sense of camaraderie between the two.

Both quickly launched into a profanity-laced tirade about being separated from his girlfriend. "Fuck," swore prisoner Both.

"You gonna be okay?" Jeremy asked.

"Well, my old lady's fucking here at the courthouse, and she's got no fuckin' money for a cab or fuckin' fuck all," Both complained.

"That sucks."

"Really fuckin' sucks."

"Well, I take it she's got – you going to Calgary too, eh?" Jeremy asked.

"Yeah."

"So she's gotta try and find a way up there?" Jeremy inquired amicably.

"Well, I don't know, like – hopefully they can bring me back, I think," Both replied. "If I don't get fuckin' remanded up there then they're just gonna kick me loose up there. And I don't know how the fuck I'm gonna get back, and she doesn't have cash to get up there and bring me back."

"That's retarded. The system's fucked, man."

"It is fucked," Both replied.

Jeremy laughed. He was desperate for his fellow priosner to like him. He told Both that his girlfriend, too, was in Calgary. JR had been transferred to the Calgary Young Offenders Centre, where she was scheduled to have a psychiatric assessment.

"Fuck. Be nice if she was coming back, she could give me a ride," said Both.

"Yeah, I doubt she'll be coming back. She – she's locked up too."

"Oh. Shitty," Both said, building up rapport with his target.

"Yeah, big time."

"What happened?"

"Huh?"

"What happened?"

"Uh – you hear about that triple homicide?" Jeremy asked.

"Yep."

Jeremy paused and gave Both a smug look.

"No shit," Both said.

"Yeah. You're looking at him," Jeremy said proudly.

"No shit. Fuckin', you're famous, brother," replied Both, acting impressed.

"Yeah, so I've heard," said Jeremy. "Me and my old lady have become legends."

The pair hadn't even left the Medicine Hat city limits and Jeremy had already implicated himself in the murders.

The two made small talk about women. Jeremy told Both about his engagement to JR, which she had accepted and he had responded to just yesterday.

"So you're that guy, huh?" Both asked. "It's all over in the fuckin' papers and shit."

"Yeah."

"There's always a reason for it, eh?"

"Pardon?"

"I did some crazy shit too, but there's always a reason for it, right?" said Both.

"Well, I don't know . . . You love somebody enough you'll do anything for 'em, no matter what the consequences and . . . so, I did anything."

The talk turned to the brutal nature of jailhouse society. "This Muslim bastard that was in the cell next to me kept harassing me," said Jeremy. "I fuckin,' man oh man, I was ready to fuckin' just tear his heart out and make him eat it. Yeah, he was pissing me off just cutting me down and cutting my old lady down. I was like, 'Oh, if I could get my hands on you.'"

"In this jail?" Both asked.

"Yeah. Here in the Hat. He's all bragging about how he's been shot so many times and crap like that, and I'm like, 'Yeah, how would you like to get stabbed?' And I'm not fond of guns 'n' that guy, I'd rather use knives. I'm all into that whole Japanese sword thing."

Both knew the murderers had used a knife and saw an opening. "Yeah. Yeah," he said, enthusiastically. "Fuckin' A. Blade's the way to go. That Leather and Steel, you ever been there?" the constable said, referring to a Medicine Hat motorcycle clothing accessories shop that also sells collectible swords and knives, along with neoprene face masks and bandanas.

"Yeah, yeah. I got all my swords from there actually," Jeremy said. "Yeah. You know like a Ninja sword." He also mentioned another Ninja weapon. "It's got like all these hidden features on it. You can kill 13 people before even drawing your sword. That's how many, like, hidden throwing stars and crap around –"

"It'd be nice to take one of those to the bar one day," Both said encouragingly.

Jeremy laughed. "Yeah, I bet. And lob off a couple heads." He then complained that he hadn't been able to read newspapers, only listen to a few minutes of radio. Both told him the media didn't have the full story.

"No?" Jeremy asked.

"Everyone's fuckin' dying to know the fuckin' deets," said Both, carefully trying not to lead with a direct question. "Sounds like a pretty cool story . . ."

"You ever watch the movie *Natural Born Killers*?" Jeremy asked pensively. "I think that's the best love story of all time and basically, I don't know . . . I guess, I guess me and my girlfriend just started our own love legacy. She says it is the next closest step to immortality."

"Some day they'll make a movie, too, huh?"

When Jeremy asked Both why he was arrested, the constable gave a cover story that he was up on an assault charge, but that it was self-defence. Here, Jeremy saw something he had in common with his new buddy.

"I dunno, I might get off on one of those charges or two of those charges cuz, one, she killed her brother," Jeremy said. "I didn't touch him. And her dad attacked me with a screwdriver, so that's technically self-defence."

The pair began talking about the women in their lives. "I treat my girlfriend like a fuckin' queen, man," said Jeremy. "I promised her that once we get outta here . . . I'm gonna save up my money and we're gonna buy one of those old castles in Germany. She loves the idea."

"There's a lot of castles over there," Both said.

"Well, yeah, man, and that's where they all, like, started. All you can find on this continent is mansions and shit," Jeremy replied. "There's no castles. Yeah, we figured we'd go and buy a castle and any of our friends that are still friends, invite them to come live with us cuz we're all, like, two people and a couple of kids, gonna live in a castle. It's like a hundred rooms or whatever."

Constable Both expressed no incredulity at the absurdity of a 23-year-old unemployed high school dropout who lived in a trailer with his mom buying a castle in Europe. If there were an Academy Award for best performance by a cop keeping a straight face in an undercover operation, Both would be a surefire winner.

"Well, that sounds cool, man," he said.

Jeremy went on: "My mom's sending up money for me. I'm starting a trust account, and once we get out we're gonna go get a ring tattooed [on] our ring finger and then we're gonna actually get wedding bands. We're gonna go have a gothic wedding."

He told Both that he was high on booze and dope the night of the murders and claimed he tried to talk JR out of it, but she'd insisted that they go through with it. "We didn't argue or anything. She didn't yell or anything. Just she . . . like she was sad. And I didn't like that. I was like, okay, well, I'm a man of my word, so – fuckin' do it."

Both contrived a story about having a buddy who once had a girl-friend who wanted him to "tune up" her parents.

"My old lady's father – fuckin', he's a big guy," said Jeremy. "Fuckin' when he came at me with that screwdriver I was scared shitless. I thought I was going down . . . I screamed cuz I thought he got me, eh, and I just stabbed and like – fuckin' yeah. I'm like – I was surprised I came out on top. I thought I was dead, man."

"No shit," said Both. "Then what happened?"

"The last thing I really remember was . . . him laying on the ground asking me 'Why?' And I said, 'Cuz you treat your daughter like shit, she wanted it this way.' And fuckin' – and that was it and then I went upstairs and I watched my girlfriend cut her brother's throat. It didn't bother her at all either. She didn't cry or anything. In fact, the next day when we were on the road fuckin' she was laughing about it. She's got a few screws loose, too . . . She's a Wiccan, eh. She practises all that witchcraft. . . . She's all spiritual and shit . . . Yeah, I gave her a bottle of my blood."

"That's cool," said Both.

"First and only person I've ever given a bottle of my blood to. And she said she . . . cut herself and gave me or got a bottle, too, but says that she thinks her parents found it and so they got both bottles of blood and shit like that."

"That's wild, man."

"I guess one of my friends spoke with a reporter or something and told them about the stuff he's seen me do. Like drinking blood. He's seen me drinking blood."

"Is that bullshit or what?" Both asked.

"It's true, man. I was drinking blood," Jeremy claimed. He also said he consumed it in food. "A friend made me blood cookies. It was sup-posed to be a white dough cookie, like a sugar cookie. When they came out of the oven they were pink. That is how much blood he put in them.

Well, the cookies were alright but I was . . . a little hesitant on eating because of STDs and shit like that."

JR also had a taste for blood, he told Both.

"Me and my girlfriend got a pretty fucked up relationship. When we're like going at it or whatever, you know, getting all intense and shit, she'll like claw my back to the point where I'm bleeding and she'll bite my neck and actually, like, pierce the skin and start drinking my blood. Fucking, I don't know, man. That's something I'm gonna miss."

The church-going Both didn't have to resort to a cover story for a response: "Whatever, yeah. I've never dated a chick like that."

"Well," said Jeremy, "me and my girlfriend are freaks, man. She wanted a corset for the longest time. She's got like, black leather hooker boots or whatever. She wears fishnet stockings and does her hair all up and has makeup on you know, gothic and shit. The one thing she was missing was the corset. I bought her a corset and I was gonna wait until my eye is healed and stuff. I was gonna give it to her, and then I was gonna take a picture of us together so my mom had a picture of us.

"You know what really pisses me off?" he continued. "There's people going around saying I'm 25, and saying my girlfriend's 12. Fuckin' utter bullshit, man. I just turned 23. And she's 13 turning 14. She's legal age . . . And they start, like, 'How the hell did you get such a young girl?' And, you know, like it's called being a lady's man. You know what they want and you give it to them."

As the long trip progressed through the flat prairie countryside, Jeremy began to complain, "My ass is starting to hurt." He told Both about his fondness for violent movies and lamented that he and JR should have just driven her mom's car to the east coast, sold it, and sailed away to Europe.

They saw an old barn with a caved-in roof and noticed a small house being moved down the highway. "Wonder where that's going? I wouldn't mind having a place like that," Jeremy sighed.

He talked more about the night of the murders, how he slipped through the basement window, how the floor creaked and JR's mother came downstairs. He told how he stabbed her, fought with Marc, then: "I went upstairs. My girlfriend did her brother."

Jeremy described how he wanted to make a life with JR. As the landscape rolled past the steel-mesh window of the van, he turned wistful. "There's a fucking nice ranch," he said as they travelled down the Trans-Canada Highway toward Calgary. "Gotta be over 500 head of cows there."

They saw a truck pulling a big recreational trailer. Shackled and caged, Jeremy saw it as a symbol of freedom.

"That'd be life, eh, be retired and just travel around and shit. Those fifth wheels they make nowadays are like living in the fucking house. You got satellite, recliner chairs, full kitchen, and shit like that."

As they entered Calgary, Jeremy marvelled at the fancy cars in the prosperous oil city and remarked about a yellow line painted down the middle of a bicycle path: "I never seen that before, though. A line painted on the sidewalk."

As they pulled into the correctional facility in northwest Calgary's Spy Hill, Jeremy noticed a sign for psychiatric services. "This would be my stop. Now I get to finally maybe correct my mental problem . . . Looks like a goddamn penitentiary."

As Jeremy was being loaded out of the van, Both bid him adieu. "Well, I hope everything works out for ya, buddy."

"Well, and good luck to you, too," Jeremy replied.

"Yeah, thanks, man. I hope you get to talk to your old lady."

Constable Both felt sick to his stomach at what he had heard, but his ride with the talkative Jeremy was a remarkable piece of undercover work. Not only had Jeremy admitted to the killings, he'd described in detail how he'd stabbed Marc and Debra. Although he accused JR of killing her brother, the body count didn't matter: if the taped conversation held up legally, the police knew they had enough to put Jeremy Steinke away for a very long time.

15

JUDGMENT DAY

"Your parents adored you, didn't they?"

More than a year had passed since the murders. JR's trial, held separately from Jeremy's because of her age, was stirring up old feelings in Medicine Hat, thrusting the community back into the national spotlight as the hometown of Canada's youngest accused killer. Most Hatters seemed to want to keep their heads down, attempting to weather another media storm as they recalled the headlines of the previous year: "Triple Murder Shocks City"; "Medicine Hat Girl Missing, Family Dead"; "Man, 23, Girl, 12, Charged in Triple Slaying"; "Suspect in Grisly Killing Was Laughing: Friend"; and "Friends Say Steinke Believed He Was Werewolf with a Taste for Blood."

But many were also eager to have justice served, and they wanted to see it happen with their own eyes. The case began the morning of June 4, 2007 and was scheduled for six weeks in Medicine Hat's grand old Court of Queen's Bench courthouse, built in 1919 and a designated provincial heritage site. Like many historic courthouses in Alberta, it is made of red brick and sandstone, designed as a symbol of strength and permanence in a new territory with a rapidly expanding and often transient population. Thick coils of cable from TV news satellite trucks snaked down the sidewalk as a public gallery made up mostly of teenagers, retirees, and parents lined up to pass through the courthouse's airport-style security and jockeyed with reporters for front-row seats.

Flanked by two sheriffs, JR was escorted into the courtroom and seated in the prisoner's box, a high-sided oak structure that shielded her from the gallery's view except when she entered and left the courtroom.

Those who came to snatch a glimpse of the notorious little girl were surprised, or disappointed. Where was Runaway Devil? Gone were the black tears and pouting, lacquered blood-red lips. Here was a freshly scrubbed teenager, long dark hair pulled back into a tidy ponytail. She was wearing a short-sleeved lavender blouse and plain, loose-fitting black slacks. She looked as though she could have been facing the judge of a county fair pie bake-off, instead of a judge and jury in a notorious murder trial.

Unlike her provocative and widely circulated Internet self-portraits in which she posed with a fake gun or with a fingertip pressed seductively to her lower lip, here was a 13-year-old girl, and an ordinary one at that. After 16 months in custody, JR's cheeks and body had become rounder. She looked compliant – not at all the lethal vixen depicted on her profile pages.

The indictment listed 90 Crown witnesses, including Jeremy Steinke, who could be called on to testify against JR. A handful of Jeremy's friends who were banned from court because they were on the witness list slipped in and snagged seats. They were soon spotted by Crown prosecutor Stephanie Cleary, who alerted sheriffs to have them removed. They slunk out through the heavy old wooden doors, which creaked loudly.

When the bailiff read out her family's names and the three charges of first-degree murder laid against her, JR sobbed. Her child's voice was small and quavering as she responded "not guilty" to each of the charges.

Before the 12-member jury was selected for JR's trial, her defence lawyer, Tim Foster, attempted to ban the public and media from her preliminary voir dire, a hearing held in the absence of the jury to determine the admissibility of evidence. Above all, Foster didn't want any leaks of his client's recorded police interrogation with Sheehan. Foster also outlined for

Justice C.S. Brooker, the presiding judge, that there had already been numerous breaches on the Internet of a publication ban protecting JR's identity. A court-ordered publication ban wouldn't be good enough, he argued, as it is not binding on international media outside Canada. The blogosphere was rife with breaches of the law regarding his client's identity. Many of these originated from Canada, including at least two produced in Medicine Hat. There were also numerous breaches on social networking websites, where teenagers with no concept of media law were exposing JR's identity daily.

Similar applications to hold in-camera hearings occurred during other infamous Canadian murder trials. Lawyers tried to block the public from sex killer Paul Bernardo's trial and from getting exhibits at serial killer Robert Pickton's pretrial hearings. Both times the request was denied. Daniel Burnett, a Vancouver media lawyer who successfully opposed a wide-sweeping publication ban in the Pickton case, suggested that technology such as blogs may force the Canadian legal system to re-examine its decades-old laws about publication bans.

"It is the bluntest and crudest secrecy tool that the courts have," Burnett told the *Calgary Herald*. "In the United States, publication bans during court proceedings are unheard of. They've been running jury trials a lot longer than we have, and it would be chauvinistic of us to think that our system is better . . . We've come to depend on publication bans and secret court orders like some sort of magic pill and we are deceiving ourselves that it is working. . . . It is unreasonable in this day and age to expect jurors to have no knowledge of a case. What you want are jurors that are able to fulfill their oath."

If jurors can't be trusted to deliver a verdict based only on the evidence presented in court, as they are sworn to do, we might as well abolish the jury system, Burnett argues. Banning the public from voir dires also denies the media the chance to hear evidence that can be reported at the conclusion of a trial, further limiting the public's access to the judicial process.

After hearing from media lawyers who fought Tim Foster's proposed ban, Justice Brooker refused to grant it. Noting that the open-court principle is a cornerstone of law, he said that excluding the press and the public is a "drastic and exceedingly rare event, and rightly so."

Known mainly for defending people accused of impaired driving, Foster, a gravelly-voiced man with a shaved head and earring, was no stranger to sensational murder cases. He had defended Chris Anton LeClaire, a 23-year-old also charged with murdering his Medicine Hat family. A paranoid schizophrenic, LeClaire was delusional and found not criminally responsible for the second-degree murders of his parents and his 21-year-old brother in 2001. LeClaire believed that the bodies of his parents and brother were inhabited by non-human impostors and felt he was "eminently at risk by these entities posing as his family members," according to a forensic psychiatrist. Foster had also represented Sheldon Zelitt, a Calgary high-tech fraudster who fled to the Czech Republic in 2001 after his company VisualLabs' 3-D products were exposed as fakes in a multi-million dollar stock market hoax.

Foster and his assistant co-counsel, Katherin Beyak, intended to mount the defence that JR was a child victim of an adult male predator, Jeremy Steinke. Although the accused murderers had discussed ways to kill her parents, Foster was determined to prove that JR never intended for the murders to happen.

The defence team seemed like perfect champions for a now orphaned 13-year-old accused murderer who was angrily referred to on blogs as "that little bitch goth princess." Foster, 47, travelled from Calgary in his new orange Hummer, blaring rock music like AC/DC. He also owned a Harley-Davidson motorcycle. But the quasi-biker image belied a soft-hearted family man with four sons who coached lacrosse and phoned his kids daily. One of his sons was the same age as JR's deceased brother, Jacob. On weekends, he would go home and sit in bed with his sons, wrapping his arms around them. Beyak, a bright young lawyer of 26, visited JR almost daily in jail. Like a cool big sister, she brought along gifts, including a book of sudoku puzzles and a copy of *Cosmo Girl*, a magazine hardly in keeping with the black goth image of Runaway Devil.

Crown prosecutor Stephanie Cleary, a prim, married mother of two, was also no stranger to high-profile and complex cases. She led the prosecution for the deadly 1992 Westray mine disaster case in Halifax, a catastrophic underground explosion that killed 26 miners. Like Foster, Cleary had also been involved in another gruesome Medicine Hat case, prosecuting 79-year-old Sofia Gawron, who was charged with chopping up her husband's body and burying the parts in their tidy backyard. A tip led police to unearth the skeletal remains of Tadeus Gawron in 1997, 17 years after he disappeared, during which time Sofia had continued cashing his pension cheques. By the time police caught up with her, she was wheelchair bound and living in a nursing home in the Crowsnest Pass on the Alberta–B.C. border. She suffered from dementia and was unable to answer questions about her husband's mysterious death. Like Anton LeClaire, she was declared unfit to stand trial.

With the voir dire portion of the trial underway, Justice Brooker was asked to rule on the admissibility of JR's interview with Sergeants Chris Sheehan and Robert Cole. The two officers had gotten what they needed from JR, but they would pay a price for it. Their tactics during the interview infuriated Justice Brooker, who ruled its contents inadmissible. Sergeant Sheehan, the judge wrote in a ruling, "engaged in a calculated process of strategic manipulation and blatant disregard for the young person's rights to have counsel present." The actions of Cole and Sheehan, Brooker said, "demonstrate a clear, calculated, and egregious course of conduct and strategy to deprive a suspect of her Charter rights and her rights under the *Youth Criminal Justice Act*. It would be serious enough if this conduct was towards an adult. That, in fact, it was against a 12-year-old youth with special rights under the *Youth Criminal Justice Act* makes it utterly deplorable."

Norm Boucher, the chief of police, defended his officers. "With statements, it's always a question if they are admissible or not. We are not the ones to decide if it goes into evidence. That is the decision of the Crown. We try to gather as much information as we can." Yet Boucher would later reassign Sheehan from the major crimes unit to a one-year purgatory as a court liaison officer, insisting it was a promotion. Cole, who was retiring, escaped without a reassignment.

"I knew from the get-go her confession was likely to get thrown out," Sheehan said later. "In my experience, any street cop who's been around for a year will tell you that if you catch a kid with a stolen bike, any confession is getting tossed. It is next to impossible to get a confession from a young offender admitted. The ones that do get in are the ones that are the perfect scenario. You start out knowing that you're fighting an uphill battle. I look at the statement in the same way I see a search: 'This probably isn't going to get in.'"

After a week of pre-trial arguments, the trial proper got underway. Cleary's opening address to the jury on June 12 detailed the evidence that she would present, which she said would prove that JR planned the deliberate killings of her family so that she could be with Jeremy Steinke. JR quietly wiped away tears as Cleary spoke. She wore a lilac-coloured, short-sleeved shirt and her long brown hair was pulled back into a high ponytail.

Neighbours Phyllis and Vernon Gehring and Sarah Penner were the first witnesses called, followed by Sergeant Secondiak. The officer struggled to maintain his composure as he described finding Jacob's body. "I saw a small boy deceased on a bed," he said, employing neutral language that did little to mask his emotions. His voice quavered: "He had knife wounds all over his body." When he finished testifying, Secondiak left the witness box and let out a huge sigh.

The next day, as crime scene investigators presented evidence, jurors were shown shocking photos of the victims. They were given no warning by Cleary or the judge – to do so would be prejudicial. Struggling not to reveal emotion, one young male juror put his hands over his mouth. Entering all the police and forensics evidence would take nearly a week.

It took 45 minutes alone for forensic pathologist Dr. Craig Litwin to describe Marc's stab wounds.

JR's paternal aunt and uncle were the only surviving family members to attend the trial. Her 76-year-old paternal grandfather, who said he forgave JR because she was "under a bad influence," did not travel from his home in Ontario. A graphic briefing by the Medicine Hat police of the murders of his son, daughter-in-law, and grandson was enough for him. "I can't live that again," he was quoted as saying. "It's too hard."

Jeremy's mother, who had attended her son's court appearances wearing his green high school football jacket, was on the witness list and thus barred from the courtroom. Jackie May had already moved temporarily east to Saskatchewan to avoid the glare of publicity. "It's still very stressful. It doesn't matter if I'm there or here. But out there, I don't get a thousand questions," she said.

May's sister and mother went to court faithfully every day. A Maple Creek, Saskatchewan high school law class attended one day of testimony. On another occasion, a mother and her 17-year-old daughter sat holding each other, listening to evidence. They asked for access to the crime scene photos, which Cleary allowed after warning of their graphic nature.

Because of the protective provisions of the *Youth Criminal Justice Act*, the media would be forced to make written applications to Justice Brooker to see the photos and other exhibits. The Act is specific on who can have access to records in a youth trial, and journalists are not on the list. It requires that a judge must hear arguments for access to exhibits from anyone who may have an interest in "the administration of justice," a broadly interpreted legal phrase.

Having entered all the evidence from investigators and experts, Cleary began calling friends and acquaintances of Jeremy and JR. They were a study in contrasts, depending on which side of the tracks they came from. JR's friends were mostly typical, fresh-faced youngsters from middle-class backgrounds, only some of whom dabbled in the goth lifestyle. Jeremy's friends and acquaintances were a collection of aimless alcoholics and drug users, many of them on medication for depression.

JR's friends were among the first called by Cleary, on June 20. Only a year before, they were just giggling schoolgirls who rode the bus together, laughed at each other's crazy dancing, gorged on mall junk food, uploaded photos of themselves to the Internet, played video games, and watched cartoons and movies at sleepovers.

Now, in the formal setting of an imposing courtroom with high ceilings, the usually talkative girls were silenced. Subpoenas had brought them here. They huddled in a witness room waiting to take turns on the stand to testify against their friend. Give evidence. Solemnly swear to tell nothing but the truth. Spill secrets.

Aubrey, Alyssa, Jocelyn, and Nora waited nervously in the room reserved for witnesses, located just outside the doors to the main courtroom, where a sheriff was posted. Lawyers and court clerks swirled around in long black robes. If teenage girls live for drama, this was not one they would have chosen. It could have been a movie or a TV show. But this was happening. This was real. The girls, all 14, looked at their toes, fiddled with rings, examined their fingernails, waiting to be summoned.

Alyssa was called first. She walked into the courtroom stiffly, passing through the wooden gate that separates the gallery from the court. She was wearing a grey hoodie and her blonde hair was pulled back into a stubby ponytail, making her look even younger and more baby-faced than she was. She stepped into the raised wooden witness podium, lips pressed into a straight line. The grey-haired, bearded judge was looking at her. The jurors were looking at her. The court clerks seemed like stern librarians. She turned her head slightly to the right, facing the strangers in the gallery. The only familiar person she saw was JR, looking straight back at her from the wooden prisoner's box. It was the first time they'd laid eyes on each other in over a year. *Look how much you've changed* they must have thought as they were drinking one another in.

Sensing the young teen's nervousness, Cleary mercifully eased Alyssa into her testimony by asking simple questions in a pleasant, welcoming tone: what are your mom and dad's names? Do you have any brothers or sisters? Where do you live? Where do you go to school? The comfort didn't last long. When she was asked to recall her friend's fury and hatred for her family, the girl burst into tears.

All of the girls cried. They recalled how they'd heard JR say she wished her family was dead and that they knew she was asking for help killing them.

Jocelyn was petrified. Her eyes were brimming with tears as she stood chewing gum nervously, waiting to be sworn in. She was dressed in a black cardigan over a white top. Her flip-flops showed off her black toenail polish. The beautiful, willowy dark-haired girl was so frightened she had to be fitted with a clip-on microphone to amplify her meek voice. She wept and shook in terror. After just a few questions and endless requests to speak up, Cleary asked for a 20-minute break so that the special-needs student could compose herself. As she was led out of the courtroom, her parents wrapped her tightly, protectively, in their arms. When she returned, her 20-year-old sister was allowed to be beside her in the witness stand for support. It helped. Jocelyn answered what she could: "I didn't really know [if JR had a boyfriend], because no one really tells me anything."

Jocelyn may have had difficulty functioning on the stand, but her testimony was guileless. She testified that she had heard JR talking to Jeremy on a cellphone on the school grounds. JR, she said, was asking Jeremy to help her kill her family.

JR's best friend, Aubrey, looked a little like Canadian rocker Avril Lavigne. Her long, shiny straight hair was light brown in the back and dyed darker around her face for dramatic effect. Her chunky bangs were stylishly side-swept. She wore blue eyeliner and red lipstick on her naturally upturned mouth. She was dressed in a Batman T-shirt and jeans with a black choker and pendant encircling her neck. Most witnesses arrive at court dressed as if they were going to church. Aubrey, wearing her usual teen uniform, looked ready for a quick trip to the mall.

"Did you ever meet Jeremy Steinke?" Cleary asked.

"Unfortunately, yes," said Aubrey, full of teen sass that made her the most audible of the girls. "On quite a few occasions."

Aubrey was the only one of JR's friends to reveal her personality. She confidently spoke her mind. She said she thought Jeremy was "really immature." She said she urged JR to pull the plug on her romance with Jeremy so she could get back the confiscated MP3 player, phone, and computer privileges that her parents had taken away as punishment. She told JR she could earn her mother's respect by following the rules, and get back to being a kid.

Aubrey's voice quivered with emotion as she recalled the time JR ditched her parents at the punk show and snuck away to make out with Jeremy in an alley. She referred to JR's mother by her first name and started to cry. How many times had her friend's mom laughed at her jokes, and cooked the girls whatever they wanted for breakfast after sleepovers? Her tears flowed as she recalled her friend saying she wished her mother was dead.

Before long, Aubrey regained her composure, locked eyes with JR, and mouthed "I love you." She hugged herself while staring at JR with a smile. As she stepped off the stand and walked toward the door, Aubrey blew her friend a kiss. The girls had been through a lot together: shared girlhood secrets and mini-battles with their Catholic school's dress code. Not even jail could douse their loyal friendship.

Nora testified last and spent the shortest time on the stand. Another dark-haired beauty, she looked like Katie Holmes from the young actress's days on the TV series *Dawson's Creek*. Nora's halting testimony was often at odds with her written police statement, which the Crown made her refer to. Her answers became more exact after that. It was as if Nora wanted to forget all the times she had heard JR say she hated her parents and felt controlled. In grade 6, the pair had been close. Nora seemed to want to remember things differently. Under instructions from Cleary, she read over her own girlish handwriting on the official police statement form. She sniffled, swiping at her nose with a tissue from a box perched on the stand. And then she answered the questions.

After each girl's testimony, Foster gently cross-examined them with the same general line of questioning. They gave nearly identical answers.

"Did you ever take JR seriously when she said she wanted to hurt her parents?"

"No."

"Because if you did, you would have told someone."

"Yes."

"It was all just talk, wasn't it?"

"Yes."

"Kids say stuff like this all the time, don't they?"

"Yes."

"You never expected in a million years that this would happen, did you?"

"No."

Foster wanted to plant doubt in the jury's mind that JR ever deliberately planned to kill her family. What teen or preteen girl struggling with the pains of puberty and independence hasn't said she hated her parents and muttered in anger the terrible words "I wish they were dead?"

Alcoholics at 18. Drug addicts. Dropouts. Runaways. Suicidal cutters. Unlike JR's obedient and well-groomed 14-year-old girlfriends, Jeremy Steinke's pals were rough around the edges. The two peer groups were a contrast in upbringing. JR's friends were conventional, suburban junior high students. Jeremy's were a motley crew. Most came from broken homes. They were drunk or stoned or depressed – or all three.

Five of them, ranging in age from 15 to 23, were called to testify. They were there to tell a tale of Runaway Devil and Souleater, but ended up unwittingly revealing sad insights into their own tragic lives.

TeJay Stadelman admitted that he spent most of his days drunk. Although his memory was foggy, he said he definitely remembered the two kissing and making out on the couch after the murders. He recounted how he was so wasted later that night that he tried selling an undercover cop some weed. He said he was arrested but not charged. "It must have been your lucky day," Foster said, drawing laughter from the courtroom.

The witnesses all admitted using substances that made their memories hazy.

Grant Bolt told how he'd never made it past grade 10. He testified that he was drinking and smoking three or four joints daily at the time of the murders. Bolt had offered police three different stories about how he arrived at the party the day the bodies were discovered. Now he told the jury a fourth version. Bolt blamed his hazy memory on antidepressant medication to curb his recent suicidal thoughts. "They make me unbalanced," he said under questioning from Foster. "They can affect my memory," he added, twirling his finger in the air.

Cam Barkley, glassy-eyed and red-faced on the stand, admitted being a hard drinker at 18: "I was pretty much drunk all the time. I'd wake up, buy some more booze and start drinking every day." That's what he did the day the family's bodies were found. At the party house, he said he drank a case of beer and a 26-ounce bottle of Hpnotiq.

Barkley gave the most confusing testimony. He told the jury Jeremy and JR watched *Black Hawk Down* with him the night of the killings. He said the couple left and returned in the small hours of the morning, hoping to stay. "I didn't want them in my house," said Barkley, who claimed he turned the pair away after noticing Jeremy was nursing a sore arm and had a swollen eye. When Foster pressed him, Barkley admitted to doing "a few" lines of cocaine with Jeremy earlier in the evening. Under questioning, he agreed that maybe the co-accused couple had stayed the night at his apartment after all. He admitted he had been both drunk and stoned.

Even Jordan Attfield, the most animated and likeable of the bunch, admitted to Foster he drank between six and eight beers the day he overheard JR asking Jeremy on the phone to kill her parents. Foster quizzed him about the group's style of dress, about their habit of wearing all black.

Attfield replied that they just did it for attention. Jeremy, he said, was in black most of the time. "I had a little more colour to me, though," he smiled. The gallery chuckled.

Jeremy's teenage female friends were among the saddest stories. Kaylee, the chronic runaway, had once been admitted to hospital and put on suicide watch for a week. Hailey, 15, also admitted to spending a week in the hospital under psychiatric watch. Both girls confirmed they had been cutters, that they voluntarily sliced their legs and arms with blades to feel pain.

Foster treated each of the witnesses with respect, showing empathy for their situations. He did not deride them in his bid to undermine their credibility by questioning their alcohol-fogged memories. Jeremy's friends responded to Foster as if the lawyer with the shaved head and earring were a friend.

Jeremy's hapless group left the gallery amused – and shaking their heads in disbelief. Their memories were hazy and their lifestyles reckless. "My view is they're not very credible, but that's up to the jury to decide," Foster said to reporters later.

Despite Foster's best efforts, the almost comical parade of characters presented by the Crown inflicted considerable damage on his client. Jordan Attfield was unwavering in his testimony that JR seemed serious in asking Jeremy to kill her parents. His testimony that Jeremy sought his help with the murders was also credible. Grant Bolt, while admitting he was stoned at the time, insisted he clearly remembered Jeremy asking for his help to kill JR's parents. James Whalley, who was at the party house the day after the murders, gave the damning evidence that Jeremy had told him that "we gutted them like a fish," and that JR had said that her little brother "gargled."

The fragile Jocelyn had also damaged JR with her testimony of hearing JR asking Jeremy to kill her family during a cellphone conversation. That plus the police evidence of JR's self-incriminating message of a plan to kill her family, of the drawing found in her locker, and of her actions in the hours immediately after the murder, including making out with Jeremy at the party, made Foster think that he might have to resort to the dangerous gamble of putting his client on the stand.

Having JR testify in her own defence was fraught with peril. The damaging effect of a cross-examination could reinforce guilt in the minds of the jury. Foster's hope was that the jury would believe her own words that she truly never intended Jeremy to take her seriously. "She always felt responsible, the question was whether, legally, she was guilty," Foster later said.

Dressed in a blue-grey smocked top and dark pants, with her hair swept neatly back into a ponytail, JR was sworn in to give evidence on Tuesday, July 4. She had listened to testimony and heard the evidence against her for a full month. At first halting and tearful, her soft voice often inaudible, she was gently asked by Foster to tell her story to a packed courtroom. Foster painted his client as lovestruck, an innocent girl swept away in a potent sexual relationship with an older man. Just a girl, not even yet a teenager at the time, whose morbid wisecracks were taken seriously by Jeremy Steinke, resulting in a "horrible misunderstanding."

Foster's tone was like that of a gentle psychoanalyst. "How did that make you feel?" he often asked. Under Foster's careful questioning, JR reasoned away her questionable and callous behaviour in the weeks leading up to, and hours after, the murders. She dismissed her online instant messages and her spiteful, macabre wishes for her family's violent demise as "just joking."

"In my group of friends, it was just the way we talked. It was just stupid talk," she explained. "Every time I said that, I never meant it. I was angry. I didn't mean it. Everybody else knew I didn't mean it."

The pair discussed "hypothetical" scenarios for killing the family, she admitted, but she never expected Jeremy to take her seriously.

"Did you ever think he would kill them?" Foster asked.

"No, never."

When Foster broached the topic of her relationship with Jeremy, JR quickly became dry-eyed and dreamy, brightening as she strolled down memory lane. Rather than an alarming coupling of an adult and a child two years younger than the legal age of consent, she warmly recalled a budding love affair. She relived the joys of their first meetings at the mall, the "flattering" poems and songs Jeremy had written for her, the secret late-night telephone calls, and the forbidden kisses that led to lovemaking with a grown man. "We made love," she said. "I loved him so much." (In Canada, statutory rape is called sexual interference. But police and prosecutors never pursued that charge against Jeremy. With so much evidence against him for the deaths of JR's family, murder was a much higher priority.)

Justifying why the two had sex while hiding out in Cam Barkley's apartment just hours after the killings, JR said, "I was scared. He was trying to make me feel better."

As Foster turned to asking about what happened inside the house the night of the murders, JR requested a break. Foster gently encouraged her to continue, and she tearfully whispered short answers that were barely audible.

She haltingly told the jury she was awakened by screaming and yelling as Jeremy carried out the stabbings downstairs. She said she snuck down the carpeted steps and saw her mother's body sprawled at the foot of the staircase. She could see her father, wearing only boxers, fighting with her boyfriend. She ran back upstairs where the family's bedrooms were, she said.

JR testified that her little brother was cowering on her parents' bed and that she joined him. "He was . . . wrapping his arms around me going, 'I'm scared, what do we do?' I didn't know what to do . . . He was panicking, he was really scared . . . I was panicking and I was really scared and I, like, I could, there was, like, I couldn't believe, like, what was happening. I couldn't absorb it. Like, I couldn't think. I couldn't do anything. I was, like, I was panicking. I didn't know what to do. And he was panicking . . . I put the crook of my elbow around, around his neck . . . he was clinging to me . . . I squeezed him, and I, I was – he's still talking. I was just, like, go to sleep, go to sleep."

"What were you doing?" Foster asked.

"I was trying to make him go to sleep. I was trying to make him go to sleep."

"Why?"

"Because it was horrible. I didn't want him to hear it."

She said the boy was clinging to her arm as she was trying to choke him unconscious.

"He's, like, 'What are you doing, JR?' He's, like, 'Aaa,' and I stopped. And he kinda stares back and comes and grabs me all over. He's still panicking. I'm like, I didn't know what to do. I felt so helpless. I couldn't think of anything."

Foster asked his client to explain how she came to be standing in the upstairs hallway with a knife at her side when Jeremy lumbered up the staircase panting wildly, a nightmare dressed in black, dripping with her parents' blood.

Here, JR said, "I forgot one part," and asked to go back over her story. She said she had earlier retrieved a kitchen knife hidden in her bedroom because, like Kaylee and Hailey, she had been dabbling in "cutting." She had sliced her own leg the week before because she was "really, really depressed." That's probably why a trace of her own blood was later found on the knife, she explained. She said she grabbed the knife before Jeremy reached the top of the staircase "to protect myself because I didn't want this."

She repeatedly testified that she was by turns "panicking" and "in shock," and that she was afraid Steinke would hurt her.

"Why?"

"Because I didn't want this to happen. I didn't – I didn't think he could – he could even – he could do something like that. Like, I thought I loved him. I thought I knew him. And he comes up the stairs and he's going, 'I love you, I love you so much.'"

She said she told her brother to go to his bedroom. Jeremy pushed past her, she said, following the boy into his room – testimony that doesn't fit with the forensic evidence of a "major bloodletting event" in the hallway outside Jacob's bedroom.

As she talked about the killing of her brother, JR began to hold herself and rocked from foot to foot on the stand. "What happened then? You have to speak up," Foster said.

"He is telling me to stab him. He says, 'Stab him, just stab him, just slit his throat.'"

"Where were you?"

"I was standing beside him. He was screaming at me."

"What did you do?"

"I was like – I was like, I can't, I can't do that."

"Did you say that or were you thinking that?"

"I think I said it. And he's like, 'You have to do this.' It was kinda like, 'I did this for you, you have to do this for me.'"

She claimed Jeremy was getting mad at her and said she feared he was going to hurt her.

"What did you do?"

"I stabbed my brother," she whispered, covering her mouth with her hands and crying gently.

"You've got to speak up."

"I went to stab my brother."

Foster asked how hard she stabbed him.

"Not very hard," she said, her voice cracking.

She says Jeremy snatched the knife out of her hand.

"What was your brother saying?"

"'I'm scared. I'm too young to die.'"

"Can you tell us what happened next?"

"Jeremy, he, he slits his throat."

"Did you see that?"

"No."

JR said she turned and was backing away, not wanting to watch, but was aware of Jeremy's motions. She went to her parents' bedroom.

"What did you hear?"

"My brother trying to breathe."

"What kind of sound was that?

"It was gurgling."

"What happened next?"

"Jeremy's like, 'He won't die!' And he stabbed him, stabbed him again."

She said Jeremy came out of the boy's room "like a zombie" and silently handed her the dripping knife on his way downstairs.

She went into the bathroom to wash the blood off her hands and the blade. She had to pack a bag and leave. She left the knife by the sink, in a pink puddle of her brother's watery blood.

The night, she said, remains blurry in her mind. She said she recalled walking downstairs, past the bloody smears Jeremy had left along the walls, and how Jeremy was "twitching and tweaking" in the kitchen.

Tim Foster hoped his client's testimony would convince the jury of her innocence. Why, he argued, would she voluntarily admit to all these incriminating actions? Why would she admit she talked about wanting her parents killed? About calling Jeremy's house after the murders? About having sex with him hours later? Because, Foster tried to show, she never intended for anything to happen.

"She didn't need to testify," Foster summarized in his closing argument. "It was difficult and stressful, obviously, for her to do that, and yet she did it. She did not have to get up on that stand in front of all these people. She did not have to bare her soul, talk about intimate details. She never had to do that. She could have sat there. She could have hid behind her lawyer," he said.

Outside court, Foster was asked how he thought JR did on the stand.

"All we ever told her was get up, tell the truth, do your best, and I thought she did," he replied.

JR had sobbed a few times during her testimony and spoken softly, but was hardly distraught. Asked about her seemingly emotionless demeanour, Foster offered that his client had been analyzed and interviewed by police and therapists so often that she probably had grown accustomed to the questions.

JR seemed almost to swoon when recalling intimate details of her relationship with her family's murderer. She had accepted Jeremy's jailhouse proposal. Was she still in love with her co-accused killer, her lawyer was asked?

No, Foster replied, his client no longer had any feelings for Jeremy Steinke: "With therapy and time to reflect, my client has drastically changed her view of Mr. Steinke."

JR, Foster said, was the victim of a predator. "She was a 12-year-old who had a sexual relationship with a 23-year-old. We can't ignore that all of this happened in that context."

The next day, Stephanie Cleary cross-examined JR. Unlike Tim Foster, she was not gentle in her line of questioning. She made no merciful small talk to put the girl at ease, as she'd done with JR's friends. She took on the tone of a stern, scolding mother as she set out to show the jury that JR and Jeremy had jointly premeditated the slaughter.

"We heard a lot of, 'I think,' yesterday, so I only want to hear today what you actually know, alright? Yes?" Cleary asked sharply.

"Yes," JR said obediently.

Cleary asked her about the messages she had sent as Runaway Devil. "That message about having a plan to kill your parents so you could live with him. You wrote that?"

"Yes."

"Those are your words?"

"Yes."

"You never took them back in writing, did you?"

"What do you mean?"

"You never said, 'I'm just joking, you know, I didn't mean it?'"

"Well, cuz I didn't have to say that because he knew that I wasn't serious."

"Right. You never wrote anything nice about your family in any of those messages."

"No."

With the burden of proof resting on the Crown, Cleary began debunking JR's story that she had never intended for the murders to happen and that Jeremy had showed up on his own and gone berserk.

"You go to the 7-Eleven [after the murders]?" Cleary asked.

"Yeah."

"They have a clerk there, right?"

"Yeah."

"It's all lit up?"

"Yeah."

"You don't ask that person for help?"

"No."

"You don't say there's people at your house who might need help?"

"No."

Cleary asked why, after Jeremy left her stranded in the house, JR didn't check to see if her wounded family could be saved. "You don't do anything to try and help them?"

"How could I have helped them?"

"You didn't even check on them, did you?"

"No."

"At this point, you don't even know if they're dead for sure."

"I wasn't thinking if they were dead for sure. I was practically sleep-walking."

"You don't call an ambulance for them?"

"No."

"You don't call 911 – 'My parents have been attacked?'"

"No."

"You don't call any of your friends?"

"No."

"You don't call any of your friends' parents?"

"No."

"You don't call anybody belonging to your parents?"

"No."

"You don't run next door?"

"No."

"You don't just sit down and cry?"

"No."

Referring to the night of the murders, Cleary walked JR through her previous testimony about hearing Jeremy killing her father downstairs.

"So you don't call 911?"

"No."

"You don't tell Jacob, 'Call 911'?"

"No."

"You see your mother lying at the bottom of the stairs with blood on her chest?"

"Yeah."

"You don't rush up to her and try to help her?"

"No."

"You see your father and Jeremy fighting?"

"Yeah."

"And you don't say, 'Stop it. Stop it'?"

"No, I was – I was so scared. I was terrified. I was panicking and I couldn't think, and I was so scared. I didn't know what to do. It didn't even occur to me to call 911."

"No. What occurred to you was to try and make Jacob go to sleep."

"Yes."

"You didn't say, 'Lie down in your bed, honey, go to sleep'? You put your arm around his neck?"

"Yeah."

"And tried to choke him?"

"Yeah," JR said softly.

"Pardon me?" Cleary asked incredulously.

"Yes."

"And you thought that somehow was going to result in him going to sleep?" Cleary said, disgust rising in her voice.

"Yes."

"So you had the one arm around his neck?"

"Yes."

"And he was clawing at it?"

"Yes."

"Because he weighed, what? Sixty-eight pounds?"

"I don't know what he weighed."

"Putting him to sleep wasn't working out so well, was it?"

"No."

Cleary noted to JR that her next act was to go into her bedroom and get a knife because Jeremy had ordered her to cut the boy's throat. "You just said, 'I can't.' Not 'I won't,'" Cleary said, asking why she did nothing to shield her brother from her boyfriend.

"I wasn't thinking straight. I was like a zombie," JR said. "I could barely function. It didn't even enter my mind to call 911."

Further in her cross-examination, Cleary asked JR about her commenting to friends at school that she wished her parents were dead.

"You were saying, 'I want to kill them,' right?"

"Yes."

"You said that so much to Alyssa, it actually affected your friendship with her, didn't it? You told her you couldn't stand being in the presence of your mother?"

"Yes."

"You told Aubrey you wanted them dead?"

"Yes."

"And you never said to any of these little girls, 'I'm just having a hard time, you know'?"

"Because they knew I wasn't serious, that I didn't mean these things, that I was venting and saying stupid stuff."

Cleary asked the clerk to show JR Exhibit 48 – the stick-figure drawing she had made of her family burning alive. "It's a little bit different, wouldn't you agree with me, than drawing your band teacher as a duck, isn't it?" Cleary said.

"Yes."

"Pardon me?"

"Yes."

"The four people in that drawing, that's you and your family, isn't it?"

"Yup."

"And the truck is Jeremy's truck, isn't it?"

"Yes."

"You were talking to everybody at this time about how much you hate your parents and how you wanted to kill them, right?"

"Yes."

"And you had a lot of those conversations with Jeremy, right?"

"Yes. . . . I said stuff like, I hate them so much, I wish they would die, I just want to kill them."

"I just want to kill them?" Cleary asked, again with incredulity.

"Yeah."

"I hate them so much I wish they would die?" Cleary said in an almost stunned tone.

"Yes."

"What else?"

"I hate being around them."

"I hate being around them?"

"Mm-hmm."

Cleary then asked her about choking Jacob. "You were squeezing his airway? . . . He was fighting you, wasn't he?"

"Yes," the girl replied coolly.

Cleary pressed on. "You didn't even try to save him, did you?" she asked.

"I was really scared," JR said, tearing up. "I thought [Jeremy] was going to try to kill me."

But Jeremy's first words to her as he appeared at the top of the stairs, Cleary noted from her testimony, were "I love you." The plan all along was for the boy to die, Cleary insisted. You couldn't hold up your end of the bargain, she said.

"There wasn't a plan."

"I'm going to suggest to you that the plan was that Jacob was supposed to die all along, and you just couldn't finish it yourself."

"There wasn't a plan."

"Well, if there wasn't a plan, wouldn't you have begged [Jeremy] to stop? He's your little brother."

The jury hung on every word. The gallery seemed shocked. Reporters scribbled furiously.

Cleary then turned to the remorseless jailhouse letters JR had written. "You don't say in any of those letters, 'This is a horrible mistake'?"

"No."

"You don't say, 'I didn't mean it'?"

"No."

"You don't say to him, 'How could you take me seriously'?"

"No."

"And, instead, you really told him, 'Ah, it's over, don't worry about it'?"

"Yeah, we can't change it – not, don't worry about it."

Cleary suggested that JR could have simply run away with Jeremy, but then the prosecutor ruled out that option: "Your parents loved you too much to let you run away, didn't they?"

"Yes."

"And they would have looked for you as long as they were alive, wouldn't they?"

"Yes."

"They adored you, didn't they?"

"Yes."

"You couldn't have left that residence with any chance of success unless they were dead, could you?"

"No."

"They would have come after you?"

"Yes."

The withering, relentless cross-examination appeared to shock JR. She left the stand looking ashen and stunned. But the worst was yet to come.

16

A MINI-KARLA?

"This is a young woman who is seriously disturbed."

Stephanie Cleary's devastating cross-examination of JR undoubtedly had a profound effect on the jury. Cleary had exposed too many holes in the girl's story to make her defence seem plausible. If there had been no premeditated plan to kill her family, why had she not called 911 while Jeremy was downstairs butchering her parents? Why had she not told Jacob to run? Why, when left alone in the house with the bodies, had she not checked to see if anyone was still alive? Instead, she'd called a cab and booked it to arrive in 25 minutes, long enough for her to take her mother's credit card, run to the nearby 7-Eleven to withdraw money from a bank machine, and run back. If she'd been afraid that Jeremy was going to hurt her, too, as she testified, why had she run to him immediately after the murders, carrying a knapsack packed with clothes, toiletries, and lavender bath beads? Why had she not run next door to the neighbours for help? Instead, she ran to her family's killer, had post-murder sex with him, and went to a party less than 12 hours later, where she'd giggled and straddled him on a couch.

Coupled with the incriminating evidence presented during the trial – her Internet message to Jeremy saying she had "a plan" to kill her parents, the drawing in her locker showing her family being burned alive as she ran toward "Jeremy's truck," the insensitive jailhouse note saying they were "legends," the apology written mockingly to "my loverdly parental units," her overheard conversations asking her lover to kill her parents – all painted a portrait of a cold, calculating murderess.

"Perhaps not since Karla Homolka described the drugging and handing over of her younger sister as a Christmas present for her then-serial-rapist boyfriend Paul Bernardo has a Canadian jury seen and heard such a galling confession," commented *Globe and Mail* columnist Christie Blatchford.

Comparing Runaway Devil to Canada's most reviled female killer was not a huge leap. At times during her testimony, JR appeared to be a mini-Karla. Homolka, convicted of manslaughter for the 1992 and 1993 murders of two Ontario schoolgirls with her husband, Paul Bernardo, had been immortalized in an infamous close-up photograph showing her cold, squinting eyes, described by her victims' lawyer Tim Danson as "empty" and "dead." Runaway Devil's eyes showed the same unfeeling coldness. Despite the hair pulled neatly back in a ponytail and the prim blue and lavender tops that she wore to court, JR evoked Homolka not only in appearance, but also through her actions: both had willingly sacrificed younger siblings for their lovers.

In his lengthy closing argument, Tim Foster asked the jury to question Stephanie Cleary's theory that JR had plotted with Jeremy Steinke to kill her family. If there was a plan, argued Foster, why did Jeremy have to sneak in through the basement window? Why not just open the back door? If there was a plan, why wasn't JR packed and ready to go when Jeremy arrived, rather than scurrying about after the murders? Why didn't Jeremy take her with him rather than running out of the house and leaving her behind? Why would he have allowed Mick and Erica to stay at his trailer that night, leaving witnesses to his actions? Why did he and JR spend the whole next day at the party house, where they could be seen? If there was a plan, why didn't they leave right away with a destination in mind?

Cleary responded succinctly by telling the jury not to be fooled by the defence's argument that there was no plan. In her closing argument, she said, "It doesn't have to be a good plan. It doesn't have to be a sophisticated plan." There just has to be a plan, no matter how ill-conceived.

Foster had asked the jury to consider that the blood evidence overwhelmingly implicated only Jeremy. It was not his client who killed the family, he insisted, "It was Jeremy who did that. It was Jeremy who had the blood of each of them on his clothing and on his shoes."

Cleary had an answer for that, too. Under Canadian law, she told the jury, "A person can be found guilty of murder even without holding the murder weapon."

As set out in law, a person can be found guilty of murder in four ways: 1) by directly committing the murder; 2) by aiding the perpetrator – that is, physically assisting the killer to commit murder, such as helping to gain entry or physically restraining the victim; 3) by abetting the killer – that is, encouraging or inciting; and 4) by counselling the killer, such as coaching on how to carry out the crime.

The jury could find JR not guilty, guilty of second-degree murder (meaning that she didn't intend for the killings to happen, as she claimed), or guilty of first-degree murder, meaning that she planned the murders and intended them to happen. They returned a verdict with stunning swiftness. The jury had been gone only four hours, including the hourlong break they took for lunch. Most observers expected they would at least deliberate overnight. But at 5:39 p.m., on July 8, 2007, after 25 days of hearing evidence, they re-entered the courtroom.

"Ladies and gentlemen of the jury," the court clerk asked, "have you arrived at a verdict? If so, say so by your foreperson. What is your verdict on Count Number 1?"

The jury foreman, a slim, dark-haired young man, rose and answered for each count. The jurors found JR guilty of three counts of first-degree murder.

With Foster at her side, JR was asked to stand by Justice Brooker.

"You've heard the verdicts of the jury," he said. "I convict you of all accounts on the offences charged. Please be seated."

The youngest person ever convicted in Canada of multiple homicide clasped her hand over her mouth and began to sob quietly.

Unlike in the American judicial system, jurors in Canada cannot be identified. Nor are they allowed to discuss with anyone their deliberations or the reasons for their verdict following a trial. Two of JR's jurors, however, began posting comments on a social networking website less than a week after the verdict. One of them was the jury foreman, who was killed on August 31, 2008, 13 months after the trial, when his pickup truck rolled on a rural highway, ejecting him from the vehicle late at night. He was 21.

He did not discuss the jury's deliberations online but wrote that the stress of the trial made an impact on him: "Effects of the trial can take up to four weeks, they said. They also gave us an envelope full of paper on how to deal with it. I'm doing alright. I'm still not getting a full night's sleep."

In another post, he added that he had wanted to be on the jury when he got his summons. "I didn't really know what I was getting myself into, I guess. I found that out on the second day. It's hard to deal with. After seeing everything and hearing everything every day, it sticks with a person. I don't sleep as much that's for sure. I think with time I'll be good."

The second juror wrote that the grisly crime scene photos put stress on the jury. Although several media reports indicated that the jury viewed the binder of photos dispassionately, the juror said they were only trying to keep it together and appear impartial.

"It hit a lot of them pretty hard. But we had to remain cool as best we could because we were constantly being watched by everyone," he commented. "The shitty thing is that there was no warning. They just told us to open the binder and, BANG, there they were. The papers, I think, had to say that stuff so that people didn't think that a decision was made on feelings. Like the final day when we got charged to make our decision, we had to walk right past the girl and the paper wrote 'and the stone-faced jury walked past the accuse with no emotion.' That's bullshit . . . there was a lot of people that had a rough time."

The speed of the verdict, he indicated, was due to the overwhelming evidence against JR.

"Truth be told, I did not feel sympathy for her," he said. "She got what she deserved. The fact of the matter is that three people are dead so she could have a relationship with a 23-year-old man. She did show emotion both ways. She cried maybe twice and then cried hard after the verdict was given. There were also times when I saw her smirking. She knew what she was doing, no doubt. We tried to give her the benefit of the doubt but the evidence was just way too strong to prove anything but guilt. I tried to feel for her but as time went on in the trial it got harder and harder to believe her story."

JR was sentenced by Justice Brooker on November 8, 2007.

"The circumstances surrounding these murders are horrific," he said. "It is difficult to imagine or conceive of a more horrific crime than this – the planned and deliberate murder of her parents and only sibling by a twelve-and-a-half-year-old young person."

The judge described Marc and Debra as "wonderful parents who loved JR and were at all times acting in her best interests. They were concerned for JR's welfare . . . They never gave up on her and I do not think that they would even now." The murder of JR's little brother, he said, was "completely incomprehensible."

Justice Brooker explained that, by Canadian law, the sentence imposed on a person of JR's age had to be the least restrictive possible while still holding her accountable for her actions. Noting that his sentencing options were limited under the terms of the *Youth Criminal Justice Act,* the judge said that the maximum custodial sentence JR could receive was six years, followed by another four years of conditional supervision in the community. In addition, he could find JR eligible to receive specialized care known as Intensive Rehabilitative Custody and Supervision (IRCS), a rehabilitation program reserved for serious violent young offenders who are diagnosed as suffering from a mental illness, a psychological disorder, or an emotional disturbance.

Although not altering her time in custody, IRCS would provide JR with the best mental help available and allow the incarcerating jurisdiction, in this case Alberta, to recover $100,000 a year from the federal government for her treatment.

Will Friend, a psychiatrist at the Alberta Hospital, an Edmonton psychiatric institution, and director of forensic psychiatry at the University of Alberta, tested JR and determined she suffered from conduct disorder and oppositional defiant disorder (ODD). According to medical literature, about 15 percent of teens may have ODD, which, according to the American Academy of Child and Adolescent Psychiatry, is a normal part of development for two- to three-year-olds and early adolescents. In the extreme, it is manifested by an ongoing pattern of disobedient, hostile, and defiant behaviour toward authority figures, such as parents, that "goes beyond the bounds of the normal behaviour of childhood." This defiance can also be directed at siblings, playmates, or peers at school. Conduct disorder is a more severe form of oppositional defiant disorder and is the childhood equivalent of anti-social personality disorder, the blanket term covering such conditions as psychopathy or sociopathy. Conduct disorder and ODD are prerequisites for a young offender's diagnosis of sociopathy or psychopathy later in life.

Because their brains are not fully developed, children and youth under 18 cannot legally be labelled as psychopathic (getting psychological gratification from violence or aggression) or sociopathic (lacking in remorse, shame, or guilt). Instead, the label of conduct disorder is used. Children and adolescents with conduct disorder, such as JR, "have great difficulty following rules and behaving in a socially acceptable way."

The terminology used to describe her disorders seemed benign for someone convicted of participating in the murders of three family members. Stephanie Cleary described JR more succinctly, calling her "seriously disturbed."

The public will never know the exact extent of the mental health issues plaguing the self-styled Runaway Devil. Justice Brooker denied an application by media outlets to view her psychiatric and pre-sentence reports, citing concerns expressed by the Canadian Psychiatric Association. The CPA opposes the public release of mental health records, saying it could harm successful treatment and put a chill on a person's participation in the mental health process.

According to the CPA's position statement on the subject, "Confidentiality is a prime condition in enabling the establishment of effective therapeutic relationship. In no other medical specialty is so much private information required for establishing an accurate diagnosis and treatment plan. Breaches or potential breaches of confidentiality in the context of therapy seriously jeopardize the quality of the information communicated between patient and psychiatrist and also compromise the mutual trust and confidence necessary for effective therapy to occur."

Roger Marceau, a clinical neuropsychologist with Alberta Hospital, also analyzed JR and reported that she may be able to become a productive member of society through treatment. He noted that JR has a "very high level" of executive, intellectual, and memory function. Marceau also concluded that she requires "significant treatment."

With JR found to be suffering from several psychological disorders and thus eligible for treatment, the court granted the IRCS application requested by both the Crown and defence. "To refuse an IRCS disposition and simply sentence JR to the maximum six years in custody followed by four years in the community under supervision would not be appropriate on the evidence and submissions before me," Justice Brooker said. "JR would not receive the treatment she so obviously needs. The chances of her coming out of such custody as a productive, law abiding and contributing member of society would be comparatively reduced." With his order, JR would be eligible to receive at least $1 million in taxpayer-supported mental health care over the term of her sentence.

When IRCS was introduced in 2003, it was expected that 50 young offenders a year would qualify for the program. As of the end of February 2009, only 47 teens had received the sentence, partly because Canada lacks the mental health resources to deal with adolescent criminals, according to critics in the field. JR would become the youngest person in Canada to receive an IRCS order.

Taking into account the 18 months she had already spent in jail, Brooker sentenced JR to four years in custody to be followed by four and a half years of community supervision, or probation, giving her the maximum 10-year sentence allowed under the *Youth Criminal Justice Act*. He also issued a warrant for her DNA samples to be taken and kept on file and made a standard prohibition against her owning firearms. He did not say anything about knives.

"JR, you can never undo what you have done to your mom, dad, and little brother," Justice Brooker said to her. "However, what you can do is honour their memory by dedicating your life to becoming the woman your parents and brother would be proud of."

With that, the gallery stood as the judge left the courtroom. JR spoke with her lawyers in the prisoner's box and managed a smile. By the time she is eighteen and a half, in 2012, she will be out of custody. Her sentence will be completed after four years of community supervision, when she will be 22. Her record will remain in a criminal database for another five years. If she commits no offence in that time, her record will be expunged. In the words of one Calgary legal expert: "She could do the disappearing act."

Reaction to JR's sentence was negative and swift. Police chief Norm Boucher, who had by now been elected mayor of Medicine Hat, acknowledged that the judge's hands were tied but doubted the 10-year term would sit well with the community. Boucher, who grew up in Quebec in a family of 14 children, had spent 30 years in the RCMP, six and a half as Medicine Hat police chief, and served in two United Nations peace-keeping missions, to Croatia in 1995 and Kosovo in 2001. He had seen his share of bad things and believed in consequences to hold youths accountable for their actions. A father of two sons, Boucher was instrumental in setting up a local Youth Justice Committee in Medicine Hat, a key feature of which requires young offenders to engage in a reconciliation process with victims and the community.

"When it is a young offender, we have to accept it because that's the law," he says of the sentence. "That does not mean it can't be changed, but for that we have to rely on the politicians. Would I have liked it more severe? Yes. Probably more severe than this."

If JR had been six months younger at the time of the murders, the worst she would have faced would have been probation. Twelve is the age of criminal responsibility in Canada. Those under 12 who commit criminal offences can be dealt with only under provincial child welfare legislation. The United Nations Convention on the Rights of the Child calls for nations to establish a minimum age "below which children shall be presumed not to have the capacity to infringe on the penal law." But the Convention does not set a specific age, and it varies greatly around the world. In England, the age of criminal responsibility is 10. In Scotland it is 8, Germany 14, Scandinavia 15. Seven is the minimum age in 10 countries, including India, Pakistan, Spain, Singapore, and South Africa. In Iran, the age of criminal responsibility is 9 for girls and 15 for boys. In the United States, the minimum age is determined by each state and ranges from 6 to 12 years among the 13 states that have set minimums. Most states rely on common law, which makes the minimum age between 7 and 14. For U.S. federal crimes such as kidnapping, damaging or destroying mailboxes, arson, assault, immigration offences, or assassinating a president, the minimum age is 10.

The orphaned JR, now under the guardianship of the director of Alberta Children and Youth Services, was ordered to serve her time at

Alberta Hospital, a 410-bed psychiatric facility of 45 buildings spread over 110 pastoral hectares on the northeast outskirts of Edmonton.

About 1,700 people a year are treated there, ranging from youths age 12 and over to geriatric patients. Those under secure custody, such as JR, are not free to walk around the grounds without a security escort, but there are no cells and no doors with iron bars, and patient rooms can be personalized. The hospital has a swimming pool and other recreational facilities and patients are given chores. JR would be required to attend school during the week, although not necessarily all day or every day. She would have sessions with counsellors and therapists and be given periodic medical evaluations.

At any time during her sentence, a judge can authorize JR to be switched from secure custody to "open" custody, depending on how well she progresses through therapy. Open custody could be served either in a less restrictive environment within Alberta Hospital or in a group home setting with no bars on the windows or locks on the doors. Under open custody, she could go out under escort, to school or counselling, for instance. Gerry Wright, head of Intensive Rehabilitative Custody and Supervision for the Alberta Solicitor General's Office at the time JR was sentenced, said JR would be strictly monitored in open custody: "Her movements would be controlled at all times. They don't have complete freedom at all. There is total control over where they go and what they do."

The bottom line for three lives taken was 18 months already served, plus another four years in custody, with the chance to be let out under escort at almost any time. Many asked whether this was just punishment. But in Canada youths really cannot be "punished" at all. Under two Supreme Court rulings in 2005 and 2006, denunciation and deterrence aren't to be considered factors in the sentencing of young offenders. Under Parliament's direction, any sentence imposed must be "the least restrictive available to hold a young person accountable" while still having "meaningful consequences . . . that promote his or her rehabilitation into society," as Justice Brooker had noted.

Herb Allard, a retired Alberta family court judge from Calgary, argues that this is the right approach. "What people forget in all of this is that time in child time is different than adult time," he says. "Remember when summer holidays lasted forever? Two months for a 12-year-old child is a long time, a year is an eternity. What we do is destroy kids during those formative years with custodial and other interventions. Kids aren't deterred like adults are. They don't have the formative notion of criminality like adults do. They know right and wrong, but in a different sense."

Recent research into the neuroscience of the teen brain confirms Allard's argument. Magnetic resonance imaging (MRI) technology has given researchers new insight into children's apparently muddy concept of right and wrong. While children and early teens certainly know the difference between right and wrong, they do not fully comprehend consequences, according to researchers at Harvard, UCLA, and the U.S. National Institute of Mental Health, who collaborated to map the development of the brain.

To their surprise, they discovered that the teenage brain undergoes an intense overproduction of grey matter – the "thinking" part of the brain – followed by a period of so-called "pruning," during which the brain discards grey matter at a rapid rate. Pruning is accompanied by myelination, a process in which white matter develops. White matter is fatty tissue that serves as insulation for the brain's circuitry, making the brain's operations more precise and efficient. This process takes place twice during a lifetime, in the womb and continuing through the first 18 months of life, and again at puberty. Teens are literally "growing their brains" during this pruning period.

"The part that warns of consequences isn't fully on board yet," says Dr. Jay Giedd of the U.S. National Institute of Mental Health.

The Juvenile Justice Center of the American Bar Association summarized the findings of Giedd and other researchers in a 2004 paper titled "Adolescence, Brain Development and Legal Culpability." The association concluded: "This fresh understanding of adolescence does not excuse juvenile offenders from punishment for violent crime, but it clearly lessens their culpability."

Nick Bala, a law professor at Queen's University in Kingston, Ontario who specializes in youth law, says that lesser penalties for young offenders are appropriate, even for those convicted of the most serious crimes. Statistically, most girls do not commit serious crimes until the age of 15.

"First of all, there are very few homicides committed by 12-year-olds, and there are relatively few homicides committed by females, and a 12-year-old is highly unusual to be involved in this type of offence. Most, although not all, of familial killings involve young people who have been abused or in a situation where there is a difficult or troubled home situation. That doesn't seem to have been the situation here. And, in some way, it must be every parent's worst nightmare with their teenagers."

Adolescence, says Bala, is a difficult stage of life. "We want to protect them as a society. In adolescence you have unpredictable behaviour, immature behaviour, high-risk behaviour, and those all come together. And on top of that, in this case, you have the exploitation by an older person. What happened is a terrible tragedy for everybody, most obviously the victims and those who loved them, but it is also a tragedy for this girl who is affected by this, as it should be.

"The case was horrific and unusual. There are adolescents, and in particular girls, who say they hate their parents: 'I wish they were dead.' It's not surprising that they can't act on their own and have to link up with someone who is an adult. I think it would have been very different if she hadn't linked up with him. In a way, it's amazing there are not more homicides by adolescents because they have such bad judgment. One of the things about 12-year-olds is that they lack the strength and sophistication to kill someone. I'm not surprised that he or she is aided by an adult."

At 12, though JR was physically mature, she was obviously psychologically and intellectually very immature, Bala says.

"But, having said that, there are people who are absolutely horrified by this. There is not going to be a moral accounting for this that will ever be satisfactory."

The most galling aspect of JR's sentence is not that her identity will remain a secret or that she will be released after a maximum six years in custody. What concerns many people is that her youth record will vanish if she commits no offences for five years after her sentence has been fully served, with probation, at age 27 ½. For someone guilty of three counts of the most serious crime known to society, this, to some, is simply wrong, even if she was only 12 at the time. "It's disturbing. You have the most heinous of crimes and the state bends over backwards to protect people like this, even if it is a young offender. I have a problem with that," says Art Hanger, a former Member of Parliament, a retired policeman, and a critic of the Canadian justice system. Fully rehabilitated or not, JR could move into a position of trust and become a teacher, a lawyer, a health care worker, a caregiver, and no one would be the wiser.

"She does not have to reveal anything about her youth record in the future unless she wants to," explains Janne Holmgren, a criminologist at Calgary's Mount Royal College and an expert in aberrant behaviour. "She is not required to reveal that she murdered her own brother and parents." Assuming she commits no offences for five years after her sentence is served, "she is granted a clean slate and she can do whatever she wants to do," says Holmgren. "She is not restricted from contact with minors. Like Karla Homolka, there are no conditions on her release and we can only sit back and watch."

17

A TRAIL OF TEARS

"You stabbed me every day, Jeremy."

Alain Hepner, one of Calgary's top criminal defence lawyers, had watched JR's trial with interest. As Jeremy's attorney, Hepner kept a keen eye on the intense publicity surrounding her case for anything that might prejudice his client's right to a fair trial. Within two weeks of JR's guilty verdict, he applied for a change of venue out of Medicine Hat. The odds of pulling a second, unbiased jury from the small city of 57,000 for the same case seemed improbable, Hepner felt. JR's defence team had been widely quoted as saying that she was a child victim and that Jeremy acted alone in killing her family. The incriminating testimony of Grant Bolt and Jordan Attfield that Jeremy tried to recruit them had also been reported in detail, as had many other trial details implicating Jeremy in the murders. One of the most damaging statements about Hepner's client came from none other than Justice Brooker in his charge to the jury: "I suggest that you will have no difficulty concluding beyond a reasonable doubt on the evidence that Steinke caused the death of each of Marc, Debra, and Jacob. That he caused their deaths by an unlawful act, that is to say, by stabbing Marc and Debra and cutting Jacob's throat as well as stabbing him, and that he intended to kill them."

Hepner, in arguing for a change of venue, cited Brooker's instruction to the jury, saying "there can be no other reasonable conclusion [than] that Justice Brooker advised the jury, and inferentially the press and the community, that Jeremy Steinke is guilty of the three acts of first-degree murder."

Hepner's application to have Jeremy's trial moved from Medicine Hat to Calgary, with a population of one million, was opposed by Crown prosecutor Stephanie Cleary, who said it would be expensive, inconvenient for staff and witnesses, and against the long-held legal tradition that justice should be served in the community where the crime is committed. She acknowledged, however, that the publicity surrounding JR's trial permeated every corner of town. "You'd really have to have been living under a rock" not to know what happened, Cleary said. The change of venue application upset many residents of Medicine Hat, including Mayor Norm Boucher, who felt Jeremy should answer for his alleged crimes locally.

The change of venue hearing was delayed until after JR's sentencing. Arguments were heard in Medicine Hat on March 19, 2008, before Justice Bryan Mahoney, who agreed with Hepner and ruled that the trial should be moved to Calgary. Nearly two years after the murders, the Crown could at last proceed with its case against Jeremy Allan Steinke.

It would take eight more months, however, for Jeremy's trial to begin. Stephanie Cleary had been appointed a provincial court judge, a new prosecutor had to be chosen, and other legal preparations made.

When Jeremy finally shuffled into a prisoner's box at the Calgary Courts Centre, it was Friday, November 14, 2008. His jury selection was held in Courtroom 1801. A cavernous room with high ceilings, it was filled to overflowing with more than 300 people summoned for jury duty. Monitors had to be set up in an adjacent courtroom to accommodate the overflow crowd, which included court staff, law students, and members of the public curious to see for themselves the self-described werewolf. Although it had been one year since JR was sentenced and two and a half years since the murders, the public's appetite for the case remained insatiable.

Two prosecutors from Medicine Hat were brought in to handle the Crown's case – lead prosecutor Ramona Robins, a rising star in the Southern Alberta Crown prosecutor's office, and assistant prosecutor Brandy Shaw. Robins, 37, had assisted Cleary behind the scenes during JR's trial and was familiar with the case. Appointed acting chief Crown prosecutor for Medicine Hat after Cleary was given her judgeship, Robins had recently scored a successful prosecution against a 32-year-old Alberta man for killing a teenage girl and dumping her body on the side of a rural road. He was a mundane killer compared to Jeremy Steinke, who would be Robins's most high-profile case in her six years as a prosecutor.

Hepner was a legal veteran and no stranger to bizarre and brutal murder cases. His list of clients included those charged with death by shooting, stabbing, suffocation, and dismemberment, including one who, if not for the modern ingredient of cocaine, might have been a character out of an Appalachian murder ballad. Dean Victor Gosse, 38, admitted to killing a 58-year-old woman during a cocaine binge in 2007, after which he chopped her up with a knife and hatchet and scattered the body parts along the banks of Calgary's Bow River. But Gosse's case, as brutal as the circumstances were, was nothing compared to the lengthy list of high-profile battles that Hepner had fought. One of only a handful of Canadian lawyers to be made a fellow of the American College of Trial Lawyers, Hepner is the kind of guy people in trouble want in their corner. He has more than 30 years of experience defending people with seemingly impossible chances of victory.

Hepner made history using the first-ever "battered wife syndrome" defence in an Alberta murder trial. A jury acquitted his client, Gladys Heavenfire, of second-degree murder for shooting her abusive common-law husband to death in 1990. They ruled that it was self-defence. When a truck driver crashed into a car, killing four elderly nuns on Easter Sunday

2003, he called Hepner, who persuaded the judge that his client had been distracted by a dangerous driver. Hepner also once defended a notorious mass murderer who slaughtered four people at a drunken party in his basement apartment in 1988. The man shot his victims – including a 15-year-old boy – slashed their throats, and defiled their bodies, including placing a rose into one victim's vagina. Two of the first-degree charges were reduced to second-degree.

Years of exposure to such mayhem had done nothing, however, to alter Hepner's gentle, genial nature. He had obtained a master's degree in psychology before taking up law, and his work with the criminally depraved paled in the historical context of his having lost relatives in the Holocaust.

Before jury selection began, Justice Adele Kent read out the three first-degree murder charges against Jeremy. Hepner answered not guilty to all three counts on his client's behalf. Jeremy showed no emotion except when the third charge was read. Told he stood accused of murdering Jacob, he silently shook his head no. The once-bullied Jeremy, who showed off at the local mall dressed in goth attire, displayed none of the braggadocio he exhibited when he boasted to fellow prisoners about the killings. He had spent two and a half years in custody awaiting trial. Now, the man who so desperately wanted to be accepted sat alone in the prisoner's box with his head bowed looking at the floor.

Ramona Robins made her opening statement on Monday, November 17. She told the selected jury of six men and six women that the murders were planned and deliberate. She laid out the evidence that would be presented – the Internet chat messages, the blog postings, the taped undercover operation with Constable Cory Both, and the friends and acquaintances who would say that JR had wanted her parents killed so she could pursue her forbidden relationship with Jeremy.

"She was the motive but he was the means," said Robins. "Mr. Steinke would do anything for JR."

The proceedings unfolded in an almost carbon-copy fashion to JR's trial. The testimony of police and forensics experts was nearly identical. Jeremy's rabble of aimless, substance-abusing friends and JR's former schoolmates were unswerving in their repeat testimony, even though more than a year had passed since JR's trial.

Sergeant Sheehan's interrogation of Jeremy was not entered as evidence. It was not needed. Jeremy's taped undercover conversation with Constable Both, which stood up as evidence, would allow the jury to hear the defendant incriminate himself in his own words. The testimony of courtroom security sheriffs Steve Durk and Sean McGuigan, who had overheard Jeremy bragging about the murders, was also strong evidence. The Crown also had Jeremy's blog posts, including the one in which he wrote "their throats I want to slit," as well as his messages to Super.Jesus that "we were thinking more among the lines of killing them" and to JR that "I love your plan." All were damning indications of premeditation. The blood evidence, and the testimony by Jordan Attfield and Grant Bolt that Jeremy had tried to recruit them, further added to a seemingly slam-dunk case for the prosecution.

JR was on the witness list, but she was never called.

Jeremy's mother, Jackie May, came to court daily, toting an oxygen tank. Her lung condition had worsened. She sat alone in the front row, where reporters swirled around her, wanting her comments. She declined their requests. There was too much at stake and May didn't want to risk saying the wrong thing. She brought three discount department store dress shirts for her son to wear during his trial, two blue, one white. Jeremy shuffled into the prisoner's box every morning and sat with his head down, barely looking up except to steal an occasional quick glance at his mother and at the gallery. Early in the trial, May was admonished by Justice Kent for talking to a juror. "I'm sorry you have to go through this," she told a female juror in the corridor. Although merely a human gesture, it was nonetheless a legal breach.

Hepner's strategy was to plant doubt in the minds of the jury that the murders were planned, which if successful could result in a second-degree conviction or, by some outside chance, one of manslaughter. The talk of killing and death was simply part of the everyday culture of death-metal music and the goth lifestyle into which Jeremy and JR immersed themselves, he argued. This strategy had failed for Tim Foster, but this was a new jury.

There was little Hepner could do to help his client with respect to the killings of Marc and Debra. Two sheriffs and one police officer had heard Jeremy admit to their murders. The physical evidence was also overwhelming that Jeremy had killed Marc. His clothes were literally soaked with the blood of JR's father, who had fallen on top of his attacker, dying. There was less hard evidence that Jeremy had killed Debra, but enough testimony that a blood type "consistent" with that of Debra had been detected on his clothes to eradicate any suspicion of reasonable doubt.

The blood evidence was not so clear as to whether he'd had a direct hand in Jacob's murder. From the day of his arrest, Jeremy had been consistent in his story that he had not killed Jacob, insisting vehemently to jailers, interrogators, and undercover officers that he absolutely did not harm the little boy.

The only forensics evidence linking Jeremy to Jacob's murder was a small amount of the boy's blood on the shoelace of one of Jeremy's size 10 Emerica running shoes. Sergeant Serge Larocque, the RCMP blood pattern expert, concluded that one of Jeremy's shoes "was in direct contact" with Jacob, a statement that Hepner challenged. He asked Larocque whether the shoe might have been "dragged through" a puddle of Jacob's blood, as if the contact had occurred after the fact. Larocque replied that the shoe would have been in an unusual position for that to occur, because the bloodstain was on top of the shoe, in the middle of the laces, between the lace holes.

"Unless whoever had the black Emerica shoes had fallen, or unless the shoe went forward," the sergeant said, bending his own fingers forward to show the awkwardness of that scenario. "To me, that's not really logical." After further questioning from Hepner, the officer did concede: "I don't know how it got on the shoe."

"You're not saying the blood dropped on the shoe? You can't go that far," Hepner pressed.

"No," the sergeant replied.

Hepner also asked Larocque why no firm evidence of Debra's blood was on Jeremy's clothing. "Would you not expect some bloodstains from her?" he asked.

"Not necessarily," the sergeant said. "It would depend on the injury."

To successfully explain away Jeremy's incriminating blogs and messages, Hepner would need him to testify. After the Crown had closed its case, and with a day's adjournment to consider whether he would call his client, Hepner decided to take the gamble.

Jeremy Steinke took the stand two weeks into the trial, on December 2, dressed in a white shirt that his mother had bought for him. For the first time, the public was able to hear the voice of the man who called himself Souleater. For someone accused of such heinous acts and who bragged of being a lycan and drinking blood, his was not a commanding, strong, or authoritative voice, but one that was surprisingly soft, high, and almost vulnerable sounding. Hepner asked Jeremy to talk of his childhood. He answered respectfully, explaining his upbringing at the hands of a hard-drinking mother, an abusive father, and equally brutal stepfathers. Hepner had brought out Jeremy's own alcohol and drug use during the trial and now had his client explain his substance abuse in his own words, leading up to the night he went in the basement window of JR house's and killed her parents. Hepner was building a case for a second-degree conviction, and Jeremy's extreme state of impairment that night could explain that his actions were impulsive.

Jeremy admitted to killing Marc and Debra, saying, "I freaked out" when JR's mom came down the stairs and turned on the light. He then claimed he tried to back away when Marc came at him, but fought wildly when Marc lunged at him with the screwdriver. "He attacked me and I went to back up and I tripped and fell and he jumped on me."

Why, Hepner asked, did he go in through the basement window that night when he never did on any of the previous occasions when JR snuck out.

"I don't know. I wasn't thinking clearly," Jeremy replied. He insisted he was just going there to meet JR and leave. "I never went over there with the intention to harm anybody."

If he'd intended simply to meet JR, why had he brought a knife? his lawyer asked, trying to anticipate every incriminating detail the prosecution might probe.

Jeremy said he had carried a knife for protection ever since he was jumped by five assailants in his early teens: "I had a habit of arming myself when I leave my house."

"You didn't need a knife to see JR," said Hepner.

"That didn't change my habits. I was going to Cam's first, so I had armed myself."

Jeremy repeated what he told everyone all along, that he had not harmed Jacob. He said he went upstairs, saw JR cut Jacob's throat, and then: "I stood there in shock and she walked past me casually into the bathroom."

He denied trying to recruit Jordan Attfield or Grant Bolt to help with the murders and explained away much of what he said in his jailhouse confessions as bravado: "I was trying to be a tough guy and gain acceptance of a criminal into a world I knew nothing about . . . I was trying to act macho, to put myself out there as a tough guy," he said. "I had been harassed my entire life and that was in the back of my mind, just trying to be accepted."

Jeremy also had an explanation for each of his damning blogs, poems, and e-mails.

"What is 'Blood Shedding Fight'?" Hepner asked.

"It's basically about a guy exaggerating on what someone would do for love."

"When did you write this song?"

"I had written it in about March. I was with JR at the time."

"The chorus says, 'I will kill, I will spill the blood for you tonight, there shall be a blood shedding fight.' That's pretty ghoulish, isn't it?"

"With the music that I listen to it's fairly common. There's a lot of songs out there from metal bands talking about death and other stuff amongst the same lines."

"Was this an omen of what was to happen?"

"No, sir."

"When you wrote this song was there any thought of doing anything to JR's parents?"

"No, sir."

Hepner asked about the blog post that said, "My girlfriend's family are totally unfair . . . their throats I want to slit."

"It's just a poem expressing my frustrations with something I couldn't do physically," Jeremy explained. "Like when you are mad at your mom and say, 'I wish you would die.' It's just talk, just verbal frustration, not something I would be able to do physically. It says about killing, something that I wouldn't do."

"One of the lines says: 'Their throats I want to slit. Finally there shall be silence, their blood shall be payment.' What did that mean?" asked Hepner.

"Just expressing frustration for something I couldn't do physically."

Jeremy also denied making the incriminating comment while watching the move *Natural Born Killers* that JR "is going to kill her brother" and explained his e-mail messages as "just venting."

"Me and my friends talked like that often."

"About killing people?"

"Yes, sir."

"That's the way you speak?"

"Yes, sir."

"Was there a plan or an agreement that you would kill her parents and JR would kill her brother?"

"No, sir. There was never any discussion about killing her family."

Ramona Robins cross-examined Jeremy the next day, beginning with his confrontation with Debra in the basement.

"The window was behind you?"

"Yes, ma'am."

"So you didn't turn and jump out the window, did you?"

"No, ma'am."

"Instead you stabbed Debra?"

"Yes, ma'am. I panicked."

Robins then turned to the horrifying last moments of Jacob's short life. "And you say JR stabbed Jacob upstairs in his bed and you saw that."

"I seen one stab wound, yes."

"So Jacob was crying, wasn't he?"

"I don't recall."

"He was hurt, wasn't he?"

"Yes, ma'am."

"You heard him crying, Mr. Steinke."

"I don't recall hearing him cry."

"When you came upstairs you got Marc's blood on the walls of the stairwell, didn't you?"

"I must have, yes."

"You said you looked into Jacob's room and you saw JR slit Jacob's throat."

"Yes, ma'am."

"So you didn't stop her, did you?"

"I didn't realize what was going on until it was too late."

"You didn't try to grab the knife from her?"

"No, ma'am."

"After you saw what happened you didn't rush to him to try to put pressure on his neck?"

"No, ma'am."

"You didn't call 911?"

"No, ma'am."

"Instead you stood in the doorway and listened to him die."

"I turned around and left because I couldn't handle it."

"You were standing in the doorway the moment that this wound was inflicted on his neck, isn't that the truth?"

"Yes, ma'am."

"It would have been very difficult for Jacob to get by you and back out of the residence for help."

"I left. And when I left, he was still making some disturbing sounds."

"So you were standing in that doorway in that hall, the only way down is behind you when she slices Jacob's neck?"

"Yes, ma'am."

"And you'll agree with me, sir, that it would be difficult for Jacob to get away from JR and run past you?"

"He could have got up and run after I left."

"But at the moment that she cut his throat, you were standing in the door. You were standing in his exit way."

"He was on the bed. Yes, I was standing in his exit way, I guess."

"You heard testimony from Sergeant Larocque that Jacob bled all over the room."

"Yes, ma'am."

"Sir, I'm going to put it to you that you went upstairs because she couldn't handle him and needed your help."

"Pardon?"

"I'm suggesting to you that you went upstairs because she couldn't handle Jacob. He was fighting her and she needed your help."

"No, ma'am."

"Sir, if Jacob had lived, he could have identified JR as a participant in her parents' murders, isn't that true?"

"That would be true, yes."

"And if Jacob had lived he could also say that he saw you and could identify you."

"Most likely, yes."

"And you didn't help Jacob at all. Instead you stopped in the bathroom . . . to look at your injured eye."

"For a brief second, yes."

"And you told the jury yesterday that this was just coincidence and no plan that JR killed Jacob on the same night that you just happened to kill her parents."

"Yes, ma'am."

"And there was no discussion of those two events happening at the same time?"

"There was never any discussion about killing anyone."

"Sir, by the time you came upstairs you thought that Marc was dead."

"I didn't know if he was dead or not. He was lying on his stomach when I last seen him."

"And he wasn't moving, was he?"

"No, ma'am."

"And so, if you had not been there and killed Marc, you would agree with me that JR could never have been able to get to Jacob because Marc would have fought her."

"Most likely, yes."

"And you know that, Mr. Steinke, because Marc fought you to the death, to his death, trying to protect his family. Isn't that true?"

"Yes, ma'am."

Robins's cross-examination supported one of the investigators' theories: that Jacob had fought his sister desperately and that Jeremy had finished off the boy. Even if he had not, Robins's questioning clearly showed that he'd aided in the boy's death by blocking his retreat, thus making him complicit in the killing.

Throughout his testimony and cross-examination, Jeremy did not use common street language, but instead used police and court vernacular. At one point, for instance, he said that he "inflicted a wound" on Debra. It was difficult to know if he had been well coached, or was simply parroting the neutral language he had heard in court. In his taped undercover conversation with Cory Both, Jeremy had also repeated many phrases that JR had written. He seemed incapable of coming up with an original thought.

In their closing remarks, Hepner and Robins pleaded their cases before the jury.

"Jeremy Steinke is guilty of second-degree murder, or possibly manslaughter, but there was no plan in effect," said Hepner. He told jurors that what happened in the basement was an impulsive reaction, and as for Jeremy's ghoulish poetry and Internet messages, "I think that was just talk from a young man with zero self-esteem who finally found someone to love him."

Robins said there could be no doubt that Jeremy was guilty of first-degree murder in the deaths of JR's parents. As for Jacob, "The easiest way to kill a child is to kill the parents first," she said. That would make the accused guilty of Jacob's death even though he may not have held the murder weapon. Blocking the child's exit further assisted in his death.

She argued that the two lovers did, indeed, have a plan. "It was all part of the love legacy that they had together," Robins said, recalling Jeremy's March 16 online message to KillMyHeart that read: "The whole point of killing them would be to start a spree across Canada!"

In their plan, Robins argued, life would imitate art, fashioned after what Jeremy called "the best love story of all time," *Natural Born Killers*.

Jeremy was not so intoxicated that he could not form an intent to kill, said Robins, because he remembered in detail what happened in the house and other events of that night. As for his upbringing, "There are a lot of abused children. There are a lot of children of alcoholic parents. There are certainly a lot of people who are bullied in school, and their lives don't end with tragic homicides," Robins said.

The jury deliberated for one day, recessed for the night, and came back the following morning with its verdict – guilty of first-degree murder on all counts. The mandatory sentence was life in prison with no possibility of parole for 25 years.

Justice Adele Kent could have sentenced Jeremy Steinke on the spot, but Robins asked that sentencing be done in Medicine Hat as final justice for the community. It would also give time, she said, for surviving relatives to face Jeremy and deliver victim impact statements.

After court, Robins spoke to reporters.

"I think what the public can take away from this is that there are heroes in this story and not just villains," she said. "You had police officers who mourned the loss two and a half years later of the terrible things they saw. The police officer from Leader, who on a slight lead that maybe these people will come, actually caught them by doing his own stakeout."

Robins also mentioned JR's father, Marc – "a father who fought for his family's life to his death."

Jeremy Steinke's sentencing in Medicine Hat on December 15, 2008 filled the courtroom with his family and spectators, including the weepy and still smitten Morgan, who had stood faithfully gazing up at the Medicine Hat Remand Centre in the days after the murders and saved Jeremy's phone messages from jail. She sat beside his sister, aunt, grandparents, and family friends. Braving the media throng, Jackie May sat in the front row as she had each day of her son's trial. Though she could do nothing to change what her son had done, or mistakes she had made raising him, she could keep loving him. The trial and its publicity had taken its toll – May wanted her own family to be able to enter victim impact statements, but they were not allowed to do so. Jeremy had been through two trials in her mind. JR's trial had effectively convicted him in the public eye, she said.

"It made me very mad. I can understand why they'd bring him up [during JR's trial], but at the same time, he didn't have a lawyer there to defend him, and it seemed like his trial, not hers," she said. The headlines and the glaring looks from locals continued to wound her. "This can happen to anybody. I hope it doesn't. I don't wish it upon anybody."

The hearing lasted one hour. Robins read emotional statements from relatives into the court record, including one from Marc's sister, Monique, who told of the devastating effect the murders had had on the entire family: "Your choices hurt us all, Jeremy. There were broken relationships because of this, lost jobs, heart attacks, drug abuse and much, much more. Both families endured so much pain."

Personally, Monique said she no longer felt safe. "I stopped going out for my daily walks in the beautiful sunshine. I feared someone would run out and stab me. At work was the same. I would wake up every morning and felt every stab wound you inflicted on Debra. She was like a real sister to me. You stabbed me every morning for at least seven months. I was living and breathing her.

"And then I felt my little brother [Marc] fight you over and over again. I nicknamed him Lovey because he was such a gentle soul. I hope you never forget him. He was just trying to protect his 12-year-old daughter from you. If she was your daughter, you would have done the same, but you will never ever know that, will you? I can't even talk about little Jacob because it's too raw still. I still have work to do to grieve him, too."

Robins continued to read, coming to a part of Monique's statement where she wrote of JR.

"My little niece, she was so sweet, you killed her, too; the beautiful little sweet princess I knew. I will never understand how in the few short months you knew each other, she could have changed so much. She was an A student. I try to get my head around that, but I never will. Maybe you could enlighten us one day, when you become a man, maybe not. As

I drive, eat a meal, do everyday things, it hits me they are all dead, stabbed, brutally, and I find myself shaking my head all the time. It's going on three years and I am still in disbelief. I'm averaging about eight cries a day now, since the trial is over. The shock has worn off, the pain continues."

Peter Doolan, Debra's brother, was the only relative who read his statement in person. With remarkable dignity and grace, he looked Jeremy in the eye and forgave him.

"I will never understand why she was taken. I will never understand the workings of sick and twisted minds. But I do understand about forgiveness. Debra taught me that. So it is for Debra's sake and through deep love for my sister, who I know is watching over us right now, that I extend forgiveness. Forgiveness of the murder of my sister, my brother-in-law, and my sweet nephew. Forgiveness. And may God help you and offer you love and light, which is how Debra signed every card and letter she'd ever send – 'Love always, yours in love and light.'"

Jeremy never had the courage to look up. He kept his head bowed and his eyes on the floor, as he had throughout his trial. Before passing sentence, Justice Kent asked if he had anything to say. Hepner, speaking for his client, said that Jeremy had told him he would undo it all if he could. It was important for Hepner to get the comment in the court record because it could be used by Jeremy in his future bids for parole. It was the only show of remorse, and it wasn't even from his own mouth.

After Hepner spoke, Kent again offered Jeremy a chance to express his own words. He shook his head. His trail of victims had extended far beyond Marc, Debra, and Jacob, but he offered no apology. He had admitted killing Marc and Debra, yet could not find it in himself to say anything to those who had offered him forgiveness, or even to look them in the eye.

Kent sentenced Jeremy Steinke to the mandatory prescribed sentence, life without parole for 25 years. "I'm about to send you away to jail for a very long time, perhaps for the rest of your life, and it's because of the horrific, unspeakable violence you've committed," the judge said. She encouraged Steinke, then 25, to take advantage of therapy while serving his sentence. "Maybe sometime in the future you can begin to repay the community for all of the damage you have caused."

The sentence brought to an end one of the most sensational murders in Canadian criminal history, rivalling the Karla Homolka–Paul Bernardo case.

Sergeant Chris Sheehan slipped into the courtroom for the sentencing on his day off and watched the conclusion with his own eyes. For the man who had led the investigation and suffered public humiliation for his forceful but inadmissible interview with JR, it was finally over.

"Justice has been done," Sheehan said after Jeremy was sentenced. "Life 25 – it doesn't get any better than that."

Legally, yes. But the most disturbing outcome of the trials is that neither JR nor Jeremy Steinke ever took responsibility for the death of Jacob.

Only they know for certain what happened in that house, and one of them is not telling the truth.

EPILOGUE

"A failure to internalize"

Few crimes are more shocking than the annihilation of an entire family by a child. The ancient Greeks, who were obsessed with murder, didn't even have a word for it, says Elliott Leyton, author of the groundbreaking *Sole Survivor: Children Who Murder Their Families* and a recognized expert in the psychology of the multiple killer.

The case of Runaway Devil is so disturbing that people want an easy answer, a tidy explanation for JR's complicity in the deaths of her parents and brother. No 12-year-old could kill her family. There must be a reason. She must have been abused. Neglected. Controlled by a predator. Brainwashed. Drugged.

Kathleen M. Heide, a professor of criminology at the University of South Florida who specializes in youth crime and juvenile homicide, says sons and daughters who kill their parents are likely to have been abused at home. This is particularly true for parricides involving a child under 18. But this was not the case for Runaway Devil. She was not in a desperate attempt to end abuse – she even admitted that her parents did not physically abuse her.

In her studies of child killers, Heide also found that there is likely to be substance abuse in the home. This, also, was not true in JR's case. Although her parents had gone through recovery for drug problems, there was no evidence that they engaged in substance abuse as parents and, in fact, they had lived their lives as models of recovery since before their children were born.

Heide says children who kill their parents fall into three categories: the severely abused child who is pushed beyond his or her limits; the severely mentally ill child; and the dangerously antisocial child. JR may be in the latter category, but her psychological assessments are sealed and only snippets were presented in court.

If JR was none of these things, how are we to understand her actions? Heide says if parents do not set rules for their children, even little ones such as doing dishes or making the bed, they could have difficulty enforcing things like curfews or age-appropriate relationships when their children become teens. If JR's parents were too lenient with her and tried to set limits when she started going off the rails, it may have been too late, Heide says, cautioning this is just a speculative scenario. Leyton, however, may have the best explanation of all: mainly, that there is no easy answer.

"In any given family annihilation, a curious social process emerges in which the courts, police, press and public embark together on a shared feeling for meaning," Leyton has written. "Typically, they struggle to construct an explanation of the tragedy that can make sense in terms of conventional understanding . . . The human being is an extraordinarily complex creature, full of evasions and creative rationalizations, and it should not surprise us that the motives underlying familial annihilations appear to be many and varied. Each human family is a unique machine that malfunctions in its own way, and families can create a rich variety of homicidal motives."

Leyton has, however, reached one remarkable conclusion, drawn from his extensive case studies: the annihilation of families by children is a uniquely middle-class crime.

"Sociologists have long made it clear that most homicides are the acts of the poor, the disenfranchised and the oppressed . . . We might thus expect familicides to come from such humble backgrounds as well, and to be driven to their acts by intolerable poverty and humiliation. . . . Our analysis of all available cases shows clearly that familicide is most likely to occur in ambitious, even prosperous, families." Working-class killers might kill their girlfriend's parents or someone else's family, wrote Leyton, but one from the middle class "is most likely to kill his own."

When Runaway Devil found Souleater, a middle-class child met her working-class tool. Together, they were like fire and gasoline. As with the horrible coupling of Paul Bernardo and Karla Homolka, the consequences were tragic.

Bernardo, who was known as the Scarborough Rapist, had never killed before he partnered with Homolka. The murders of Homolka's sister and two schoolgirls might never have happened had the two never met, as the murders of JR's parents probably would not have occurred had she not found Jeremy Steinke. Perhaps there is a peculiar chemistry unique to team killers, a subject that criminologists have pondered, digested, and categorized – without any tidy conclusion. As Leyton asserts, the human being is, indeed, a complex animal.

In searching for an answer, perhaps it is not necessary to turn to experts and psychoanalysts. The best explanation may come from Judith, an attractive, street-savvy former addict who has her own theory about why her good friends Marc and Debra and their eight-year-old son were slaughtered.

JR, she says, was not a victim and Jeremy Steinke was not a predator. Despite their age differences, they were equals. Emotionally and physically, 12-year-old JR was more like a 16-year-old. And Jeremy, although 23, had the emotional maturity of a post-pubescent teenager.

"I think with her mentality and his mentality they kind of met in the middle," Judith says. "Because of his lifestyle and upbringing and insecurities, he wasn't 23. And she played him. I know because I've been there.

She gets this attention from this boy and, well, you get tunnel vision. After that, nothing else matters. You're sexy. You're a 'woman.' I can relate because I was fighting with my mom at home and I had a boy interested in me when I was 14. That's all that matters. School doesn't matter. She started getting attention and it was power-tripping. This boy was giving her attention, and she's standing taller because she's getting this attention. I think it's as simple as that.

"Steinke, he didn't know how to handle her. A part of me feels for him because he loved her. He truly loved her. With his mentality, I would even buy it that he was not going there to kill anybody. He was going there to scare them, thinking he would grab his damsel in distress and they would run away. I can see him thinking that. I truly believe he was coming from the heart and JR was on this huge power trip."

Judith also understands the cocaine-fuelled rage that was ignited in Jeremy by whatever JR told him in her phone call on the night of the killings.

"When you are in the drug world, it's bravado," says Judith. "[When I took drugs] I was not the person that I am. It wasn't me. I was in situations where I had to stand up for myself and prove something."

Judith took counselling to deal with the loss of JR's family. She wrote letters to Debra as a form of therapy and attended a victims of homicide support group. She still goes to therapy once a week and carries a picture of Debra. "I try to take quiet time to be with her and . . . nothing's feeling right. Nothing's feeling natural. I sleep with the house in lockdown and with my bedroom door locked. I don't do well with knives out.

"I see Jacob. That's the hardest thing. I see Jacob. Here and there you see little boys, and your mind tries to go there and heal in the heart, and I can't. It is a little boy's nightmare come true. But I really am grateful that he didn't get left behind because they loved each other so much, Deb and Jacob. Hopefully he didn't have to be afraid too long.

"I'm trying to find where to put this in my heart and in my head. It's just too big and too bizarre and I haven't done too well with that. So I stuffed it. I'm okay with that, for now. It will come back."

Separated from their violent past by only a thin coat of paint, "death houses" usually sell for far below market value due to so-called crime-scene stigma. Such was the case for the dream home that JR's parents bought in the fall of 2003, where an excited Debra put everyone's names on their bedroom doors as the family was moving in. The house, which had been held by a public trustee pending a verdict in JR's trial, sold in August of 2007 for $219,000. The money could not go directly to JR, as it is considered proceeds of crime. Instead it went to JR's paternal grandparents, who planned to set up a trust fund for her future education.

A land title on the property shows it was purchased by JR's parents in the fall of 2003 for $169,000 with an original mortgage of $144,485. The 1,014-square-foot four-level split house, built in 1977, had been listed for $239,900 – about $50,000 below market value – after being extensively remodelled. The blood-smeared drywall in the stairwell walls had been cut away, removed, and replaced, new carpet installed, and rooms repainted.

While there are no laws in Canada requiring that sellers divulge that a property has been a crime scene, realtors often do so out of good business practice. The MLS listing on the property stated in capital letters that the house was the scene of a violent crime in 2006. Photos showed new carpet in the basement where Marc and Debra were murdered. The railing broken during Marc's fight with Jeremy had been repaired and the upstairs bathroom remodelled. No photos were posted of the bedrooms.

Death houses can also become macabre tourist attractions. The Clutter house in Holcomb, Kansas, made famous in Truman Capote's 1966 book *In Cold Blood*, still attracts bus tours. In Ontario, the St. Catharines "house of horrors" where Paul Bernardo raped and killed two schoolgirls with Karla Homolka was bulldozed.

The Medicine Hat home of JR's parents has not attracted similar attention, although it was broken into at least twice after police finished their investigation. Intruders may have held a séance, judging by four votive candles that were left on a baking tray on the floor in Jacob's bedroom.

Kacy Lancaster and Jenny, who wiped the blood from Jeremy Steinke's truck, were charged with being accessories to murder. One year after the crime, Jenny pleaded guilty to a reduced charge of obstructing justice and was sentenced to 20 months' probation. The pretty teen, who once pawned her belongings for drugs, eating only when she could afford to do so, came to court with her father at her side, mature, sober, and clearly changed by the experience.

Kacy, after nearly three years of house arrest while awaiting trial, also avoided jail time by pleading guilty to obstruction of justice. She was sentenced on March 19, 2009, to a one-year conditional sentence, to be served at home, one street over from the house where JR's family was slain. Crown prosecutor Ramona Robins agreed to the lesser charge against the former Blonde Vampire because of the difficulty in proving beyond a reasonable doubt that she had deliberately cleaned the truck in an attempt to obliterate evidence or that she had intentionally spirited away Jeremy and JR to avoid arrest. She called Kacy's involvement in cleaning and hiding Jeremy's bloodied truck an "error in judgment."

In an impassioned, heartfelt statement filed with the court, Kacy wrote that she was a "changed woman" who was "utterly humiliated" by her mistakes. She was the only player in the murders to voice responsibility for her actions and express remorse at what she had done. "This is not who I am. . . . I am mortified that my name will be tied to this forever. The sorrow that I feel for the victims, and all the people who were affected by this, makes all the hardships I have had to overcome seem insignificant. There is not a day that has passed that I have not wished I could change it all."

Kacy, who had been like a den mother to the goth mall kids, took up cooking and baking during her three years of house arrest. Feeling guilty that her single mom had to support her, she upgraded her high school education and took a college-level course in microeconomics, working toward a two-year management studies diploma program. Her hazy, pot-smoking days behind her, Kacy admitted she had made bad choices in friends and vowed to be more cautious in her relationships. "One day I would like to own my own business. Eventually, I would like to own my own home. I can't wait to be able to work again, save up money to make my dreams come true."

Robins felt that Kacy was sincere. "The victims' family, all they ever asked was for her to tell the truth. I am satisfied that she took responsibility for her poor and criminal choices and believe she has chosen to change her life as a result of her involvement in this tragedy," Robins said.

Three years after the murders, the Internet – which was used by Jeremy and JR to communicate their evil intentions – continued to be a form of therapy for those affected by the killings. People continue to express their feelings on blogs, in chat rooms, and on websites. Among them is JR's best friend, Aubrey, who emerged online in August of 2008 after remaining silent for months.

"Just because I don't pour my feelings into a blog every day, doesn't mean I don't miss her, too," the pretty 15-year-old blogged on a social networking website. "It doesn't mean I'm not hurting just as much, and probably more, than you are. I spent every other day in that house with that family, and basically every day with her. And because I don't advertise it all the time doesn't mean I don't wake up every day pretending they just moved away, or something regular and not scary."

On JR's fifteenth birthday in the fall of 2008, many of her friends posted loving birthday wishes to her on websites.

Morgan's affection for Jeremy continues to deepen. Before his trial, she moved out of her parents' home and took up residence at Jackie May's trailer, where she could take Jeremy's phone calls undetected. When

Jeremy and JR's relationship crumbled in custody – each blamed the other for what happened – Morgan became Jeremy's new girlfriend. Eight and a half years his junior, she remains too young to visit him in jail without her parents' permission until she turns 18, in the summer of 2009.

Morgan is everything JR was not. Unlike the come-hither goth vixen image that JR flaunted on websites with crimson lips and short skirts, Morgan has a more natural look, with glasses and blonde hair she sometimes wears in braids. She rarely uses makeup, favours jeans and baggy hoodies, but has added earlobe spacers to her multi-pierced ears. Like JR, she was unhappy at home, but she holds down a job in a café where she is well liked.

"I have always liked him more than a friend, but a certain crazy bitch was in the way," she jokes. "Although JR is/was my friend, I never liked the way she made Jeremy feel – stressed, angry, fed up – and he deserves far better than her. He did eventually realize her true intentions . . . and mine."

Morgan says she and Jeremy are planning a jailhouse marriage that will take place when she is 18. "My folks are not really supportive. They say, 'You will do what you want and we will support you, but we will not help you,' basically meaning they won't sign the papers to let me go see him."

She insists Jeremy is still the same person she has always known – sweet, caring funny, and loving. "The world has labelled him as a monster and he's so far from that."

Morgan apparently does not share the concerns expressed by an aunt of JR's who asked not to be identified in a victim impact statement read at Jeremy's sentencing. In it, she said: "I am afraid for any young girl who might fall under the charms of someone like Steinke."

Although the movie *Natural Born Killers* figured prominently at both trials, there was never any suggestion during the proceedings that Jeremy and JR were motivated to kill by the type of music they listened to. That came as a relief to Cradle of Filth lead singer Dani Filth in a January 2009 interview with *Calgary Herald* music writer Heath McCoy. "People can find blame in anything. 'Oh, they have songs with a bit of violence and a dark side so that must be the immediate problem.' [Heavy metal] is an easy target. It's a very easy scapegoat. You may as well blame testosterone," Filth said.

Young people in every generation are fascinated by the macabre, according to the 35-year-old Filth. So-called death metal or black metal, he says, is the modern-day equivalent of Edgar Allan Poe short stories, Mary Shelley's *Frankenstein*, various works of Lord Byron, or films by Alfred Hitchcock.

"Most of my stuff is like dark fairy tales. It's Poe-esque, Lovecraftian. They're classic horror depictions. We're no different than hundreds of years of poet laureates like Byron and Shelley and anybody else that's been affiliated with the dark arts. We've got quite a lot of fans, fortunately. You can't be responsible for each and every one of them. You can't tell if someone living next door to you is a powder keg waiting to blow [no matter] what music they're into. I mean, you get gang killings and shootings and rape and murder associated with hardcore rap as well, don't you? It depends on the person. Some people, their rationale isn't good no matter what they're listening to. Some people take things literally."

Filth was quick to defend his fans, stressing that nobody should condemn all of them for the actions of two disturbed people. "I know that most [of our] fans are intelligent, well-to-do people. They have day jobs. They're accountants, lawyers." As for himself: "I'm a nice guy, believe it or not. I have a 10-year-old daughter and a very nice house."

On October 27, 2008, a year after she was sentenced for murdering her parents and brother, Canada's youngest multiple killer had her sentence reviewed by Justice Brooker in the same Medicine Hat courtroom where she was convicted.

JR, who had just turned 15, appeared by video conference from Edmonton, flanked by a caseworker and a psychiatrist. Gone was the demurely dressed girl with her hair pulled back in a ponytail who sat in the prisoner's box at her trial. Those who attended the hearing saw the return of Runaway Devil. She was dressed in black, her hair worn straight and long, looking like the old JR of her Nexopia and VampireFreaks pages. The court was told that JR was doing well in therapy but had a "failure to internalize."

"She seems to be participating well with a very high level of conduct," Tim Foster told Justice Brooker. Her psychiatric report, however, indicated the need for ongoing therapy, and it was recommended she be kept in secure custody, according to snippets of the publicly sealed documents that were read in court.

Her "failure to internalize" was not explained at the hearing, but an expert on aberrant behaviour says the term generally means that someone lacks remorse. "With youths, being seen as incapable to internalize or have appreciation for the grave crime committed, can be called lacking empathy," said Janne Holmgren, a criminologist at Calgary's Mount Royal College.

A second review was held in Medicine Hat on February 25, 2009. "She is on board with treatment and is happy things seem to be going well," JR's lawyer, Katherin Beyak, told reporters. "The treatment team feels that she is doing well and that she has made progress in terms of addressing the issues which led to the offence, as well as on a broader scale."

Her new therapist, who specializes in adolescent psychiatry, also told the judge she seems to be doing "very well" and is making good progress. JR, appearing by video with her therapist and two caseworkers, was pleased with what she was hearing. She turned to her therapist and flashed a smile and then just as quickly turned back to the camera and wiped it from her face.

It is difficult from the small amount of detail provided to the courtroom to determine what the future holds for Canada's youngest multiple killer. The intensely protective *Youth Criminal Justice Act* sets out myriad restrictions on who can have access to legal records of young offenders. Often, access to these records requires a hearing before a judge with notification given to Crown prosecutors, as well as the lawyers and guardians of the young offender. For this book, a special court hearing was required to obtain the stick-figure drawing JR made foreshadowing her family's demise. Calgary lawyer Scott Watson, appearing for the authors on February 5, 2009, said the graphic image should be be reprinted. Beyak opposed its release, as did lawyer Todd LaRochelle, representing Alberta's director of children's services. "Having this disturbing image published is certainly not in the best interest of the child," LaRochelle said. Justice Brooker disagreed, and granted the authors exclusive use of the image.

"It's not sensational as would be a crime scene or autopsy photo. It may have played some role in the decision of the jury and may be of interest to those who wish to know more about the case and read the book," the judge said. Access to other records requires similar legal applications.

JR's caseworkers, psychiatrists, and jailers are prevented from speaking publicly about her except in a controlled courtroom environment. Patrick Baillie, a Calgary forensic psychiatrist who is not involved in JR's treatment, believes she can be rehabilitated through treatment.

"I believe that she has a good potential for positive change. She was, from a forensic point of view, very young when she committed the crime and, I suspect, not fully aware of the consequences that would flow from the behaviour. I doubt very much that she seriously believed she and Jeremy were going to run off to Europe and live happily ever after. I do not believe that at the moment she wished for her parents' deaths she was fully aware of what that would mean. Further, there is no significant history of misconduct prior to the homicides and while that does not lessen the seriousness of the behaviour, it does speak to the degree of change needed in the future. In short, she was not a pervasively antisocial individual with entrenched non-compliance. She was a 12-year-old student with some adolescent rebellion that massively snowballed into acting out with her much older lover."

As JR matures, Baillie believes she will struggle to come to grips with her role in what happened. "She did not kill her mother and her father, but she did make the comments that led to the plan with Jeremy." He believes the evidence that she killed Jacob is strong, yet thinks her "failure to internalize" will change as she gets older. "Yes, she has to accept some accountability, but, in my opinion, that accountability is lessened by her relative youth."

"Maturity usually helps with the development of better internalization," Baillie explains. "Life is complex and sometimes maturity is needed in order to see that complexity. From a developmental perspective, many 12-year-olds don't yet have a full appreciation of how actions have consequences. Certainly, some do, but brain development experts will tell you that the frontal lobes, responsibility for planning and self-control, continue to develop until we're in our early twenties."

For Baillie, the vast professional help that will be given to JR as she completes her sentence will enable her to recover and lead a relatively normal life as an adult.

"She has resiliency and tons of maturity that will come her way. She's bright and she doesn't have a long history of misconduct. There aren't any major mental health problems or marked substance abuse problems. And she's likely to be relatively unrecognizable when released. In short, the opportunity exists, if JR makes a few positive choices, for her to move forward with great success. She'll have to work at it, but the tools will be available."

Baillie thinks it is highly unlikely that she will ever again commit such a serious crime. Statistically, females have low rates of recidivism, the term used in criminology to describe repeat offences.

"In terms of the public's concern about her potential for engaging in other murderous behaviour, that risk really is quite low, from an actuarial perspective, and is certainly something that her case workers and the courts will continue to monitor," says Baillie. "I have little doubt that when she is released without conditions, she is unlikely to pose a significant threat."

Considering that a supposedly rehabilitated JR could one day move into a position of trust, society can only hope that her treatment is effective, as Baillie believes, and that she becomes, in the words of Justice Brooker, "the woman your parents and brother would be proud of."

JR, however, foretold a different outcome for herself. In the closing words of her Nexopia profile, she made a haunting, prescient prediction before the murders.

Following several lines of poetry that read "Trust these words are stones, my cuts aren't healing," she posted, in large type:

"Welcome To My Tragic End."

Acknowledgements

The authors would like to thank the following: Trena White for her clarity, Beverly Slopen for her advice and guidance, Scott Watson and Katherine Donahue of Parlee McLaws for their counsel, Leah Hennel for making us look presentable, and Clint Yarshenko and Robin for their hospitality. In addition, Ramona Robins and Chris Sheehan for their assistance on the workings of the criminal and legal systems. Gloria Remington, Melissa Remington, Rachel Crook, and the Zickefoose and Borger families for their patience, interest, and input. *Calgary Herald* managing editor Monica Zurowski and editor-in-chief Lorne Motley for their willingness to give us ownership of a story, and our colleagues at the *Calgary Herald* for their diligent reporting in the days immediately following the killings: Emma Poole, Deborah Tetley, Sarah Chapman, Renata D'Aliesio, Tony Seskus, Leanne Dohy, Sarah McGinnis, Sean Myers, Tim Fraser, and Michelle Lang. And, lastly, "Judith." Without her eloquent insight, the victims might not have had a voice.

Index

A NOTE ABOUT THE TYPE